# MOTOR CYCLES

### FROM 1950 TO 1988

# MOTOR CYCLES

## FROM 1950 TO 1988

## Steve Wilson

Patrick Stephens Limited

This book substantially comprises material first
published in 1992 in
BRITISH MOTOR CYCLES SINCE 1950
Volume 6 – Triumph Part Two: The Bikes;
Velocette and Vincent-HRD

British Library:
A catalogue record for this book is available from
the British Library

ISBN 1 85260 571 5

Library of Congress catalog card no. 96 78555

Patrick Stephens Limited is an imprint of Haynes
Publishing, Sparkford, Nr Yeovil, Somerset,
BA22 7JJ

Typeset and printed in Great Britain by
J. H. Haynes & Co. Ltd, Sparkford.

# Contents

## Acknowledgements

Thanks for very extensive help to ex-Meriden Triumph experts Hughie Hancox, Harry Woolridge, and most particularly John Nelson, as well as to others too numerous (and in some cases, too reticent) to mention.

Grateful thanks to Graham Sanderson of the late *Motor Cycle Weekly* for kind permission for use of photos; and now thanks to *Classic Bike* and *The Classic Motor Cycle* magazines for kind permission for the use of pictures which are currently copyright of EMAP National Publications Ltd. Thanks also in this department to affable Cyril Ayton of *Motor Cycle Sport*, and several others.

Outstanding work at the keyboard was once again rendered by The Boss typist, Sandra den Hertog. Finally, last thanks to the original journalists and road-testers, artists and photographers, without whose painstaking original work this volume would not have been assembled.

# Introduction

This book originally appeared as part of Volume 6 of my *British Motor Cycles Since 1950* series. So the first thing to do is apologize for the inevitable references within it to Volume 5 of that series, which concentrated exclusively on the history of the Triumph Engineering Co. during the period — its length being a measure of the way in which the Triumph name and fortunes dominated the development (and decline) of the British industry at that time.

The material contained in Volume 5, however, is really only a background to the essential year-by-year information contained in this book. If you want to read that background, I'm afraid there's a problem — at the time of writing (1996), Volume 5 is out of print. It is now a case of searching the specialist second-hand book dealers; or better still, encouraging the publishers to do a reprint as a companion volume to this one!

For those completely unfamiliar with the Triumph story, briefly it goes like this. In 1936 talented designer Edward Turner was moved to the company from Ariel by his boss Jack Sangster, after Triumph split away from its car-making side and Sangster had bought the motorcycle business. Turner rapidly made the Triumph Engineering Co. into a runaway success story. A principal component of this was his sensational new, fast and compact parallel twin-engine design, first seen in 1937 in the 500 cc Speed Twin.

After the Coventry works had been blitzed in 1940, Triumph moved to a purpose-built green field site at Meriden, between Coventry and Birmingham. There, after the war, Turner put all his production into twins, though from 1953 these were joined by the diminutive 150 Terrier and 200 cc Tiger Cub singles. Success followed success. There was the expansion of the twin to 650 cc with the Thunderbird for 1950, an early example of a prompt response to the demands of the American market. Turner cultivated this above all the other British manufacturers, who had continued to rely on traditional export markets in the Commonwealth and Empire, which then contracted dramatically, early in the '50s.

At Triumph in the '50s there were the sporting 500s, the T100 Tiger and the dual-purpose TR5 Trophy, which like everything that flowed from Turner and his 'pencil', chief draughtsman Jack Wickes, were as pretty as they were quick. There was the world motorcycle land speed record achieved by a twin carb 650-engined streamliner at Bonneville Salt Flats, Utah, in 1956; so that when the first production twin carb 650 roadburner was released for 1959 as the T120, naturally it was named the Bonneville.

Meriden's production was held at a ceiling of around 20,000 machines, built by a workforce of just over 1,000. This kept build quality good, demand healthy and profitability even more so. The machines may have had their weak points but these were far outweighed by the twins' mixture of smoothness and pep, practicality and charisma. Since the book was written I have been privileged to ride several well-sorted pre-unit Triumphs, and their lovely character was quite a revelation. The Fifties were indeed Triumph's decade of splendid maturity.

At the top level, however, things had been moving. Sangster had sold the company to the BSA Group in 1951, and then executed a sort of reverse takeover in 1956 by ousting the Chairman of the BSA Board, Sir Bernard Docker. He appointed Edward Turner as head of the Group Automotive Division, but Turner largely preferred to carry on concentrating on his Meriden fiefdom, which continued as an outstandingly profitable part of the BSA Group.

With the '60s an immediate change came. The home market, after its 1959 peak, slumped dramatically. Japanese competition began to emerge, in both Europe and America. To reduce costs and streamline production, for 1963 Triumph's big twins adopted the unit construction of engine and gearbox which Turner had initiated in 1957 for the smaller ones. The result was a performance gain, but at the cost of much of the old smoothness and charm. Turner himself went into semi-retirement; Bert Hopwood and Doug Hele ran Meriden, the latter's work ensuring that big Triumphs now handled as never before.

Their immediate overall BSA Group boss became Harry Sturgeon, who initiated a sales fight-back which centred on the Triumph-developed US market and involved doubling Group motorcycle production in the two years from 1964 to 1966. This also meant doubling Meriden's workforce. By 1968, it had grown to 2,235, and they were producing 37,059 machines. To put the sales profile in perspective, of that total, 25,047 went to the US, 4,299 to Canada, 3,559 elsewhere abroad, and just 2,143 were sold at home.

As academic Steve Koerner has pointed out,

the dependency on the US market with its tight selling season meant that delays could not be tolerated by the sales-hungry Group management, and this gave the closed-shop unions at Meriden, already part of a tradition of militancy associated with the Coventry area, major negotiating leverage with management which they did not hesitate to use. As the decade progressed, wage rates spiralled higher and higher, with stoppages increasingly disrupting production.

Koerner's MA thesis, *Trade Unionism and Collective Bargaining at Two British Motor Cycle Factories* is clear on the number of unreported stoppages at Meriden, and includes a telling anecdote. In 1966 Works Manager John Walford complained to Bill Lapworth, the Coventry District Secretary of the TGWU, about the way in which Ray Alsop, Meriden's powerful TGWU convenor, was undermining management's authority by calling union meetings whenever and wherever he felt necessary, without reference to the

*'They always seemed to come out of nowhere.' Triumph twins like this Metropolitan Police 1968 650 Saint were the Forces' favourites.*

*Opposite: Two '50s icons — Wurlitzer Model 1015 jukebox, and '56 TR6 Trophy 650.*

supervisors. Walford wanted things done by the 'Blue Book', the CSEU/EEF collective agreement which laid down procedures for processing disputes between parties. But Lapworth recalled how during one of the many unconstitutional stoppages at Meriden, when Alsop had been confronted by an official accusing him of violating Blue Book procedures, he had replied cheerfully 'Oh, we threw the Blue Book out of the window here years ago'. Management, desperate for US sales, had permitted and even encouraged this.

Mismanagement by a new set of BSA Group executives then led to the missing of a series of American selling seasons, and a desperate attempt to recoup matters with a revamped range for 1971 which incorporated many technical hitches and again missed the US season. Though Meriden weathered the storm, the Group as a whole foundered and in 1973 was merged with Dennis Poore's Norton-Villiers to form NVT. Poore attempted, partly because of the record of high wages and industrial unrest, to close Meriden and shift Triumph production to their traditional rival, Small Heath. Militants at Meriden organized a workers' sit-in late in 1973 and then a co-operative which, with the advent of a Labour government in 1974 became, tortuously, a reality in 1975. But — always under-capitalized, and tied to the increasingly antique 750 Bonneville twins with their 40-year-old engine design — the co-op, despite brave efforts, went under in 1983. A few more traditional Triumphs would be made until March 1988 by Devon-based Les Harris, who had been licensed to do so by the new owner of the Triumph name, John Bloor. And there the scope of this book ends.

The lack of history, as stated, is perhaps not crucial, as the machines themselves are at the heart of the Triumph story, and here you will find them described in detail. The other obvious parameter of the current work is its 1988 cut-off date. You may be surprised at the lack of a fresh section dealing with the ongoing success story of John Bloor's Hinckley-built Triumphs. In the post-war period Triumph may have dominated the industry, but now, with the recent shameful demise of the rotary Norton enterprise, the industry at present virtually *is* Triumph.

But even if publishing production considerations had allowed it, one would have been straining to find any significant continuity between the old Triumph and the new. In fact multi-millionaire builder Bloor deliberately emphasized the lack of it, even down to a subtle

but definite redesign of the Triumph logo (which incidentally thus became easier for his company to keep a complete lock on commercially). Like almost every step Bloor has taken, this was well-judged. It was a sad but necessary disassociation from the by-then proverbially leak-prone, unreliable and increasingly antiquated image of a design which, though well-loved, had arguably been prolonged well beyond its natural span.

The bikes that Bloor produced (in the factory which his own company had built too) were very different. New Triumph hit the ground running with modern machines, assembled by the most advanced CNC-controlled production methods. To come from nowhere in a highly competitive market-place the new motorcycles naturally had to reflect, and in some instances borrow, design features from their Japanese rivals, as well as sourcing components from Japan and elsewhere.

But distinctive features of the modular range on offer, in particular the 3-cylinder engine configuration, soon gave new Triumph an identity of their own. And as Dave Minton points out in his book *Triumph: The Return of the Legend*, a recent paper presented by two designers to the SAE (Society of Automotive Engineers) revealed domestic input in the form of Hinckley collaboration on cylinder head development with British racing car specialist Cosworth, and on piston and rod design with Ricardo Consulting Engineers, a connection echoing the 'Riccy Triumphs' of the 1920s.

Since 1994, too, there has been a softening of attitude at Hinckley to the traditional Triumph company and its enthusiasts. Bloor spearheaded his relaunch in America with a pair of retro-styled triples, the Thunderbird and the Adventurer, whose names also echoed, though not very appropriately, past glories. I have ridden a Hinckley Trident, and while wonderfully forgiving and powerful, its top-heaviness and sanitized exhaust note held few charms. Even an old fogey, however, could recognize that most of its features were necessary for the company to survive in the over-legislated modern world — though disposable income patterns mean that the Hinckley products' owners too are fairly old 'young men', with an average age of 39. The best of British luck to them, and to the company which bears such a proud name.

Wantage
Oxfordshire
September 1996

# How to use this book

The book is arranged in the following way:
**1** Detailed consideration of the major categories within the factory's road-going output during the period.
**2** These are followed by a table of *production dates*. Here, though production generally shifted during August and a new machine would be on display in November at the annual show of, say, 1950, I have followed the makers' intentions and referred to it as the 1951 model or model for 1951. Next come such necessarily brief *technical specifications* for each machine.
**3** A final section gives details of the marque's *engine and frame numbers* (where available), and *colour schemes*.

The following further points should be borne in mind. The *production dates* quoted are in general those for availability in the UK rather than for export. *Weights:* all weights quoted in the technical specifications are the weight dry (unless otherwise stated). They have usually derived from

*Motor Cycling* magazine's Buyer's Guide section, and occasionally inaccuracies have come to light, either from a failure to update or from optimism by the factory which supplied the figures. *Speed:* top and cruising speeds for most models are to be found in the text not the specifications, and are approximate figures. This is because not all machines were road-tested, and not all those tested underwent timed runs at MIRA. Also the author feels that top speeds on road-test machines were not always representative, as they could feature non-standard high-performance parts fitted by the factories. *MPG:* petrol consumption figures are also approximate, being subject to the variables of state of tune, prevailing conditions and the hand at the throttle.

*Owners Clubs.* For up-to-date information on Owners Clubs, please phone the BMF (British Motorcyclists Federation) in London on 0181-942-7914.

**Triumph: The pre-unit twins — The 3T, 5T Speed Twin, TR5 Trophy, Tiger 100, T100C, 6T Thunderbird, Tiger 110, TR6 Trophy and T120 Bonneville**

Triumph twins covered so many years and model changes that in the space available it has not been possible to include the customary year-by-year summary of changes after each section, which is provided for other marques in these volumes. The changes will be found detailed in the text, and to assist reference, as each model year commences, the year has been printed in heavy type. As much information as possible is included, but even further detail may be found in Roy Bacon's *Triumph Twin Restoration* book. John Nelson's *Bonnie* and *Tiger 100/Daytona* and Harry Woolridge's *Speed Twin*. The guidelines of this work remain to indicate significant changes between different years and models, and to provide information useful for keeping a machine on the road today; it is hoped that these have been met reasonably successfully.

The Triumph pre-unit twins represented a major design revolution in the motor cycle industry, and in 1950 were entering on a decade of splendid maturity. Their combination of looks, performance, comfort, economy and reliability made them the market leaders of their time, and today, in the light of Classic retrospection, their consistently high build quality, smoother power and transmission, and often their reliable magneto ignition, together with an indefinable rightness, make them preferred by many to their better-handling, marginally faster, but mass produced and often harsher unit successors.

At the beginning of our period the 650 Thunderbird, a great all-rounder, was launched, but partly due to the continuing restriction to 'Pool' low-octane petrol in the UK, as well as to a 500 cc upper limit in many of the European competitive events of the day, the sports cutting edge was to remain with the 500 Tiger 100, alloy-engined from 1951. This would remain so until the major change year of 1954, which saw the introduction of the swinging-arm sports 650, the T110, still with iron head and barrels but with 'big bearing' crank and tuned engine, as the balance slowly shifted towards the US market and its own forms of competition.

So in **1950** the all-twin Triumph range came in three capacities, a 350, three 500s and the new 650. The development to that date plus the general description of the twin-cylinder engine will be found in *British Motor Cycles Since 1950*, Volume 5.

The 3T 350, launched in 1946, featured an engine differing from the other two in several respects. As on the military side-valve 500 TRW, its three-piece crankshaft was held together by an unusual method. The

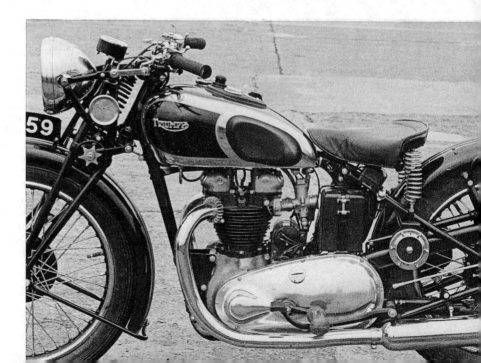

*The pre-war Speed Twin for 1937 — girder forks, big chrome headlamp, but otherwise similar to post-war.*

**Left** *Post-war Speed Twin for 1948, with Mk I spring wheel at rear.*

**Below left** *3T unit 350 engine — note single rocker cover, unlike twinned inspection caps on the others.*

mainshafts and big-end journals were integrated with two outer webs, and the one-piece con-rods had plain big-end bushes. On assembly, the rods and bushes were fitted over each end of the journals, which then pushed into each end of a hole in the central flywheel. They were held in place by clamping bolts engaging, like cotter pins, with recesses machined at a right-angle across the journals.

The timing side main bearing was a white metal bush, while the drive side was a ball race as on the 5T. The plain timing side bush could cause low oil pressure when worn, since it allowed oil to leak between the bearing and crankshaft on that side, reducing or stopping the supply to the big-ends. The 3T's rocker boxes, in a feature of the aborted wartime 3TW, were cast in one with the cylinder head, with a single cover retained by a large knurled nut for each pair of valves. This differed from the other twins' characteristic separate rocker boxes, each valve with its own cap, which vibration often unscrewed and detached. The 3T's rocker box spindles and the rockers themselves also differed from the 5T's.

By 1950 the 350 was offered as the 3T deLuxe, in an all-black finish, but with a $3\frac{1}{2}$-gal tank with slightly different chrome bands from the others' 4-gal item, a slightly smaller rear mudguard, a different saddle, a $3.25 \times 19$ in rear tyre to match the front, an 85 mph speedo (the others were 120 mph) and gearing lowered by the use of the 500's side-car 19-tooth engine sprocket. Otherwise cycle parts were as the 5T, including the nacelle. At just 325 lb dry weight it was 40 lb lighter than the 5T, but with power a lowly

*1949 3T de luxe—the last year of chrome tanks, first year of nacelle.*

19 bhp at 6,500 rpm, and top speed just under 75 mph. Plus points were quite a tough, understressed engine, relatively vibration-free until 70 was reached, where speed wobbles could also feature. The 3T never achieved the popularity of its unit 350 successor, and would be dropped after 1951 due to demand for the 500.

The basic 500 model was the Amaranth Red 5T Speed Twin. Several major changes had occurred for the engine, electrics and cycle parts since the model's launch in 1937. To begin at the top end, pre-war rocker boxes had drained by external piping, but from 1946 until 1950 draining was by drillways through the head and the one-piece iron cylinder block to the crankcase. When rebuilding an engine of this type, it is important to check that your head gasket has small holes in it in addition to the $\frac{3}{8}$ in diameter head bolt holes, or rocker feed oil will not drain down into the sump. The first few 6T 650 Thunderbirds had used Speed Twin castings as they were, but with the block bored out it was found there was insufficient metal for the drillways. So for 1950 to '54, the 500's and 650's surplus oil drained down external pipes to the fore-and-aft pushrod cover tubes, and thence via the tappet guides to the crankcase.

Another recent innovation had come in 1949 with the replacement of the tank-top instrument panel by the headlamp nacelle. The previous oil gauge was replaced by a plunger button attached to the piston valve of the oil pressure release valve, down to the right on the timing cover (except on the 350, where it was fitted to the front off-side crankcase). When oil pressure was at the requisite 50 psi, the mushroom-headed button protruded on its spindle to tell you so; though after a while the spindle could be a leak point, and dirt would upset its working. The dual-plunger oil pump still featured plungers of different dimensions, with the larger one being for scavenge; it was still (and would remain) vulnerable to dirt which could score the bores, cause the non-return valve balls to fail to seat, and eventually stop it working. All this had potentially disastrous results and for this reason, as well as because of its crude filtration system, regular oil changes, at 2,000 miles or less, are even more vital for a Triumph twin than they are for other Brits. One bonus for the Triumph pump was that it was less liable than the gear-type pumps of other manufacturers to let oil past it and cause wet-sumping.

In contrast to the 3T, the 500 and 650's crankshaft had its two crank flange journals and shaft assemblies bolted together with six $\frac{1}{4}$-in ground high-tensile bolts, which passed through to sandwich a central cast-iron flywheel assembly between the flanges of the crank halves, with balancing taking place after assembly. The balance factor of all these $1\frac{7}{16}$-in big-end journal cranks was to be 64 per cent, until the new crankshafts for 1954/5. This three-piece crankshaft, introduced for the 650 and adopted by all the 500s, ran on a large MS11 $1\frac{1}{8}$ in bore caged ball race on the drive side, and on the timing side a double-lipped roller race of similar dimensions to, and interchangeable with, the ball race it had already superseded in 1949; by 1950 a chip shield was fitted to this roller race. These arrangements in the main worked well, though tuned motors or regular thrashing did stress them.

*5T Speed Twin for 1950 — painted tank with styling bands, and this one also fits a spring wheel.*

Since the new 650 ran on the same crank as the 5T apart from its 82 mm throw compared to the 5T's 80 mm, there were some instances of breakages with the early Thunderbirds. They would occasionally fracture on the drive side, splitting through the web, but Harry Woolridge confirms that this was not an epidemic and only occurred with high mileage, with the use of very heavy side-cars, or when someone 'used it as a 650', i.e. at full tilt all the time, rather than as the bored-out 500 which it was; Service reckoned anything over 6,800–7,000 rpm was crank-breaking range. Plenty of examples, which would include Police machines, went round the clock on their original mains.

During the year, from engine no. 713N, the crank was revised to accommodate strengthened H-section con-rods of RR56 Hiduminium alloy, with their steel big-end caps now retained by high-tensile bolts inserted from the rod side, with ground location diameters and lock nuts. For this year the 5T's rods differed from the 6T's. Both still featured the white metal big-ends, however, with the con-rod eye metal-sprayed and running directly on the crankshaft. While specialists such as Robin James Engineering can arrange respraying of the rods if desired, by now most con-rods will have been machined to accommodate big-end shells, something Triumph themselves were to do for 1955. If converting early rods, though now no longer available, Austin A30 shells (Glacier B4144M) used to be approximate equivalents, though machining work is involved.

Post-war the twins' electrics had changed from a magdyno to a separate magneto for ignition, mounted behind the cylinder. The magnetos were either Lucas K2F or, until 1953, sometimes a BTH model, the KC2, and except for the TR5 Trophy they featured auto advance. A dynamo for lighting was mounted ahead of the cylinder block, and for 1950 for all the twins this became the Lucas E3L, as previously fitted on the TR5 Trophy. As with the previous dynamos, this was driven by a gear from the exhaust cam. The gear was fastened by a single bolt, and was small enough to pass through a hole in the back of the timing chest. Hence by taking off the clamping band and a single acorn nut, the dynamo could be removed for competition purposes and blanked off by a cover plate, which was a welcome feature to many part-time sportsmen.

To return to the basic 500, the 5T Speed Twin, compression ratio was 7.0:1, with power output 27 bhp at 6,300 rpm, giving a top speed in the mid-80s. But this roadster's big attraction was the lively acceleration, helped by a 365 lb dry weight, responsive flexibility and relative smoothness. There were also the Triumph looks, enhanced by the '5-bar' tank-top parcel grid, the characteristic Amaranth Red finish, and by the nacelle, which on a practical level made it less of a chore to remove the petrol tank, which was now minus the wiring harness to the previous instrument panel. The nacelle contained a horn, the headlamp switch, ammeter and cut-out button, plus the Rev-o-lator speedometer, with four extra concentric scales in the dial to indicate approximate rpm through each gear. Adjustment of the 6-in headlamp was managed by mounting screws in three elongated holes which could be loosened off and tapped to the correct alignment.

An integral part of the nacelle's line were the characteristic swept-back Triumph handlebars. These bars would become even more individual as other makers shifted to $\frac{7}{8}$ in diameter, but Triumph stuck with dimensions of 1 in, reduced to $\frac{15}{16}$ in at the twistgrip end, and with their own twist grip with its angled metal guide for the throttle cable immediately beneath it. While the swept bars in conjunction with seat, slightly waisted tank and footrests gave a comfortable, elbows-in riding position, they did leave an awkwardly big stretch for the fingers from the handlebar grips to the clutch and front brake levers. Many testers commented on this, but it was never rectified. Another unusual Triumph feature was the way that the left footrest on all pre-units was attached directly to the middle of the primary chaincase. This apparently vulnerable arrangement hardly ever damaged the cases in practice, in the event of

a fall, as the malleable iron of the footrest bent first. But on rebuilding, the correct footrest distance piece behind the chaincase has to be in place, or when the footrest nut is done up the case can crack.

Speed Twins were the world's most popular Police mounts at this point, and growing up in this era I certainly equated Police bikes with maroon Triumphs. Wheels were 19 in, with 7-in brakes front and rear (with one exception), giving a respectable stopping distance of 30 ft from 30 mph.

The exception in rear brake size, as on all the other models, was if the optional sprung hub was fitted (for its history, see Volume 5). The sprung hub, alone of all Triumphs, fitted an 8-in rear brake. Available since 1947 and adding some 20 lb to machine weight, for 1950 from frame no. 7439 it was offered in Mk II form. The original hub design had had each of its detachable sides fitted with a caged, angular-contact, large-diameter ball race. The left side acted as the rear wheel sprocket and brake drum, the right side being

*Triumph features for 1950: 1. Telescopic forks; 2. Parcel grid; 3. Instrument 'nacelle'; 4. Vokes air cleaner; 5. Prop stand; and 6. Spring wheel (the latter two optional extras).*

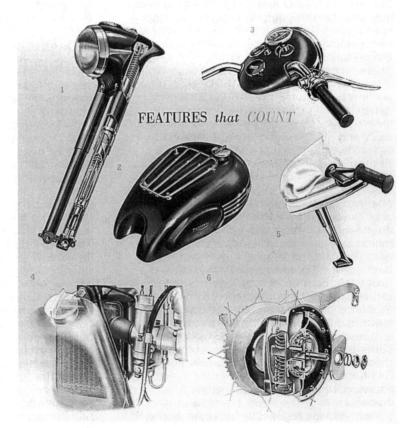

FEATURES *that COUNT*

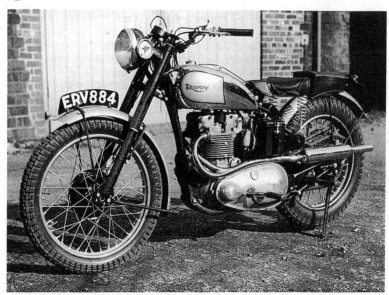

*Handsome TR5 Trophy. This brand new one was the first to be sold in Portsmouth.*

plain. The hub and sides ran on a central assembly built up from two castings, which housed the guides and springs, with on each side two compression springs below the spindle and a single rebound one above it. Dismantling a sprung hub was and remains a dangerous business without the proper tools, as the compressed springs leap for freedom. The wheel spindle passed through a square section block, which was curved slightly to match the central spring-box castings. It was located by a short arm keyed to one of its ends and registering in a slot in the frame.

The Mk I with its curved slipper blocks, and turning on ball-bearings, was lubricated via grease nipples, but the Mk II replaced the ball-bearings with deep-groove ball journal bearings, and the slipper blocks with two case-hardened steel rollers, with lubrication attended to on assembly and good for 20,000 miles. External identifiers were the absence of grease nipples and the raised rings on the back plate. In practice, while the Mk II did deal with the problems of locating the block in the casting, both variants still suffered from problems of spindle location and wheel support, all aggravated as the system wore, and leading to rear-end weaving when cornering, though Hughie Hancox believes that the Mk II hubs wore very little and were much maligned, being blamed incorrectly for weaving which was actually caused by a combination of the forks, frame, and tyres of the day. It was really only side-car men who

benefited from the sprung hub's $2\frac{1}{4}$ in of movement, with many solo riders preferring the standard rigid frame, which was the only other thing that was to be available until 1954. It should be noted that models fitted with the sprung wheel used the gearbox-driven auxiliary speedometer drive, while rigid models had continued with the rear wheel speedometer drive box until 1950, when the gearbox-driven arrangement was adopted as standard.

The other two 500s were the dual-purpose TR5 Trophy and the sports T100. The TR5's general history will be found in Volume 5. For 1950 it featured the alloy head and barrels with cowling attachment bosses and forward-facing exhaust ports, with exhaust pipes retained by bronze threaded rings screwing into the head, rather than by the roadster's stubs; all this was as on the Grand Prix racer. The TR5 fitted a single carburettor against the GP's two, and a siamesed high-level exhaust system, with the lightweight silencer carried on the left. The contours of the high-level exhaust system produced the need for one engine component unique to the TR5, differing even from the TRW whose cycle parts otherwise resembled it, namely the primary chaincase inner. This was recognizable by a scalloped flange which ran round the front where it attached to the crankcase, the object being to provide clearance for the high-level pipes. These early barrels had their liners cast-in so that, unlike their successors, they could not be removed and replaced, only bored out to +.040 in, though they wore slowly.

These rigid TR5s with the early square-barrelled alloy engine are now acknowledged by many as the best of the bunch, true all-rounders which could be ridden as everyday transport and then used as competitive sporting mounts at the weekend. The standard compression ratio of 6.0:1 provided an ultra-flexible engine, but there were also options of 7:1, 7.8:1, 8.25:1 and 8.5:1, so that Trials, scrambles, grass-tracking and even short-circuit road-racing, especially with the increasing range of available engine and gear options, were all meat for the Trophy, whose name derived from honours won in the hectic 1948 San Remo ISDT, another field in which it continued in private hands to distinguish itself.

A delight to ride, the TR5 was also one of the handsomest of all Triumphs, with the last production Triumph chromed petrol tank until the 1982 Royal Wedding T140. The tank, with Silver Sheen panels lined in Triumph blue, held $2\frac{1}{2}$ gal, and had a quick-release filler cap, twin taps and a 'four-bar' parcel grid. Slim light alloy sports mudguards, which also gave more clearance off-road against mud, and a separate black QD headlamp, contributed both to a handsome appearance and, together with the alloy engine, a commendably low weight at just 304 lb dry. Other vital statistics included a 31-in seat height for the special saddle, which was adjustable front and rear, 53-in wheelbase against 55 in on a standard 500, and ground clearance of $6\frac{1}{2}$ in from its special light frame, which had a shorter downtube and boxed-in front engine plates; the roadster frame's front downtube passed in front of the dynamo, but the TR5's headed straight for it, then stopped and bolted to the engine plates. One problem in these years for the TR5 was well as other single-carb Triumphs adapted for off-road use was the lack of space between carburettor and seat tube, which made it impossible to fit either a thick fibre heat spacer or a large enough air filter. Otherwise, TR5 electrics were by waterproof magneto, and a wide ratio version of the new-for-1950 gearbox was offered as standard. Wheels and tyres were 3.00 × 20 front, 4.00 × 19 rear, both with 7 in brakes. The sprung hub was optional, but made the TR5 tail-heavy. After 1951 there were different wheel and tyre sizes for the

rigid rear wheel, at WM3 × 19 in, and the sprung hub at WM3 × 18 in.

For seriously fast road work there was the Tiger 100. Catalogued as having polished heads, ports, rods and internals (though Hughie Hancox says that in fact nothing was polished on Production), plus a standard compression rate of 7.8:1, though higher options were available, the stock 1950 T100 otherwise differed from the 5T mainly cosmetically, with its handsome 4-gal tank with the new four-bar styling strip and polished Triumph name badge picked out in black, finished in Silver Sheen like the mudguards with their blue-lined black raised central stripe. In almost every other respect it resembled the 5T, though claimed power output was 30 bhp at 6.500 rpm, and it remained the fastest standard roadster 500 twin available; one enthusiastic user, Triumph expert Hughie Hancox, would regularly record nearly 60 mph *average* journey times from Coventry to Ripon, Yorks – yet the model also returned a commendable 70 mpg overall. While tuned T100s already existed in all forms of competition, it would not be until the following year that hot production versions began to be available.

Top of the line for Triumph in 1950, however, was undoubtedly the new 6T 650 Thunderbird, the name itself being a touch of Turner genius. This model's background will be found in Volume 5. With the introduction of its engine, as well as the new crankshaft mentioned already, the gearbox for all the twins had been substantially strengthened and modified to give easier engagement of the proverbially crunchy intermediate gears. The foot-change and kick-start mechanism remained the same, and there was little external clue in the gearbox shell, but both the layshaft and the gears themselves were altered, with the size of the pinions increased and each having a greater number of teeth than previously. The mainshaft selector fork was modified, and a new layshaft one fitted. In addition the oil pump's capacity was stepped up by one-fifth with an increase in the diameter of the pump's feed plunger and thus of the oil pump body. The 6T's clutch featured extra (fifth corked driving and sixth steel-driven) plates. The Triumph box could still be crunchy in the morning when going into first, and between second and third, with a pause necessary for down-changing. It was always wise first thing to undertake the time-

*1950 T100 Tiger.*

honoured ritual of spinning the clutch by kicking the cold engine over with the ignition off and the clutch lever pulled in; another dodge was to start up and with the engine running in neutral, pull the clutch lever in three or four times. But the Triumph gearbox was never to be a source of any real problems, being both smoother and tougher than most, and in this period the wet, four-spring clutch was a decided improvement on that of their main rivals BSA, which used six springs, asbestos inserts, ran dry and was prone to slip and drag. The Triumph gearchange was still 'up-for-up', at that stage unusual for a British bike.

Gearing was raised for the Thunderbird, with the engine sprocket going up from the Speed Twin's 22 teeth to 24; changes in the engine sprocket were how all the pre-unit twins adjusted their gearing, with the same 18-tooth gearbox sprocket being used by all from 1950, as well as by the unit 650s. Two other points, one minus, one plus, regarding the 650's transmission are noteworthy. The minus point concerned the primary chain, which behind the 6T's handsomely polished chaincase remained a .5 in × .303 in single strand item. Though the chain ws the same 78 pitch length as the 5T's, with 80 links for side-car gearing, and adjusted in the same way by moving the gearbox rearward, since indeed the two machines until 1952 shared the same frame, the extra power of the 650

could lead to rapid chain wear. The positive point helped with this, and contributed to the earlier pre-unit's exemplary smoothness. This was the efficient engine crankshaft shock absorber, used until the introduction of alternator models. In this system the engine sprocket ran free on a sleeve splined internally to the crankshaft, and on its outside splined for a slider. The slider and the sprocket had matching cam ramps, and a spring held them together. If the sprocket turned on the sleeve, the ramps forced the slider in along the splines and up against the spring, providing the shock absorption. Neale Shilton claimed to have seen 40,000 miles out of his rear chain on a pre-alternator twin, and noted that chain life was reduced after the alternator and its attendant clutch shock absorber had been introduced. And Hughie Hancox believes that transmission longevity and smoothness on pre-'54 machines can be even further enhanced by the old factory trick of fitting the later clutch with its own rubber-segmented shock absorber, so that there is then an absorber effect at both ends of the transmission sequence.

Otherwise much of the two iron engines on the 650 and 500 machines were in common—tappets, valve guides, rocker box spindles and rockers beneath their hexagon-headed caps. The 650's head was distinct, however, for while it was fastened by the same eight holding-down studs, it was no longer spigoted, and was fitted with a solid copper gasket. Finning was more generous, with four fins on the cylinder head at the exhaust port. Compression was as the 5T at 7:1 for low-octane British Pool fuel (though 8.5:1 export versions were available for the USA), and the extra cubes produced 34 bhp at 6.500 rpm. Combined with a dry weight of just 370 lb due to the use of the 5T's cycle parts topped with a 4-gal tank, the new 650 was capable of just over 100 mph. The Thunderbird in this first year came in one of Edward Turner's less successful colour schemes, the blue-grey 'Thunder-Blue'.

Its character, by comparison with the smaller twins, centred on the increased power giving better pulling from lower down the range, from 30 mph in top at least, with good torque giving acceleration in top gear from as low as 20, on up to 80 mph. A fine all-rounder, unchallenged for years by any other production 650 save BSA's A10, compared to its 500 predecessor the Thunderbird proved better with a side-car and better two-up with luggage. There may have been a marginal penalty in imprecise low-down carburation and a certain loss of smoothness compared to the 500, but vibration was completely

tolerable below 75, and other compensations were easy starting and realistic all-day 65 mph cruising, with the iron engine subduing Triumph mechanical chatter that later alloy efforts would amplify, and the large diameter exhausts and 'bottle' silencers producing a very distinctive 'pokka-pokka' sound. Despite the charisma of the later sporting pre-unit T110s and T120s, the Thunderbird was Meriden publicity man Ivor Davies's favourite Triumph, and Hughie Hancox rates the rigid 1952/3 models as the best of them. Titch Allen pointed out that the Thunderbird 'seemed to suffer less from [good year/bad year] ups and downs than any other machine I can recall . . . it remained a firm favourite with the more mature riders, who valued torque more than fancy bhp figures'. Royce Creasey's rule of thumb in his seminal 'Alternative Biking' article was that the 'simple and very stylish . . . pre-unit Thunderbird was the definitive British feet-up chopper and that everything since is an unfortunate attempt to make it go fast'.

Despite the 100 mph potential, the practical upper limit was around 75 mph, not just because of the roads, petrol and tyres of the day, and because of vibration, but due to the handling of the rigid frame and Triumph forks. The unsprung, brazed-lug frame for the twins, with its unusual tapered single front downtube, came in two major sections which

*New for 1950, the 6T Thunderbird 650.*

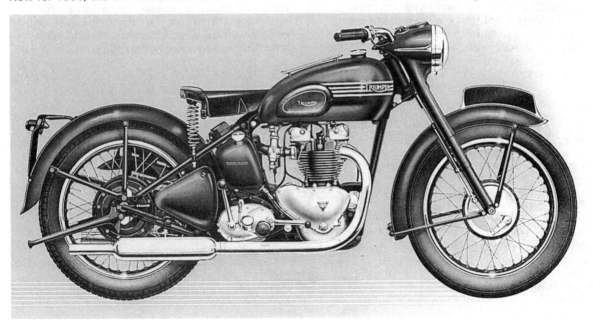

were bolted together along with the engine, gearbox and engine plates to form a relatively rigid structure. For 1950 it came with a lug for the optional prop stand, and an optional and rather thinly padded and uncomfortable 'twinseat' in place of the saddle. The slim Triumph fork with its long springs, enclosed inside the stanchions, giving 6 in of movement, has already been discussed in Volume 5. Modified to suit the nacelle, and comfortable, these forks continued to contribute to handling which, if less than perfect, was at least predictable and could be learnt. Up to certain limits, if the power was kept on through bends it might wobble or dip, but would invariably get through safely. Once the machine had been learned it could be cornered hard, with fairly restricted ground clearance for all but the TR5 setting a natural limit.

**1951** saw the 5T and 6T largely unchanged, while the sporting vanguard, as mentioned, was represented by the 500 cc Tiger 100. As part of an effort to provide a substitute for the Grand Prix racer, the T100 was now offered with new die-cast alloy barrel and head, distinguished from the previous ones by their closer-pitched fins, a more rounded shape and by the absence of the generator-set bosses. Early versions of these barrels had cast-in steel liners, but by the end of the year pressed-in centrifugally spun cast-iron liners were used, and unlike their predecessors these were replaceable.

The head too was close-finned alloy, with splayed exhaust ports, larger inlet valves, cast-in Meehanite iron valve seats, and steel screw-in exhaust pipe adaptors. Pistons featured taper-faced second compression rings, and despite a slight drop in compression to 7.6:1, output was increased to 32 bhp. The new head came in either standard single-carb form or, in a significant Triumph roadster first, with twin Amal Type 6 carbs with remote float chambers on parallel inlet tracts for the T100C. Pre-unit twin carburettors were not just for show. The 'C' stood for 'Convertible', and the twin-carb set-up for 1951 to '52 was only available as part of a £35 race kit which included suitable cams, high compression (8.25 or 9.5:1) pistons, valve springs, a 1-gal oil tank in place of the standard 6-pt, a rev counter and racing pipes, megaphone silencers, etc. Only for 1953 was the T100C offered as a complete package. With the full kit, the 500's output rose above 40 bhp and top speed to 120 mph, and in the hiatus period to about 1954, before the featherbed Manx became privately available and the 500 Gold Stars had achieved winning form, the Tiger 100s were a competitive if somewhat fragile option, as evidenced by a 1952 victory in the Senior Clubman's TT — and economically so, as even with the kit they cost £100 less than the Grand Prix. The increased performance — and even a standard 1952 T100 returned over 80 in third gear and a top speed of 92 mph on test — highlighted stresses on both handling and engine internals, including the crank and main bearings. Mechanical noise and high-speed vibration also increased.

*Tiger 100C seen here in complete 1953 form, for that year only.*

Other internal changes to the T100 included Duralumin pushrods to match the new block. All-steel pushrods, incidentally, should only be used with iron head engines, or the different expansion rates will cause problems. For this year only, alloy tappet guides differed from the 5T's by being circular for their whole length; also for this year only, the T100s fitted the TR5's pushrod tubes with its boss. In common with the rest of the range, a new type of tappet was adopted, interchangeable with the previous but now with the foot tip induction-brazed on, to reduce wear. The crankshafts for all the 500s had their crank assembly and flywheels modified, and the 6T's stronger rod was adopted by them all. The T100's clutch also took the 6T's extra pair of plates, with a deeper clutch centre and longer springs to match.

Other distinguishing marks for the sports 500 T100 were manual control for the magneto, a dualseat as standard, and modifications to the frame. This reverted at the front to the 1948 type, identifiable by a top seat tube clip on the left, to permit the introduction of a new additional front headsteady. At the rear the T100 frame was also modified to take stronger rear wheel and chain adjusters. Additional lugs were fitted to take the race kit's higher level rear set footrests, and the tool box was moved to a higher position above the upper chain stay. These rigid model tool boxes, normally fitted between the chain stays, could sometimes be difficult to keep closed; the T100's now featured a quick-release lid fastener. For the T100, 5T and 6T, and in a separate version for the TR5, a new, welded oil tank was fitted with a more angled filler and a bayonet-type cap in place of the previous screw-on version. The same kind of cap was now fitted on the petrol tank also, and the T100s this year featured twin petrol tank taps, as well as styling strips altered to alternate black and chrome, with the tank badges having 'Triumph' painted in blue on a silver background.

The TR5 also adopted the new alloy engine, though with a 6:1 compression ratio and cams the same as the other pre-unit twins' it still made for a more tractable engine, even if marginally less so than its predecessor. Its cylinder head and that of the T100 were modified in the exhaust ports to adopt pipe nuts instead of the normal port adaptors, and a new exhaust system was fitted to suit the new engine with its splayed exhaust ports.

The 6T's most notable change was to a lighter, more attractive Polychromatic Blue finish, Thunderbird Metallic. Internally it adopted cam wheels with three keyways, to give more precise vernier adjustment to the cam timing for performance work. The carburettor's bore size increased from 1 in to $1\frac{1}{16}$ in. And this proved to be the 3T unit 350's last year. Demand, particularly in the States, was for the larger machines, and a new small Triumph was coming in the shape of the Terrier single for 1953. Meanwhile all models were claimed to have their 7-in front brake's cast-iron drum made more rigid.

**1952** saw the 6T Thunderbird adopt an SU carburettor, Type MC2, in the interests of petrol economy. The SU instruments suited the 650 and would be retained until 1959. To accommodate it, the inlet manifold was revised, and a forged lug with a round 'eye' in it was incorporated in the seat-pillar tube. This allowed a connection between the carb and a new type of Vokes 'D'-shaped air filter, which was also available for the roadster 500s. This 'hole in the frame' is a quick identifier for dating a genuine 1952-8 6T chassis. The SU carb, in place of a choke, fitted at its base a bent flat metal mixture control lever, which when raised enriched the mixture and was then pushed down for normal running. The same thing would appear on the T140E with its Amal Mk IIs in the late 1970s.

For all models fitting it, the nacelle was enlarged and its fork covers modified to accommodate a 7-in pre-focus 'block'-type Lucas MCF700 headlamp, with an elegant underslung pilot light attached to the fork covers. Petrol tanks now featured plastic petrol pipes and a raised welded central seam, with the four-bar styling strips altered to suit. There was another new oil tank and a D-type air filter, and a minor modification to the oil pump. With the new tank, servicing the D-shaped filter would mean removing the battery and battery carrier. The rigid rear wheel's brake drum and 46-tooth rear sprocket were now integral, where previously the sprocket had been a bolt-on fixture; this was a bore for competition riders, who were deprived of a quick way of altering the gearing.

Within the gearbox of all but the TR5, the layshaft second and top gears and their mating dogs were altered. The roadster's rear brake pedal was reduced in width, the battery carrier reverted to the 1938 style, a multi-coloured Lucas wiring harness was adopted, and the electrical system changed from negative to positive earth, which it remained for Triumphs until the late '70s. The previous bolts for the sump plate and its filters were altered to studs and nuts. The T100 changed the front portion of its two-part rear mudguard, and modified its left-hand footrest. It also changed back to the 1950-type pushrod tube, and reverted to the use of the 5T-type tappet guide, adapted to fit its barrel, though the TR5 retained the previous type. The TR5 also modified its frame, with fork crown geometry being revised to give greater trail.

The **1953** range was principally notable for the first adoption of alternator electrics and coil ignition. In typical Triumph fashion this was first tried out on the cooking 500 5T, only later appearing on other models. Turner's

characteristic cost-paring was the main motive, and the price of the Speed Twin was lowered, to highlight the advantages to the customer as well, of doing away with the magneto, dynamo and CVC. The Lucas RM12 alternator in A, B and finally C series was mounted inside the primary chaincase, with the rotor carried on the end of the engine shaft and the stator mounted recessed in the outer half of the chaincase, which was modified to suit, with an inspection cap. Within the chaincase, the crankshaft was lengthened and given a stud to retain the rotor on its end. Current passed to a distributor mounted in the same position as the previous magneto, horizontally behind the cylinder block, with its drive shaft projecting into the timing chest and driven by a pinion in the same place as the former magneto pinion. No voltage control was considered necessary, and there was just a simple full-wave two-plate rectifier mounted under the saddle to convert AC to DC current. In case of

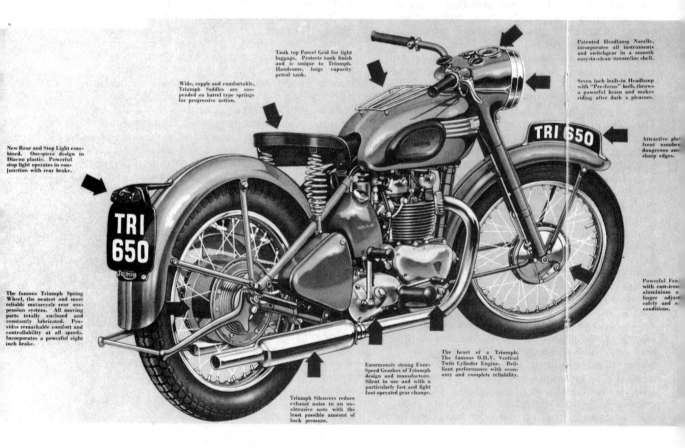

Tank top Parcel Grid for light luggage. Protects tank finish and is unique to Triumph. Handsome, large capacity petrol tank.

Patented Headlamp Nacelle, incorporates all instruments and switchgear in a smooth easy-to-clean streamline shell.

Wide, supple and comfortable, Triumph Saddles are suspended on barrel type springs for progressive action.

Seven inch built-in Headlamp with "Pre-focus" bulb, throws a powerful beam and makes riding after dark a pleasure.

New Rear and Stop Light combined. One-piece design in Diacon plastic. Powerful stop light operates in conjunction with rear brake.

Attractive pla_ front numbe_ dangerous an_ sharp edges.

The famous Triumph Spring Wheel, the neatest and most reliable motorcycle rear suspension system. All moving parts totally enclosed and constantly lubricated. Provides remarkable comfort and controllability at all speeds. Incorporates a powerful eight inch brake.

Powerful Fro_ with cast-iron aluminium a_ finger adjus_ safely and s_ conditions.

Triumph Silencers reduce exhaust noise to an unobtrusive note with the least possible amount of back pressure.

Enormously strong Four-Speed Gearbox of Triumph design and manufacture. Silent in use and with a particularly fast and light foot operated gear change.

The heart of a Triumph. The famous O.H.V. Vertical Twin Cylinder Engine. Brilliant performance with economy and complete reliability.

a flat battery an 'Emergency' switch position brought the alternator's full output into the ignition circuit. The front engine plates were modified to deal with the absence of the dynamo, and as mentioned the transmission shock absorber from that year on all the twins moved from the engine sprocket to the clutch, models so far without an alternator carrying a distance piece. In addition the 5T's nacelle was modified to suit the inclusion of an ignition switch, and a new wiring harness was fitted. For those models retaining magnetos, the BTH units and automatic advance were both discontinued.

The 5T's price incentive was advisable, as motor cyclists did need some convincing about the new arrangement. These early alternator systems were less than perfect, with their inaccessibly mounted distributors, and the unsatisfactory 'switch-controlled' output, i.e. the lighting switch had to be used to bring into the circuit four out of the six stator windings, so that the alternator output was stepped up. Though coil ignition made for easier starting, the wiring, particularly for the basic requirement of ignition, became more complicated. Mounting the alternator on the crankshaft made the vital stator/rotor air gap vulnerable to any play in the bottom end, and exposed the windings—which would not be resin-encapsulated until 1968—to the mess and vibration of the chaincase, where a loose primary chain could also occasionally slice through the alternator leads.

The distributor too presented problems, with its one set of points and one coil distributing the sparks car-fashion via a rotor arm within the distributor cap. The problem was that the distributor shaft bushes were of minimal dimensions, and suffered from a lack of both lubrication and rider attention—not unreasonably, as the system was touted as needing 'no maintenance except to the battery'. The bushes were located well beneath the points plate, and only a little play, passed on via a not very rigid auto advance unit, could quickly disturb the recommended 15 thou points gap, and cause uneven running.

The problems should not be exaggerated, as most alternator systems worked reasonably well most of the time, and were relatively cheap to replace when they didn't. But it is noticeable how Triumph bowed to riders' preference and retained magneto ignition on their top pre-unit sports models, and that both BSA and Norton retaining it on all their 500–650 twins into the early '60s gave them a definite edge in contrast to some electrical blues for Triumph. Today the situation is a little better, for while refettling a magneto can be an expensive and sometimes uncertain business, interchangeability of all Lucas alternators means that any system can be progressively uprated to 12 volts, a higher output and electronic ignition, as there are electronic conversions available even for distributors.

Otherwise, as mentioned, 1953 saw the T100C semi-racer, with twin carbs, 8:1 compression ratio pistons, and the famous E3134 sports cam profiles as standard. By contrast, in an attempt at subduing the alloy engine's clatter, the standard T100 and the TR5 at engine no. 37560 came with E3275 cams, with quietening ramps and different tappet clearances. The roadster twin's rear petrol tank support was modified, and all models fitted with a Lucas Diacon Type 525 stop/tail-light, with the shapely oval of the Triumph rear number plate, in which the upper bridge piece served as a lifting handle, modified to suit.

**1954** was a major change year. The rigid Triumphs, despite the interim measure of the sprung hub, were looking increasingly anachronistic in a field where twins from Royal Enfield and AMC had been offering swinging-arm suspension for several years, Norton would shortly come up with Featherbed-framed Dominators, and perhaps most potently, BSA's previously plunger-sprung A7 and A10 were to be offered in sturdy Gold Star-derived swinging-arm frames. Triumph responded stylishly, including the first appearance of an ultra-characteristic Triumph colour, Shell Blue Sheen, reportedly a Jack Wickes inspiration, on a machine that offered full rear springing, coupled with a striking yet historically consistent restyle, plus a performance leap which from now on put the 650s as the sports cutting edge of the range. The Triumph frame may have had its faults, but that did not stop the new T110 being a hit with the fast young public from the start.

The T110's background will be found in Volume 5. The engine, which featured both an iron head and barrels, was significant in introducing a stiffened-up crankshaft with increased shaft diameters, and con-rods of increased section (though still white metal lined) in new crankcases. Though the Thunderbird this year, like the 5T, fitted an alternator for ignition and lighting, the T110 retained a manually controlled magneto for ignition and the dynamo for lighting. Its inner primary chaincase also featured a new breather pipe boss forward of the footrest hanger rod, and the previous semi-circular cast guard round the gearbox shaft was now shaped a little. The timing side crankcase half was modified to suit a more substantial main bearing arrangement, namely an additional $1\frac{1}{8}$ in MS11 ball race with a clamping washer between this and the timing gear. This was the 'big-bearing' motor, and pretty well mandatory for tuned twins. The big-bearing motors are identifiable by their small crescent-shaped bulge on the timing cover. Though with regular oil changes the older small bearing type were perfectly adequate for

moderate road use and could give high mileages, earlier engines could and can be converted to the bigger bearing and stronger shaft, at the time by means of the Service Dept. offering later cranks with turned-down timing-side main journals to fit the earlier RM10 bearing, and today by means of a timing side bearing with the same outside diameter as the earlier cases, but with a larger internal diameter to take the bigger crankshaft. New flywheels were also adopted for both 650s, with the balance factor on these $1\frac{5}{8}$-in big-end journal cranks increasing from 64 per cent to 70 per cent.

This big-bearing arrangement was also found on the T100 (but not yet the 5T) and on the 6T. The latter now featured a revised primary chaincase as on the 5T, since as mentioned it too now adopted the Speed Twin's all-alternator electrics, with both fitting a Lucas RM14 three-lead alternator, an RB107 regulator, a revised spring set in the distributor, and a combined light and ignition switch in a suitably modified nacelle. For those machines with magneto ignition, the Lucas K2F became the type with the brushes in the rear of the points plate.

The T110 featured a new shell-moulded iron cylinder head with modified ports, new E3325 cams based on the 'Q' sports cams developed by the Americans, larger inlet valves, increased oil circulation, a single Amal Type 29 carburettor but with a TT pattern float chamber, and since higher octane petrol was now available in the UK, pistons giving a compression ratio raised to 8:1. All this gave 42 bhp at 6,500 rpm, with searing acceleration and a top speed for unbreathed-on motors of comfortably over 100 mph, with 110 and more reserved for race-kitted or further tuned machines. From now on problems of rapid wear of the under-lubricated exhaust camshaft would worsen; Hughie Hancox says the cause was owners setting the exhaust valve clearances too close, thus not allowing oil between the foot of the follower and the back of the cam, and hence incurring premature wear.

The T110's new swinging-arm frame, which was also adopted for the T100, had a wheelbase at $55\frac{3}{4}$ in, less than 1 in up on the previous frame. It had been kept compact by bringing the gearbox in closer to the crankcase and by fitting a shortened primary chaincase, a 70-link primary chain, and new rear chain plates, with the previous lower

*1954 swinging-arm Tiger 100, similar to the T110.*

chainguard deleted. The gearbox adjuster was revised, with the gearbox clamping screw and adjusting screw now more accessible. The gearbox shell and inner cover were modified to suit, with the previous gear indicator pointer and scale dropped, and a new pedal. The extra stresses of the higher output engines would have their effect here, and oil leaks from along the mainshaft and out over the rear end became familiar. The rear brake pedal too became a single forging for the pedal arm, pivot bush and rod arm, with the rod end no longer forked but bent and secured by a split pin, and the whole assembly modified at engine no. 51200.

The frame was still a brazed cradle, single front downtube design, but now with a swinging-arm pivoting on the saddle tube. Front fork springs were increased to 20 in length, and the rear units, though initially flawed as we shall see, were the best make from the start, three-position slim Girlings, with their poundage stiffened in mid-year from 110 to 125, so movement was reduced from 4 to $2\frac{1}{2}$ in. The rear fork arms were bushed at their far ends and pivoted on a spindle pressed into a frame lug at the base of the saddle tube, with side play controlled by shims on the right side, with lubrication being via an inaccessible grease nipple. Rear wheels

in the swinging-arm featured revised head angle spoking, and now turned on ball races as opposed to the rigid's taper rollers; there was also now an optional QD rear wheel. The new frame raised all-up weight a little to 395 lb dry, and featured the first-ever Triumph centre stand.

It also dictated an attractively compact restyling of the other cycle parts, with a new oil tank (claimed to be 6 pt but in fact 5) which combined with it into one unit the air cleaner, battery case and tool box. Topping this was a new one-piece rear mudguard, and as standard, a new and much more comfortable two-level design of twinseat, though the 6T's optional seat remained as previous. A valanced front mudguard, with stays formed in one and riveted to the guard, became optionally available. Along with the rest of the range there were new silencers, said to be developed form the Terrier, with a characteristic 'teardrop' shape, and giving a delightfully throaty exhaust note. On swinging-arm models they were attached to the rear frame pillion footrest support bracket, and in mid-year from frame no. 51200, this was modified on the left-hand side. A final and overdue addition to the T100 and T110 was a new 8-in SLS front brake, with a scalloped drum-side spoke flange for that year only, and with an air scoop and rear vent.

The T110 was a sales hit, with the 6T

somewhat relegated to a cooking, side-car hauling role from now on, but some problems were not slow in emerging on the new model. The engine's iron head proved a real drawback. Overheating of the cylinder head was an endemic problem with the Triumph twin-cylinder design, since the forward-mounted exhaust pushrod tube obscured, in Bert Hopwood's view badly so, the cylinder block from cooling air. The high-speed T110's engine overheated quickly when thrashed, with the oil, at 5 pt rather down on quantity, actually boiling on long fast runs. The iron head then distorted and warped, leading to oil leaks, blown head gaskets, and loss of power from imperfect combustion, often also with poor carburation due to lost rocker caps. The heads were still the eight-stud design, and prone to cracking between the valve seat edge and the studs, though often enough the cracks caused no trouble. There were partial cures to all this, however, and as will be discussed, later heads and barrels can be substituted. But for the moment the T110's iron head's shortcomings were soon known and derided by the fast boys, especially when BSA and Norton shortly offered alloy heads on their sports twins, and on the smaller unit machines, Triumph's only answer would be to paint their iron ones silver!

A more instantly perceptible problem was the spring frame's handling, with the unbraced swinging-arm turning the saddle tube into a torsion bar and inducing hairy weaving on high-speed cornering. 'A good engine let down by inferior frame design', was one 1954 owner's verdict, and he went on to mention that an unpleasant side-effect was excessive vibration, citing two broken mudguard stays and a split petrol tank in six months; both the fixing and the inner wall of the oil tank were other stress points. Bob Currie too recalled the T110's harsh power delivery, especially from low rpm. A final design fault associated with the swinging-arm frame concerned its rear fork spindle. Frequent greasing of the swinging-arm was and is no mere formality, since if lubrication was neglected, the fork arm bushes and spindle wore badly, increasing handling problems, and ultimately seized, after which they were and are extremely difficult to remove and replace. This layout lingered until 1963 for the 650s and for all the lower-capacity twins to the end. A final problem

was caused by the early Girling units, which only had rubber bushes at their bottom ends, and when these wore and the metal unit bodies could touch the swinging-arm, damping and handling deteriorated rapidly.

For '50s' speed merchants, however, these considerations were outweighed by the Shell Blue T110's good looks, free-revving nature and sheer pace. 'Triumphs always attracted ear-'olers', as one ex-rocker recalled, and they were the type to relish the hairy edge of the handling, and to master it, partially, with technique — in *Classic Bike* another ex-rocker, Jerry Clayton, recalled using advice from a book by John Surtees on how drift could be countered by moving body weight to the inside of the bike to keep it as upright as possible, and at length found that he could put his '57 Thunderbird with T110 internals through Dorking's 'Deceptive Bends', a well-known rocker testing-ground, at 90–95 mph in third without laying himself open to 'irretrievable situations'. For the next three or four years the T110 was about the fastest available roadster outside the Gold Star, and was a much more practical street bike than the big BSA single, easier to start, with a less temperamental clutch, and with the stomp to out-accelerate a Goldie from the traffic lights. At £240 in 1955, the T110s were also £10 cheaper than a 500 Gold Star. Ultimately though, as the production race results testify, the Gold Star continued to have the edge, and it was partly to beat them that even quicker and stronger 650 Triumphs were developed.

Meanwhile for 1954 the fast 500 got the swinging-arm frame for its all-alloy engine, and with the big-bearing bottom end, the 1954–8, and even more the '59, T100s held together well, and are in some ways the most desirable pre-unit 500s. Though the emphasis on the 500 as a racer was diminished, with the T100C deleted and the full race kit no longer available, the twin Amal Type 276 carburettors were still optional extras, even if the cams were now the standard touring ramp ones. For the T100 and for the still soft-tuned TR5, the stronger crankshaft and con rods were now fitted, with a single MS 11 ball journal bearing in place of the previous roller bearing on the timing side, all as on the T110. The T100's internals were no longer polished, however. Its engine balance factor was altered by means of balancing weights from 68 to 50 per cent, to suit the new frame. However according to John Nelson, an urgent need was soon discovered to introduce a form of sludge trap within the new crank journals, and the previous, heavier balancing weights were reintroduced for the T100. After early traps consisting of a vented tube within the central chamber, all models settled on a permanent sludge trap tube pressed into, and located within, machined counter bores within the cranks themselves. Externally the TR5, still in a rigid frame, adopted for that year only a version of the 'teardrop' silencer with a top-mounted mounting lug. For the T100, a 3-gal tank was offered as an option for the next two years.

**1955** saw the previous year's progress consolidated, and Triumph reacted swiftly to the T110's cylinder head distorting problem with an interim solution, a fifth, cooling fin, located by the exhaust pipe clamp. The head was still iron.

All models went into the swinging-arm frame, and engines, gearboxes and cycle parts were adapted to suit, with the rear left engine plate modified on all. The larger dualseat became standard for all, bar the TR5 which had its own narrow competition twinseat. Amal Monobloc carburettors were generally adopted; as with the previous carburettors, the air level/choke was located under the seat, for the previous models on the frame above the tool box, but in this case down on the carburettor, worked by a spring-loaded plunger rather than the more conventional and convenient cable and lever on the handlebars. This was part of Turner's drive to keep the handlebars clean, but it led to riders complaining that they were expected to have double-jointed hands, and for many of the unit models a bar-mounted lever was adopted early in the '60s.

The swinging-arm frame now got side-car lugs and a new prop stand. The kick-starter ratchet spring, sleeve and plunger changed, with its quadrant now made of nickel-steel chrome to cope with extra effort from higher compression ratios — the T100's rose to 8:1 that year. The oil tank was modified in internal construction to overcome the inner wall cracking problem. A rear brake torque stay was fitted so the rear fork incorporated a torque-stay lug for the T110 as well as the others. The silencer clips were now linked to the frame on either side by a strip stay, which was modified in mid-year from frame no. 64324. The front fork stem was stiffened a

little by replacing the previous $\frac{5}{16}$ in clamp bolts in the lower fork crown by $\frac{3}{8}$ in items. The 6T, 5T and T100 replaced the underslung pilot light of their nacelle legs with a chromed horn grill, in some cases the change taking place in mid-year. The T110 battery/tool box lid changed to one that suited all the models, with a screw rather than the previous sometimes unreliable Oddie fastener. The rear light became the Lucas Diacon Type 564 with integral rear reflectors. The sports model's 8-in front brake lost its scalloped spoke flanges, which had proved fracture-prone.

The 5T's engine now came into line with the other big-bearing motors, although there was what Harry Woolridge claims to be a rare example of Meriden using up old stock, as some 5Ts continued to be produced with the original small crankpins into the 1955 season — though even then, says Woolridge, their engine numbers and details were faithfully recorded at the factory.

For the full-alternator 5T and 6T, a thinner stator was employed on the RM14 alternator, and it was now attached to the inner rather than the outer primary chaincase. The inspection plate in the chaincase cover was therefore deleted, with a new streamlined cover bearing either a cast-in 'Speed Twin' motif or the Thunderbird's dart-like logo, as appropriate. The plates of the rectifier were reduced in size, and for the 6T a new version of the distributor was fitted, with advance reduced from $15°$ to $12\frac{1}{2}°$.

With the spring frame the TR5's character also changed, as in addition it now fitted what was virtually a T100 engine. American influence was growing, and in the UK scrambles were beginning to be the popular sport, with the Triumph Trials effort starting to angle towards their small singles. While still fully equipped for the road, as was company policy, and though it could still be ordered in Trials trim, the TR5's engine as standard now ran at 8:1 compression, with the T110's E3325 performance camshafts. Its pushrod covers were now as the other 500s, since the cylinder head was now the T100's, which meant that the TR5's exhaust pipes now had the screwed-in adaptors with clamp fixing in place of the previous castellated nuts screwing directly into the exhaust ports. Its exhaust and silencer were modified to suit this and the new frame. The gearbox shell was the T100's, and inside it the previous wide-ratio gears were replaced by the

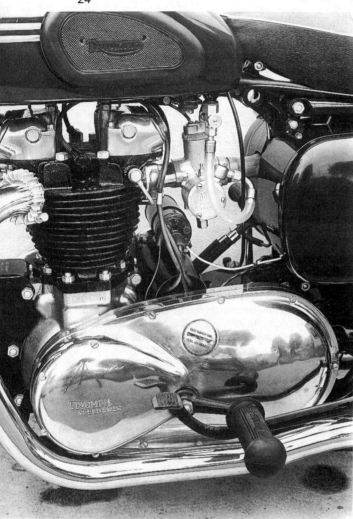

swinging-arm rear suspension was excellent and coped with moorland jagged rocky outcrops ... The Gold Star may have had marginally better road holding at really high speed, but the Triumph's was very good indeed and in every other respect it was even better than the Gold Star'.

**1956** saw Triumph definitively tackling the T110's iron head problems with a new, die-cast, light alloy cylinder head with cast-in air passages. Due to its shape, this was known as the Delta head, and it also eliminated the external oil pipes by draining oil directly into the pushrod cover tubes. Valve inserts were of cast-in austenitic iron, and instead of each valve lying in a separate chamber in the head, both inlet valves were in one chamber and both exhaust valves in another. The pushrod tubes, now with thicker cover-seals at their top ends and lacking bosses for the previous drain pipes, seated on the underside of these chambers rather than in the rocker boxes. Each of the latter was redesigned, with an extra middle holding-down stud. A heat-insulating washer was provided between the carburettor and the manifold. Compression ratio was raised to 8.5:1. The new head certainly provided improved cooling, and though it still proved prone to cracking, performance was boosted, with a steady 90 mph available without complaint and 110 mph just within reach at the top end. Yet fuel economy too remained at an admirable 70 mpg overall.

In all the twins there were a couple of significant internal changes, the first being shell-type big-end bearings in place of the previous white-metal type. These were Vandervell babbit metal steel-backed thin wall type. Rods with a larger big-end eye were necessary to take them, and the increased weight of the rod assemblies meant adjustment of balance weights to retain previous balance factors.

The engines of the various 500s also underwent some significant modification. On the T100 and TR5, the alloy barrels' liner spigot depth was reduced from $\frac{3}{16}$ in to $\frac{1}{8}$ in, with the spigot bore depth into the head correspondingly reduced. Primarily this was done because when the head gasket compressed, the head was sitting on top of the spigot instead of on the barrel/head face. The factory found that after a few hundred miles of running with the head sat on the spigot, the latter broke off. When the head

standard cluster. Ignition was via a K2FC competition magneto. The petrol tank became a Shell Blue-painted 3-gal one in a similar style to the other models, with a four-band styling strip and knee grips, and a twinseat to suit.

Many regretted the passing of the softer, likeable, truly dual-purpose model, with its off-road agility and lightness of handling, but the new one was still a serviceable tool. The factory supplied the new swinging-arm models to selected contestants in the 1954 ISDT, and privateer David Miles recalled in *Classic Bike* how, 'wet or dry, the Triumph coped with the conditions superbly ... very powerful and responsive, with excellent handling, particularly on rough going ... The

**Left** *1955 Speed Twin engine, showing new primary chaincase and Amal Monobloc carb, plus distributor detail.*

**Right** *A 1956 6T Thunderbird.*

was removed to see why it was blowing, the ring of broken-off spigot would be sitting in the head recess like a big thick piston ring! By altering the spigot in this way, previous engines only had to have their barrels changed and the heads could be left alone. A side-effect was a slight improvement of the combustion sphere, as the deep combustion chambers, together with wide valve angles, were limiting factors to the twins' performance for a long time. The new heads would not fit earlier barrels, but the earlier heads could be adapted to the new barrels. In addition, from this year the 5T adopted the 6T's cylinder block and thus also the 6T's crankcase with a mouth which would accommodate 650 barrels. The new 500 iron barrel would not fit earlier 5T cases or any pre-unit T100 or TR5 cases, which retained the previous mouth. The 5T's inlet manifold was also altered. The TR5 engine adopted the T100's 5TA-type tappet guide.

In the gearbox, for all models, the layshaft bushes, previously phosphor bronze, were now of sintered bronze to aid lubrication. The composition of the clutch shock absorber rubbers was changed, and clutch plates were modified, with the driven plates becoming solid instead of pierced, and the drive plates now with bonded-on Neolangite segments.

The cycle parts for all models saw some improvements, starting with a modified hydraulic bump stop in the front forks intended to prevent bottoming under heavy braking. At the other end, rear suspension units now fitted 100-lb rate springs with revised bleed and bump stops. In the frame's headstock, the top ball-race was changed to

the type already in use on the lower race, and lock stops became adjustable. A further side-car attachment lug was fitted at the base of the seat tube. The petrol tank now featured rubber bushes for its revised rear mounting, and fitted a chrome strip to cover its central welded seam. The TR5 adopted these changes, fitting a 3-gal welded-seam tank also available as an option for the T110. All models adopted the four-bar parcel grid to blend with this. A centre stand giving greater ground clearance was introduced, and the changeover from the underslung pilot light to the horn grille was completed by the T100 and the T110: with the light in the headlamp, at least the rider in the saddle could check with his hand if it was working. The wiring harness was now enclosed in a pvc sheath, and on the handlebars the previous threaded integral horn push was replaced by a chrome Lucas combined dip-switch/horn button on the clutch lever bracket clamp.

Finally there was a newcomer which would displace the TR5 before too long. This was the 650 TR6 Trophy, and despite the similarity of nomenclature it was a very different beast to the previous 500, being essentially a dual-purpose version of the T110, and though available in the UK, fairly clearly aimed at the wide-open spaces of the USA, where it was known, rather unfortunately, as the Trophybird! It fitted virtually the T110 engine with its Delta head and E3325 sports cams and an initial compression ratio of 8.5:1, though this was dropped to 8:1 the following year. Its primary chaincase, however, was as on the T100/TR5, since lighting was via the easily detachable dynamo, and its oil tank was the TR5 type with a safety retaining chain. Ignition as standard was by Lucas Wader magneto, with a competition mag as an optional alternative. The styling pointed the way forward into the next decade, with sports mudguards, the 3-gal petrol tank, the TR5's slim dualseat, and a separate, chromed headlamp shell. The latter incorporated a flaw, as its quickly detachable connections proved rather too ready to detach themselves spontaneously and plunge the rider into dangerous darkness! The front brake was 7 in, the rear tyre a large section 4.00 × 18, and the exhaust system siamesed and running like the TR5's above the primary chaincase on the left. With a 370-lb dry weight this was definitely the stuff to give the troops in America, where on the West Coast in 1957's prestigious Big Bear Run enduro, TR6 Trophies took no less than the first 12 places!

For **1957**, the most noticeable change to the whole range was visible on the petrol tank, with a more flamboyant era (and a burgeoning American market) recognized by the striking chrome-grille 'mouth-organ' tank badges, with the Triumph name picked out in white against a black background. Together with a chrome medial strip, this also permitted two-tone colour finishes, which Triumph more than anyone else got right, and which were echoed cleverly by mudguards in one colour with a gold-lined centre stripe in the other.

This was the year of the first unit twin, the new 350 3TA, but it also saw the T100 take the cutting edge position in the tuning stakes for the last time. As an optional extra, it was offered with a twin-carb head, made from the 650's Delta casting (and thus eliminating external drain pipes), but in this version featuring splayed inlet as well as exhaust ports, not the previous parallel inlet design. With increased diameter inlet valves, this ran with E3134 racing cams and 'R' followers, racing valve springs, bronze valve guides, and Monoblocs now easier to accommodate with the splayed inlets, on screwed-in steel adaptors locked with large nuts, and with no filters. 9:1 pistons were fitted, with the chromed second ring dropped in favour of the previous tapered version, for better oil control. As John Nelson has recorded, this 500's twin-carb head 'created an almost uncontrollable demand for a similar-ported 650 cc version from both American coasts'. Meanwhile a twin-carb T100 was tested at 105 mph.

Otherwise there was a further mass of detail changes for the pre-unit twins, which in total added up to some significant modernization and attempted problem-solving. The 5T, 6T and TR5 7-in front brakes, though their actual shoes and brakes were unchanged, fitted a patented full-width hub with cooling fins, a new slightly larger back plate, and a chrome-plated cover plate. For the T100, T110 and now the TR6, which moved up to the 8-in size brake, there was also a new drum and hub, still in the single-sided form, but with a back plate modified, like the new design, to take a front wheel spindle adapted to suit a change in the front fork ends. Previously with a plain hole on the right-hand leg and split on the left, these now changed to bolted-on split ends on both legs. For increased rigidity, the brake anchor-plate mounting brackets became induction-brazed, as did the mudguard stays. The optional valanced front mudguard was no longer available. Wheel spokes became straight and butted, and rear wheel spokes, previously a known fracture-prone item for Triumph, particularly when used for side-car work, also increased in size. From engine no. 08563, the rear suspension units changed for the last time to 110-lb springs, which gave 3 in of movement, and in an effort to curb rear end weave, the previous rubber-bushed top and bottom mounting bushes now became the rubber-bonded Metalistic type.

On the chassis, as an option, there was a new 'Easy-Lift' centre stand developed for the Police, while the regular stand fitted a longer foot peg. There were new rear chainguards, with the swinging-arm modified accordingly, giving improved shielding from greater enclosure at the rear and a deeper flange; they were now hinged on a new bracket at the front, and bolted up independently at the rear rather than as previously, using the rear suspension unit's lower clamp bolt. Bolted to the base of the seat-tube, the silencer support stays, another fracture-prone item, were now made of stronger section. The petrol tank in 3 or 4 gal was new to accommodate the new badges, and the mounting pads welded to its rear were extended sideways to the tank edge to reduce stress. Ribbed front tyres became standard for all except the 5T. The TR6 Trophy frame was adapted in response to American requests, with a new steeper steering head lug and rake angle to suit the US dirt, as well as a 6T-type malleable iron lug set halfway down the seat-tube, to permit a pipe from the single carburettor to pass through to a more substantial air filter.

In the T110/TR6 engine, oil drainage from the valve pockets in the cylinder head was improved, and the compression ratio for the Home models reduced from 8.5 to 8:1. From January the TR6 became available in the UK with the export specification of a rev counter, which was driven from a modified timing cover. The 6T's iron cylinder head also underwent minor modifications, and the 5T's camshaft was altered. A new kick-start cotter was fitted, and more significantly, to reduce the well-known oil leakage from the gearbox, new sleeve-gears with bushes to suit were fitted, with the mainshaft high gear bush now extended through the primary chaincase oil retainer plate into the chaincase itself to divert the oil into there, with the chaincase's oil retainer disc plate now of larger bore to suit. These measures were still not fully successful. The vane-type clutch shock absorber was altered again, this time with a new mix of rubber.

**1958** saw the T110's apotheosis, and appropriately enough it was the year the tide turned in the production road race battle against the Gold Stars, with overall victory for the 650 Triumph at last in the Thruxton 500-miler going to Dan Shorey and a young Mike Hailwood, after an epic struggle against Bob McIntyre on the big Royal Enfield. For this year only the T110 was offered with an optional twin-carb head. And on either version of the Delta head, the cracking problem was tackled. The combustion sphere was reduced in size, with reshaped piston crowns and smaller diameter head inlet and exhaust valves to suit, which gave more metal between the valve seat and the holding-down stud. However, as John Nelson observed, this 'really was a pity as the engines, perhaps understandably, never seemed to run quite as well afterwards', and the previous type are favourite today with classic racers.

Otherwise, as the unit 350 got into its stride, the year's main innovation for the pre-units was the Slickshift, which used gear lever movement to disengage the clutch automatically. In road tests then, great store had always been set on clutchless changes, so Turner had decided to build them in. This dubious benefit was fitted as standard, with a new oval chrome-plated inspection cap which went on all gearboxes, whether Slickshift or not, in place of the previous hexagon-headed gearbox filler plug. The older type of box had also had a carrier for the clutch outer cable cast into its shell, but with the later one there was an abutment on top of the adjuster.

The Slickshift worked by a foot-change quadrant ramp operating on a roller thrust pin fixed to the clutch operating arm. The clutch lever mechanism had been swung round so that its pivot shaft was now vertical. The roller imparted the gear pedal movement to the clutch, which necessitated a shorter clutch pushrod with a chamfered end. An over-riding action was incorporated so that the clutch could be operated in the normal way for stopping and starting. However, trying a conventional change on the move, and not knowing what to expect, could make you believe you had broken the transmission. With practice, you could startle bystanders by pushing the gear pedal gently down into first until it engaged and then, by gently letting the lever up, drive away in an impressive manner without touching the clutch lever. But most riders lacked patience with the device, and disconnected it by removing the roller thrust pin.

A more useful innovation to counter leaks from the gearbox was a sealing rubber sleeve within it, under light compression, fitted between the boss of the kick-starter and the gearbox end cover. And in the engine, all the pre-units embodied a garter-type oil seal in the drive-side crankcase half, improving crankcase breathing and preventing oil transfer between crankcase and chaincase.

Evidence of the smoother unit styling began to appear in the pre-unit range. The 8-in front brake on the sports models got a full-width hub similar to the previous year's 7-in one, but with the chromed end cover louvred for the 8-in version only. The back plate now located onto a lug on the fork leg, the brake shoes were changed, and the straight-butted front wheel spokes now became the thicker kind as fitted at the rear. The front forks on all but the TR5 and TR6 had new sliding members with more substantial brazed-on lugs, to support the new central bridge piece of a deep-section '21'-type valanced mudguard which dispensed with front stays, though the rear stays remained and as before could function as a front stand. It should be noted that, as on the unit models, this front mudguard alone had to brace the fork legs, and if it is replaced, a substantial brace between the bottom sliders has to be

provided. The TR models' front blade changed, and it fitted two loop stays. The roadster's rear mudguard too became a deep-drawn single piece item.

The pre-units' nacelles (the 5T and 6T were the same, the T100 and T110's slightly different), like the unit 350s', now incorporated separate, grommet-ringed holes for the various cables, and the clutch and front brake cables now featured knurled finger-adjusters at the handlebar ends. The oil tank filler cap was repositioned in a more upright position less likely to foul the leg when kick-starting, but was still prone to seeping oil. Unusual optional Neiman-type steering-locks were fitted in the right side of the steering head, which embodied a socket into which a complete lock body could be inserted and locked in place with its key. And in place of the previous $1\frac{3}{4}$-in ones, all models now fitted exhaust pipes of $1\frac{1}{2}$-in diameter, with for this year only new 'straight-through' teardrop-style silencers to suit. The T110's exhausts were modified with a slight bend to give an upward tilt to the silencers.

All the 500s had their crank balance factor increased to 70 per cent, but this was the last year for the 5T and TR5, the latter gazumped by the TR6, while the former's Speed Twin name would reappear the following year on the unit 500 5TA. Meanwhile the tuned 650's greater power had revealed the literal breaking-point of the three-piece crankshaft, as well as over-stressing the clutch. It was the development of the one-piece crankshaft, the availability of the twin-carb head, and a strong demand from America, that produced the supersports T120 Bonneville. The story of its development can be found in Volume 5, but here it can be said that Edward Turner's resistance to it, as well as stemming from a proper sense of a design being pushed to its limits, probably also came from his desire to have coincided the launch of the ultimate 650 with its inevitable conversion to unit construction. But in the event it would take another four years and the combined talents of Turner, Hopwood and Hele to bring that about satisfactorily, and in the meantime there would be some fine if flawed Bonnies to

*Left* Proud newcomer. The early
1959 T120 Bonneville, in
Tangerine and Pearl Grey.

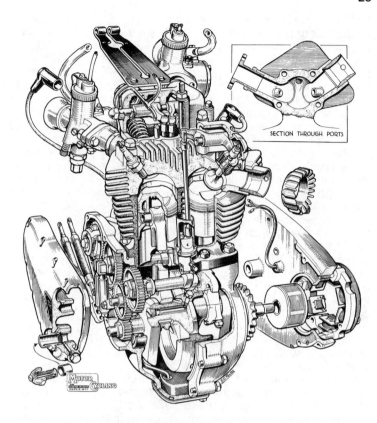

SECTION THROUGH PORTS

MOTOR CYCLING

*Right* Powerplant. T120 650
Bonneville engine, seen here in
1961 form, so with alternator.

mesmerize the speed-minded public.

Only decided on too late for the **1959** catalogue, the first T120 Bonneville 650 was an evolution rather than a new design, and showed its derivation from the T110 very clearly, for it fitted the nacelle, plain fork shrouds, the swept-back touring handlebars, full valanced mudguards and a black two-level touring-type seat with white piping. It made up for this, however, with an ultra-flamboyant finish, the petrol tank, with the 3-gal one as an option, being Pearl Grey upper and Bright Tangerine lower divided by a gold stripe, plus Pearl Grey mudguards with a Tangerine central stripe edged with gold lining, and only the frame, oil tank and battery box in sober black. Even the Yanks thought this scheme represented over-egging the pudding, and by early 1960 the colours had changed to a more characteristic Azure Blue, with Pearl Grey oil tank and battery box and a single-level sports seat with a grey stripe round its base.

The heart of the new Bonneville was the new crank, which was also fitted to the rest

of the B-range. That was how 650s (and the last pre-unit 500) were known by the makers from that year on, with the smaller unit machines making up the C-range, and the Tiger Cubs the A-range. The crankshaft was forged in one piece, with $1\frac{5}{8}$ in diameter journals. A central cast-iron flywheel was threaded over the outer crank cheek, pressed into place and centrally located by three $\frac{7}{16}$ in radial bolts, which passed through the outer periphery of the flywheel into threaded holes located in the crankshaft itself. Con rods were of H-section alloy, with the shell big-end bearings. Like the 650, the T100's version had straight-sided crank cheeks, with a $2\frac{1}{4}$ in wide flywheel (which sent the crankshaft balance factor back to 50 per cent, also as on the 650s, until the Bonnies changed in early 1962 to 71 per cent and then in mid-'62 to 85 per cent, which would remain standard on all T120s).

For this first Bonneville, E3134 inlet and E3325 exhaust camshafts, 8.5:1 compression distance and the Delta-derived twin-carb head with a pair of $1\frac{1}{16}$-in Monoblocs, unfiltered and both served by a centrally rubber-mounted remote float bowl, all went to produce 46 bhp at 6,500 rpm, four more horses than the T110. On a standard Bonnie top speeds may not have been much up on the alloy-head T110, with the average T120 being good for around a true 108 mph, and a Clubmanized one with the race kit about 115. But the joy of it was, probably thanks to the educated mixture of cams, top-end power had not been achieved at the loss of tractability or mid-range power. As easy to start and ride as ever, the T120 could still manage from 25 to 105 mph in top gear, its exhaust note was assertive without aggression in town, and it could cruise at 85 and have power on tap from low down, with very quick acceleration leading to upward changes at 50 in first, 70 in second and 88–90 mph in third. Weight until 1962 was up a little at 404 lb, and petrol consumption, in a 1960 test, down to an overall 52 mpg, but these were small prices to pay for the exhilaration of the Bonneville.

The T120 wisely came without the Slickshift in its gearbox, though the cover was in common with the other models, and the over-stressed clutch came in for some attention, with all models using a different grade of Neolangite friction material in the plates. For all the 650s, a gearbox level oil plug was fitted, and a boss added just behind the layshaft bush housing of the gearbox inner cover. At engine no. 023111 an additional gearbox adjuster was fitted. At 023941 the gearbox camplate periphery became induction-hardened, and at 024029 the same treatment began to be used on the clutch sprocket centre bore. Both these measures were responses to the stresses of US competition. The T110, TR6 and T120 now fitted an 8-pt oil tank as standard, incorporating a froth tower, with a drain tube from it discharging to atmosphere. Within the engine, the form of the piston skirts was modified for quietness and to increase the bearer surface. With the 8.5:1 alloy-head engines of the early Bonnevilles it was found that, when subjected to the heat and flat-out speeds of US competition conditions, pistons were liable to crown collapse and skirt distortion. The thickness of the piston crown was increased as far as the current dies would allow, and thickened further when the dies were replaced. And some problems with the radial bolts in the new flywheel breaking were overcome in mid-year by increasing the interference fit of the flywheel bore and the corresponding crankshaft spigot diameter by 0.0025 in.

In the cycle parts, all models were given an alteration to the angle of the front brake cam lever which improved the leverage. The

**Left** *TR6 Trophy for 1959 — in many ways a single-carb Bonnie.*

**Above right** *Alloy-engined pre-unit Tiger 100 for 1959, its last year.*

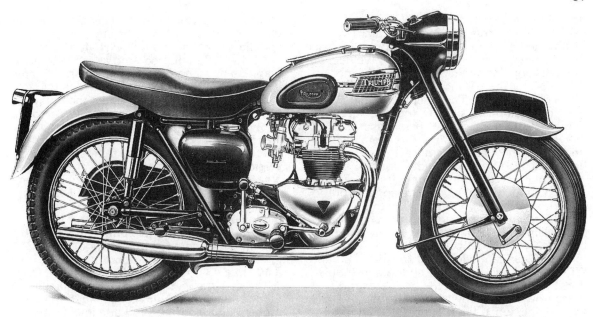

chromed covers fitted to the left side of the 8-in front full-width hubs became plain, and on the T120, from engine no. 021941, to combat a problem of the front mudguard blade cracking at that point, the guard was spot-welded to its centre mounting bridge, which was all the forks had by way of a brace. The T120 now fitted the 'Easy-Lift' centre stand. The previous year's 'straight-through' silencers were dropped in view of upcoming noise legislation, and the earlier internally baffled absorption-type, axial entry/exit, still 'teardrop' shape, were reintroduced. From engine no. 024137 a more robust Lucas regulator was fitted, and all the magneto machines could be had with optional Lucas Wader or standard instruments, with or without manual control, as well as the racing variant.

The T120 resembled the TR6 in some ways. Since its electrics were magneto ignition/dynamo lights, it fitted the latter's crankcases. The T120 also fitted ball-ended control levers, and in mid-year changed from the customary pull-backs to a straighter, though still rearward slanted, sports handlebar. The other 650s were adjusted to the T120's presence, with the T110 no longer available with the twin-carb option, and a suitably geared T110 was tested that year in *Motor Cycling*, pulling a sports side-car, which it did with greater acceleration up to 70 mph than almost any

other outfit tested. The iron-engine Thunderbird, already a side-car favourite, traded the all-gold finish it had sported for the last couple of years (countering BSA's Golden Flash?) for sober charcoal grey, and it also dropped the SU carb and adopted the T110/TR6 manifold and a Monobloc. Its alternator became a circular RM15 instrument.

These first T120s were reckoned by some to be among the very best Triumphs. One owner preferred his to the later 1961 duplex frame that he owned, observing that although the '59 frame looked identical to the TR6's, etc., 'somehow, the Bonneville got it right'. But he did allow that while the '61's seating position was more jockey-like, its ride was 'more reassuring'. For the T120's extra performance highlighted the 'whip-iron' unbraced swinging-arm frame and the high-speed wobble and weave it induced. So in typically Triumph fashion, Meriden set out to remedy matters for **1960**.

In that year, with the T100 finally replaced by a poor substitute, the unit construction T100A, all four 650s adopted a new duplex frame of brazed-lug construction, still with single top and seat tubes but now with twin front-down members. The steering-head was steepened from 64.5° to 67° to tighten the steering, and this reduced the wheelbase to $54\frac{1}{2}$ in. There was new engine plates to suit, and an extra plate to cover the gap between the down-tubes. Though the sub-frame carrying the saddle and rear mudguard was still bolted on, and nothing was done to brace the swinging-arm, there were also welded-on tubular loops on the rear frame, with one variation for the 6T and T110 and another for the TR6 and T120. These replaced the previous combined silencer/footrest support, which meant a change to the silencer clip stays; the exhaust pipe brackets were also modified. The T120's racing extras, such as rear-sets, also had to be redesigned to suit.

In conjunction with the new frame, and in a long overdue move, came redesigned front forks to reduce spring friction, with an increased volume of damping oil, and what was claimed to be internal two-way damping. The design was basically similar to that found on the C-range models, and for the T120 and TR6 carried a C-type strip bridge and tubular front stays to suit, with the bridge support boss now moved down and onto the leg centre line, while the 6T and T110 adopted the 3TA guard. There were two new types of fork crown to suit, with the 6T and T110 continuing with the U-bolt handlebar-clamp type, but on a new crown with revised clamp nuts, and the T120 and TR6 fitting new bar clamps. There was also a new steering damper plate, which located to the frame without a bolt.

The TR6 was 'export priority' that year, which virtually meant export only, and the distinction between the sports T120 and the cooking T110 and 6T was now very clearly drawn, since the latter two adopted versions of the smaller unit model's 'bath-tub' rear enclosure, while the Bonnie shed its T110's trappings. For the Bonneville was now offered with a separate chromed headlamp shell, with the easily readable speedo on a bracket behind it, rubber-gaited front forks, a two-level seat, and new sports mudguards. The Bonnie had emerged. The headlamp shell carried an ammeter, but like the TR6 the light was designed to be quickly detachable for competition, with the same dangerous pull-out connections, so the light switch was mounted below the right nose of the dualseat, in what testers found was an awkward position for the rider. One optional extra was a rev counter kit, and with the demise of the dynamo whose drive had worked the previous type, the new kit involved a complete timing cover with a rev counter drive integrally cast in it, with gears driven from the exhaust camshaft pinion

retaining nut. This proved a leak point, but one which could be cured by fitting a rocker spindle oil seal over the driveshaft holder.

As the T120 adopted auto advance for its magneto as standard, a further clean-up came about with the elimination of the dynamo from the T120, T110 and TR6. In fact the duplex downtube frame will only accept alternator (not dynamo) engines. An RM15 alternator was fitted for lighting purposes, which meant that the Bonneville and the others adopted a version of the 6T's inner primary chaincase and crankcases, with the T120/TR6 varying from the T110, and the outer cases for all varying from the 6T's. Left-hand exhaust pipes were modified to suit. In the gearbox, the T120 got its own gearbox plunger spring, and its gearing was altered by the change from a 24- to a 22-tooth engine sprocket, as well as from a 46- to a 43-tooth rear wheel sprocket. Due to the new frame, the remote float chamber for the Monoblocs was now suspended from a rubber diaphragm by a rod attached to the steel plate cylinder head steady. The object was to prevent petrol surge, but in practice this persisted, particularly with 1961's increased vibration, creating misfiring under hard acceleration. Oil tanks were redesigned, with new mountings and with the anti-froth tower removed to the rear.

The black seat with white piping on the T120 was as on the bath-tub models but bolted down not hinged, and being low set, in conjunction with fairly high footrests, gave that 'jockey-like', potentially cramped but actually suitable riding crouch, the footrests being far enough back for all but the highest speeds. The front guard was the previous TR6's; like that model, it abandoned the shapely chrome surround for the front number plate in favour of a plain plate. The '60s were coming, and though the '50s' twins may have had the edge in sweetness of line, the Bonnie — angular, purposeful with its jutting lamp, raked front downtubes and splayed ports — looked as if it was racing to meet the new decade even when it was standing still.

Destiny was less immediately inspiring for the 6T and T110, as they were lumbered with Turner's notions on enclosure, in conjunction as mentioned with the flared front mudguards, though the result was shapely enough. The 6T had its silencers revised, with a mute in the tail, and the T110 and T120 also adopted mutes. The 6T fitted the 3TA's nacelle including its chrome strips, and fork legs to

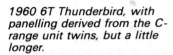

*1960 6T Thunderbird, with panelling derived from the C-range unit twins, but a little longer.*

suit, as well as an optional black and ivory two-tone colour scheme. The bath-tub panelling itself concealed an interior rear mudguard and was topped with the two-level dualseat, hinged on the left to suit; all were the same type as for the 3TA, but in different proportions, the pressings themselves being half an inch longer and with different fixing points. The two not-very-quickly-detachable panels were joined by means of bolted-together flanges at the rear of the bath-tub. On previous models these had been turned in to hide the bolts, but in an effort to improve accessibility, they were now turned outwards, and the rear number plate modified to suit.

Minus points of the panels started with a fatal lack of charisma — in Titch Allen's words, the '59/'60 Thunderbird 'had lost its masculinity'. They also made rear wheel removal a long job. In addition, despite that year's provision of four brackets beneath the bath-tub to facilitate fitting a luggage rack, the difficulty of doing this, plus the way it destroyed the looks of the rear end and made panel removal even harder, meant that luggage-carrying capacity was effectively curtailed. Within the panels these single-carb models adopted a box-shaped air filter. The wheels of both models went down to 18 in, so the T120's forks had slightly longer legs and stronger springs. The 6T's and T110's gearbox adjusting screws now faced outwards, due to the panelling. The 6T's distributor became the Type 18D2. For all the 650s the fuel tanks were now rubber-mounted at three points, and retained like a Wideline Norton by a rubber-lined, chrome-

plated strap running along the top, with badge and styling band on all but the TR6 altered to suit. The 6T/T110 oil tanks, which incorporated the froth tower changes, were further modified, being slimmer, with filler caps set to the rear, different mountings, and feed and return pipes set beyond the rear mounting lug. Centre stands on all 650s fitted a new spring and connecting link, though the latter differed for the 6T/T110, which also fitted side stands.

The new frame had marginally heavier steering and had to be put into bends a little more deliberately than its very light predecessor, but that was no bad thing, as front end lightness at speed had previously been one of the worrying handling features. The new one felt more reassuring and was still easy to ride, and due to its continuing compactness and low weight (BSA sports pre-unit twins, for instance, were some 20 lb heavier than the T120), exceptionally manoeuvreable and flickable through S-bends. One aspect where other twins surpassed it was in passenger-carrying: A10s for instance seemed to sit better on the roads with a pillion aboard, but Bonnies gave of their best solo. The Triumph still weaved when cornered hard, however, and as always both the rear end and the front fork action, despite the new design, reacted badly to bumpy corners at speed, though ground clearance was good, as was handling in the wet. The 7-in rear brake was good and could be locked up, but the 8-in front, though a good one of its kind and for its time, while working adequately at low and medium speeds, faded fast under hard usage and was not really up to 100 mph plus performance. One area where the new chassis was found to excel, however, was in damping down parallel twin vibration and providing a notably smooth ride.

So the duplex innovation appeared successful, but in a few instances, usually in US competition, the new frame's downtubes fractured immediately beneath the steering-head lug. An unfortunate fatality resulting from this (see Volume 5) led to the fault being tracked down and rectified before the following year.

**1961** therefore saw the frame strengthened by the addition of an extra tube, a lower tank rail running horizontally from the top of the duplex downtubes to a point on the top tube beneath the rear tank mounting, and thus triangulating the steering head. This effectively stopped the fractures, but cruelly had a couple of unfortunate side-effects. The first is relatively well-known, as the stiffened frame now transmitted a great deal more vibration, and while this does not seem to have been too bad for the rider, only obtruding seriously above the 4,000 rpm mark, according to John Nelson it caused fractures 'in almost epidemic proportion' of the new chromed petrol tank retaining straps, of which he says five variants of design and material had to be tried before the problem was cured. It also led to worse frothing of the Bonnie's remote float chamber and hence misfiring as already mentioned, and for 1961 the T120 simply fitted two standard Monoblocs, though the production racers knew the performance benefit of the chopped carbs and remote float set-up, and would re-install it for themselves, with the previous dodge of a brass shroud round the needle jet. A second less commonly known effect of the bracing strut is that it made it a bit more difficult to get the engine in and out of the frame, and to work on the top end.

As well as the additional frame tube, the steering-head angle altered again from 67° to 65°, where it remained until 1965, being marginally less steep to suit US cross-country competition, though without affecting high-speed road running. The gearing for all the 650s was changed again by the use of a 21-tooth engine sprocket, and in the gearboxes, Torrington needle roller bearings superseded the previous bronze bushes at either end of the layshaft. Also, gearbox adjusting screws

were now fitted on both sides of the top clamp instead of on the right only. The left side clamp, being flanked by an engine plate, proved very inaccessible. The clutch plates featured improved Langite facings again. The intention, not entirely fulfilled, was to reduce the plates' tendency to stick, especially if heavier than SAE30 oil was used in the box. A synthetic rubber O ring was fitted to prevent oil seeping past the stem of the oil pressure indicator button, a well-known leak point. The 650 alloy cylinder heads now had their cylinder fins tied with cast-in vertical buttresses linking the fins outboard of the plug positions, to counter ringing. There was also a 'flat' machined on the large diameter of the exhaust valve cast-iron seat insert, to allow a greater thickness of aluminium and hopefully help with the persistent cracking problem.

These applied to the 6T, now alloy-headed like the other three, because some shuffling of the big twin variants was taking place. This would be the T110's last year, and the Thunderbird began closely to resemble it, adopting the alloy head with its larger inlet valves and, initially, the T110's E3325 cams, though in mid-year these changed to E4220 'Dawson' cams. Both 6T and T110 gearing was lowered. The 6T fitted the others' Stellite-tipped composite pushrods in place of its previous alloy ones with pressed-on ends, and from engine no. D11193, new valve springs. Meanwhile the TR6 Trophy remained in its dual-purpose export-only form until mid-year (one was ridden by Steve McQueen in that year's ISDT), but then changed to the TR6SS sports tourer, essentially a single-carb version of the Bonneville.

Often preferred by discerning riders, it would remain in this form from then on, and as the TR7 750 almost until the end. Behind this change lay the fact that the warring East and West Coasts of the USA (see Volume 5) would no longer agree to take the same specification twin as each other, or, as the home market slumped and the US sector became the decisively dominant one, to be dictated to on the matter by Edward Turner. The results were the 1961–7 T120C (competition) and R(road) models in either East or West Coast versions; they are beyond the scope of this work which confines itself to home models, but some can be found described and illustrated in John Nelson's *Bonnie*. The 1961 T120's style meanwhile

*1961 6T Thunderbird, with the range's strengthened duplex downtube frame and alloy head.*

became a little more like the previous TR6, with a 4.00 × 18 in rear wheel and both the 3-gal petrol tank and a magneto with automatic advance as standard. (This applied to the T110 as well.) Like all the 650s, the Bonneville fitted a folding kick-start.

The 6T's compression ratio was raised to 7.5:1 (and the T110's to 8.5:1). One other benefit for the 6T was adopting the other machine's 8-in front brake, and on all models, this and the 7-in rear brake were now improved, with the shoes being made fully floating and friction strips being resited at the trailing end of the shoes. The same shoes could be retrofitted on previous brakes, and both front and rear shoes were now common on all models. Many considered this was Triumph's, and indeed the industry's, best 8-in SLS brake, and while still falling short of the 650's performance, it worked well in the wet. To further assist the T120's front end, its fork now fitted an aluminium damper sleeve between the bushes within each leg. In the electrical department, the T120/T110 RM15 alternators got different windings more suitable for use with a magneto, to reduce output and prevent battery overcharge. The ammeters became stronger, and the stop light

switches Neoprene-sealed. From frame no. D9660, the T120's tool box was modified.

A *Motor Cycle* test of a silver and sky blue '61 Bonnie was most enthusiastic, finding the brakes superb, the clutch light and strong, the power tractable, the new frame rock steady and the performance as exciting as ever. The headlight seemed a little disappointing, the suspension hard, especially at the rear, the oil filler cap liable to seep oil, and the twin carbs needing careful synchronization for slow idling, which even then was 'never wholly satisfactory'. An interesting test was also carried out on one of the new 40 bhp TR6SS models, which with dry weight down to an excellent 363 lb proved good for 105 mph maximum. Yet the bike gave 68 miles to the gallon of four-star at a 60 mph average, and a good range was further ensured by the discovery that the '3-gal tank' actually took $3\frac{1}{2}$ gal! With an aircleaner, a less hairy inlet camshaft (the E3325, like its exhaust), and on the test bike an autoadvance magneto which would be standard for 1962, this was a very flexible machine. Its silencer, still unmuted for that year, had a flat hard note under acceleration. Obviously the single-carb overcame the synchronization problem, but the Triumph twist grip with its 90° metal 'elbow' for the cable as it left the grip was found to 'make throttle delicacy just off tickover impossible to achieve', though 30 mph in top remained easy and smooth. That 'jockey-like' riding position was judged better for medium-sized riders than for the tall, who would have appreciated lower footrests. True to form, the detachable plug in the headlamp socket came loose, lights were only adequate and the horn a joke. Overall however this was a versatile all-round roadster.

**1962** was the last year of the pre-unit 650s, and while the factory brought the new unit engine up to production, the old one was adapted once again to suit US requirements, which in this case meant a wider and heavier flywheel, and hence greater flywheel inertia. The tuned pre-unit 650s were already notable for their outstanding, scrambler-like low-down grunt, and this gave them even more, as well as better 'bite' for the rear wheel when it returned to earth after jumps. For the first 1,200 or so machines, a new flywheel with a balance factor increased to 71 per cent was introduced, which, after what Hughie Hancox believes was an intermediary phase at 75 per cent, changed at engine no. D17043 to an 85 per cent balance factor, since the existing crankshaft with its straight-sided balance weight cheeks was replaced with a new crankshaft with pear-shaped cheeks.

Otherwise for the T120 and TR6, a new oil tank was fitted with rubber-bushed anti-vibration mountings. Despite the already firm rear end, the rear suspension unit springs were uprated to 145 lb/in. The speedometer became the 140 mph type, and the TR6 adopted T120 valve springs. The Bonnie had both its carburettors fed by one of its petrol taps by means of a connecting pipe between the float chambers, so that the second tap could be used to provide, for the first time, a reserve; though riders soon found that at high speeds, for best results both taps had to be kept open. The fifth and final type of petrol tank strap was fitted, and the T120's black twinseat with white piping got a grey top and lower rim trim band. The T120 and TR6SS, like the other models, adopted the RM19 alternator, featuring a larger diameter rotor with straight, unrecessed sides; for them it was modified to provide a reduced output, while the 6T's outer primary chaincase cover had to be altered to give more stator clearance.

That was not all that changed for the last pre-unit Thunderbird. It had become the last remaining Slickshift model, so when the 6T deleted it for this year, that was the end of the unpopular device. The Thunderbird still sported a full bath-tub, this year in two-tone black and silver, and both it and the TR6SS, for this year only, adopted a right side siamesed exhaust system, with the left pipe crossing just above the engine plates to join the right and flow into a revised silencer, which for the 6T was a large, resonator type designed to comply with tough German noise regulations. The T120 and TR6SS quick-release headlamp harness was dropped. The horn for all became the Lucas 8H; and though still located beneath the seat, there was a new, more fully weatherproof light switch.

That was the end of the pre-units, and while Meriden cleverly retained enough of the 650 internals and appearance in the new unit 650s to maintain historical integrity and make the changeover a relatively painless one, the bigger unit twins were indeed a different ball-game to the pre-units, and debate still goes on as to whether the advantages that came with the new twins over the years offset what was lost with the old. That is a matter which has to be decided personally, but it may be worthwhile in conclusion to consider how most of the pre-unit twins can be improved and made more reliable by the use where appropriate of later production parts, or after-market goods and conversions.

An initial word of warning is that though many Triumph parts look similar, in fact they changed frequently over the years and great care has to be taken to ensure they are actually interchangeable. 'Every time Triumph made a new bike, they changed everything', Harry Woolridge once grumbled to me, and outside the top end, and main bearings, there's little interchange between pre-unit and unit 650s. There were several exceptions—according to John Nelson, the oil pump driving block, the gear change selectors, the rockers and tappet guide blocks stayed the same from 1938 to 1983. All clutch plates are said to be interchangeable, and the clutch bearing was the same from the beginning. Despite different part numbers, the exhaust valves from a 1970 650 Bonneville would fit a 1949–62 Thunderbird as well as the 1954–7 TR6 or T110.

But much else is a maze, and the ultimate

*1962 T120 Bonneville, last of the pre-units and handsome with it.*

way out of it is to enlist the services of one of the accredited Triumph experts, who include several ex-Meriden men, especially for timing and balancing an engine. The latter can be the greatest single aid to smooth running, and for Triumphs some experts favour static balancing over the dynamic method.

Hughie Hancox and Fred Cooper are men with justified excellent reputations for work in the pre-unit field. One tip from Cooper is his preference, if performance is being pursued, of starting with genuine Triumph components rather than after-market products, and then lightening them.

The bottom end is the starting point for reliability, and though the original 'small-bearing' crankshaft gives good service if driven sensibly and if — an essential in many respects — the oil is changed regularly, a 'big-bearing' conversion for the timing side mains is a sound move, and an essential for higher revving, as is the conversion to shell-bearing big-ends. Next up is the move to a one-piece crank, either the 1959-on pre-unit one or stronger versions from later models, with their single-lipped roller main bearing on the timing side, which reputedly has a longer life, though the standard caged ball-bearing is said to give a smoother ride. Any 650 crankshaft can be used in any 650 case after suitable machining, as though of different sizes and weights, the important dimensions were the same. With any crank, one worthwhile measure is the conversion of the timing cover to take an oil seal, and Hancox and others offer this service. This is a modification whereby the bush is removed,

and a housing is turned in the bush hole to accept the oil seal/circlip assembly from the later unit 650 twins. The crank end runs in the seal and prevents oil pressure loss. A steady 80 psi is provided once the engine is hot, and without it, if the small end timing side bush is worn, pressure soon drops and the big-ends can be damaged. The modification can be carried out on all 500 and 650 pre-unit twins. A further reason for doing this is that if 'small-bearing' cranks are reground, undersize timing side bushes will be required, and these are no longer available; the conversion overcomes the need for them.

Moving up, if regular very hard riding is intended, Triumph's alloy con-rods were never the strongest, and alternative rods from Morgo or NRE (Nourish Racing Engines) can be fitted, or for racing, the ultimate (and pricey) American steel Carillo rods. Pistons can be had from Nourish also. Part of the iron barrel pre-unit twin's lightness was achieved by using a similar block for 500 and 650s, and the factory, who made their own pistons until the mid-'60s, recommended that in either case they could only be overbored to 0.040, to avoid overheating and seizure. Hepolite, however, provided replacement larger oversize pistons, so the advice does not seem to have been universally heeded. The standard pre-unit 500's 63-mm pistons had been very hard-to-come-by items in recent years, though this could change shortly. If smooth running rather than flat-out performance is the aim, original compression ratios should not be much exceeded, with 9:1 the optimum for really fast road work. Anything over 7.5:1 needs four-star petrol.

With standard Triumph pistons, or their Hepolite replacements, one of a Triumph's two most rapid-wear components were the rings, and the state of these should be checked regularly. One dodge for the 650 is the substitution of original, tougher rings from a BSA B31 single, after the grooves have been suitably opened out.

Barrels and heads came in for a lot of swapping about in the past, so it is well worth checking their dimensions. One reason for this was that the Bonneville in its time, like the RD350 LC later, used to be *the* bike to steal, and would then often be cannibalized for Tritons, racing bikes or hybrids. As well as 650 barrels on 1956-on 500 bottom ends, the most popular dodge was fitting the unit 650 barrels and nine-stud or even later 10-stud heads, both of which overcame the cracking problem, to the pre-unit bottom end. Though a 650 will not take a Triumph 750 top end, there were and are also big-bore kits to various capacities, of 680, 750 and beyond, from ARE, Morgo or NRE, as well as the Nourish NRE (originally Weslake) eight-valve heads, so check what's there if in doubt. Though café racers and Tritons (see Volume 5) are still built, originality is likely to be more desirable for pre-units today than maximum performance.

The top end is proverbially where power is developed in a Triumph, and an instant tune is the fitting of new valve springs and guides. However, if non-standard, these should be fitted by an expert, as the thickness of valve spring cups, for instance, is crucial, and mistakes like the fitting of similar-looking Trident valves and springs in a twin can be disastrous. (The same goes for fitting variations in camshafts, cam followers, cam bushes and their attendant valve timing.) For the cylinder head, due to its basic geometry, also contains the second big-wear point for Triumphs, namely the valve guides. The stems get pushed hard against the guide wall and wear it oval. The same basic geometry limitation, coupled with the oil system scavenging problems, can lead to rapid wear of the camshafts, especially the exhaust ones, so these should also always be checked. Cast-iron valve guides are considered to last longer than phosphor-bronze ones, and full ranges of long-wearing components can be supplied and fitted by specialists, notably Norman Hyde and Mick Hemmings. Still on the head, the earlier push-fit exhausts could work loose and ream out the hole, and the later screw-in exhaust stubs often loosen and wear rapidly; this can be prevented by inserting locating screws, or stripped threads can be reclaimed by some of the specialists.

The oil pump with its vulnerability to particles can be replaced by a more reliable Morgo item with increased capacity and closer tolerances, but this still follows the twin-plunger pattern, and even better is the four-plunger type introduced on the late Meriden 750 twins. The standard filter system is crude, and a car-type filter as on the Commando can be fitted to the return line, though this can lead to the pump taking aerated oil, which could possibly interfere with the scavenging, something that at high speed the Triumph pump finds a hard job. The Kirby Rowbotham system, tested in vintage racing, is said to have the answer to these problems, though some machining is involved in fitting it. A final bolt-on goodie for pre-units is a cast-alloy sump plate with magnetic drain plug from Unity. Recommended oil is monograde SEA30 in winter and SAE40 in summer, though Triumphs will also run on multi-grade 20/50.

Oil leaks were something for which Triumph twins became rather notorious. The ultimate defence against them in general, as well as careful construction, is a good engine breather system. Many choose to blank off the standard breather, a timed disc at the end of the inlet camshaft, and plumb in a new large opening, in the timing cover for example, with a suitable fitting for a large diameter hose, which is then run to the rear of the machine. However it is worth remembering that the breather system is delicately balanced; Norman Hyde once experimented with a breather in the timing side of a twin's crankcase, and wrecked the primary transmission. Otherwise several potential trouble-spots (cylinder head, tacho drive, oil pressure button, gearbox mainshaft, etc.) have already been mentioned, and in addition there were often leaks from the primary chaincase from behind the clutch, since primary chain tensioning by moving the gearbox prevented the use of an efficient seal at that point.

But the most famous ones were the pushrod tubes. Once again, the problem often stems from several similar-looking but differing seals, or from heads being interchanged without the appropriate pushrod tubes or tappet guide blocks, all three of which have to be treated as one unit. The rubbers should not be squashed, and sharp edges on the head itself should be smoothed out or they will cut these seals.

The pushrod covers themselves can also often stand some work against friction and engine noise, with any excess 'proud' material on the inside of the tubes being dressed away, especially at their top end, though the pushrods themselves should never be touched. Another measure against chatter involves the rocker arms, a source of much top-end din, where the standard Thackeray coiled washers can be replaced with machine-hardened spacers, available in steel from Unity or bronze alloy from Mick Hemmings.

In the pre-unit gearbox the kick-start quadrant and spring, as well as the gearshift selector springs and the sides of the selector forks, are the quickest parts to wear, so should be checked first. EP90 and EP80 oils should not apparently be used in the pre-'61 boxes, as they will do the bearings no good. Earlier gearboxes can be converted with advantage to the 1961-on Torrington needle rollers; despite a shorter overall length layshaft being employed on the new arrangement, the conversion needs only two additional bronze thrust washers to replace the previous two bushes and 'welch' washer. EP oils can then be used in the gearbox, but if so, the later camplate plunger should also be fitted, as it has a larger hole to allow for the change in viscosity. For the sports roadsters, later unit five-speed clusters can be persuaded into the pre-unit box with the help of some machining, but five-speed clusters are much in demand and hence in very short supply. They also have to be accompanied by a compatible selector mechanism. Further back in the transmission trail, both 500s and 650s will accept the unit duplex primary drive sprocket, exchanging a little smoothness for greater strength and longer primary chain life, though the pre-'58 drive side crankcase will have to be opened up to accommodate the sprocket.

On the electrical side, while Triumph engines can seem happiest running with the ignition timing over-advanced, this practice if persisted in will wear out the bottom end rapidly. Changing to a 12-volt system is a sound move for stronger lights. 12-volt JG conversions for magnetos can be got from Dave Lindsley, and Kirby Rowbotham

provides electronic conversions for magnetos. The latter can overcome the fact that while the standard K2F instrument provided reliable ignition, it was difficult to get an even tickover with the ignition timing correct on both cylinders. As to alternators, though all were interchangeable, note that the later two-lead stator (the earlier was a three-lead item) will not function satisfactorily on pre-Zener diode systems, as the switching which controls them requires all three leads for it to work properly. The later ('68-on) stators with resin-encapsulated coils end the problem of their vulnerable exposed predecessors, but keeping the rotor firmly attached to the end of the crank can still be a worry, which can be tackled by a Royce Creasey modification as detailed in *Classic Mechanics* during 1985. Finally, Triumphs seem to like NGK plugs, and the B-suffix ones can improve the spark from a weak magneto.

On the cycle side, as with all older machines, much of the tinware is now hard to come by, in particular cycle parts such as the three different types of nacelle and their matching fork bottom quarters, or genuine Triumph number plates, or the '59-'60 flared front mudguard for the T110/6T, this being the only one Brian Bennett does not replicate. Weak points on Triumph's original specification were wheel spokes, because of the way they were laced, exhausts, and silencer and their brackets, with the silencers cracking circumferentially just behind their mountings, so these are all further points to check. One useful after-market conversion is Hamrax's Triumph front fork oil seal conversion, which both helps oil tightness and allows seals to be replaced with a minimum of fuss.

All these tips can help ensure a more reliable machine, but what of the traditional judgement that Triumphs vibrate, leak oil and don't handle? Oil tightness may never be perfect, and in this respect the machine's worst enemy will probably have been its previous owners, but with care and the foregoing advice, matters can be improved. The vibration tag essentially came later. In this era, as a *UMG* reader brought up by a father with Tiger 100s and Thunderbirds recalled, 'Triumphs were supposed to be smoother than others', and before outputs climbed past the 40 bhp mark, very often were, being helped by factors like the early selective assembly of timing gears, the pre-'53 engine shaft shock absorber, and by build quality generally. Pre-units were certainly generally smoother than unit bikes, though there were exceptions: with the early T110s, as mentioned, the ride could be harsh, and interestingly a recent *Classic Bike* comparison test of a '61 and a '70 TR6 found the chunky, scrambler-type power delivery of the pre-unit, even before the heavier '62 flywheels, carried a slight penalty in terms of more noticeable low frequency vibration than the unit bike, though the latter's high frequency shakes were worse.

Of the handling, opinions have to be subjective to some extent, and at the time were definitely sectarian. Regular readers will know that the author grew up riding Norton twins, and Triumphs were automatically dismissed, probably unjustly, as beyond the pale in the handling department. An interesting comparison ride between a Dominator 99, an A10 and a '61 T110 recently appeared in *Classic Motor Cycle*. Journalist Tim Holmes found that after the A10, the Triumph 'felt as though it needed a very steady hand' and would be 'quite glad to see you off ... decidedly skittish. A good road-holder still, but nervous and twitchy.' Light and lithe, 'you can just flick the front end around ... but it seems also that the front end can flick you around', though he found that the engine was punchier than the BSA, revving out very willingly. All that summarizes my own view of the Triumph twins I have ridden so far.

Yet the following year in his own *BBM* magazine Holmes was testing a 1962 T120 recently restored by Hughie Hancox, a model with the same frame and almost identical forks as the '61, and found it steered well, held its line, didn't wobble and could even be braked when cranked over. The difference in point of view was not necessarily journalistic licence, but probably accurately reflected the high standard of Hancox' work, which I have not yet been lucky enough to sample. As Tim wrote, 'With one as well restored as this you get a picture of how the original was—everything, throttle, clutch, gearbox—working together so smoothly.' In a longer-term view, an owner told *Classic Bike* that he ran a 1959 Thunderbird for 12 years, and found it handled acceptably if he replaced the front fork bushes at regular intervals and adjusted the swinging-arm end float to the bare minimum. Attention and if necessary refurbishment of that awkward-to-

maintain swinging-arm does seem to be an important factor. For the rest, the popularity of the '50s' Triumphs showed that there was nothing fundamentally at fault with these versatile motor cycles, and an example 'put together properly' can make a desirable and a practical roadster today.

## Triumph: The pre-unit twins — production dates and specifications

### Production dates (post-war)
3T — 1946-51
5T Speed Twin — 1946-58
T100 Tiger 100 — 1946-59
TR5 Trophy — 1949-58
T100C Tiger — 1949-58
6T Thunderbird — 1950-62
T110 Tiger 110 — 1954-61
TR6 Trophy — 1956-62
T120 Bonneville - 1959-62

### Specifications
**3T**
Capacity, bore and stroke — 349 cc
(55 × 73.4 mm)
Type — ohv twin
Ignition — Magneto
Weight — (1950) 325 lb

**5T Speed twin, T100, T100C, TR5 Trophy**
Capacity, bore and stroke — 498 cc
(63 × 80 mm)
Type — ohv twin
Ignition — 5T (1946-52) Magneto, (1953-58) Coil; rest Magneto
Weight — 5T (1950) 365 lb, (1955) 380 lb; T100 (1950) 365 lb, (1954) 375 lb, (1958) 385 lb; TR5 (1950) 295 lb, (1955) 365 lb

**6T Thunderbird, T110, TR6, T120 Bonneville**
Capacity, bore and stroke — 649 cc
(71 × 82 mm)
Type — ohv twin
Ignition — 6T (1950-53) Magneto, (1954-62) Coil; T110 (1954-59) Magneto, (1960-61) Coil; TR6 (1956-59) Magneto, (1960-61) Coil; T120, Magneto
Weight — 6T (1950) 370 lb, (1959) 395 lb; T110 (1955) 395 lb; T120 (1959) 404 lb

## Triumph: The unit 350 and 500 twins – The Twenty-One/3TA, 5TA Speed Twin, T100A Tiger, T100SS Tiger, T90 Tiger 90, T100 Tiger, T100T Daytona Super Sports, T100S Tiger, T100R Daytona, T100C Trophy 500, TR5T Adventurer Trophy Trail

The 1957 348 cc Trumph Twenty-One, though of small capacity, was a highly significant model. It introduced the one-piece crankshaft and the use of Triumph-style unit engine construction. It also, with its 'bath-tub' styling, initiated and encouraged the trend to enclosure for British four-stroke motor cycles over the following five or six years. Not for nothing was it billed as 'The Machine with a Wheel in Tomorrow!'.

The background to the Twenty-one will be found in Volume 5. It only became known as the 3TA for 1959. 'Twenty-one' in 1957 signified the 21st anniversary of the Triumph Engineering Co., and in America, 21 'cubes' (cu in) equalled 350 cc. In the expansive United States, a 350 rather than a 250 motor cycle was then thought of as a suitable size for a learner. The capacity therefore sold well,

and in the process encouraged the novice in brand loyalty to Triumph when he bought a bigger bike.

That was one attraction which the 350 capacity held for Edward Turner. But at a time when the performance of American-tuned sports T110Ss were stretching his original twin design to breaking point and he could be heard asking somewhat desperately, 'What more do they want?', the little 350 represented a return to another, sane, admirable side of his design work, already indicated by his 3TU prototype machine (see Volume 5 again). This was a desire to provide reliable and affordable practical transport for as wide a range of riders as possible, and in the process to keep them as dry, quiet, clean and tidy as he could. 'The bath-tub was done', as Jack Wickes put it, 'with a view to making a device you could hose down.' But the two aspirations, appeal to young learners and to the sensible, would prove incompatible, with both American and British youth dumping the enclosure as quickly as possible.

With better materials, some design improvements and some weight loss, the new

A 'Twenty-one' 350 for 1958, with matching legshields and windscreen.

18.5 bhp 350 offered 80 mph performance, not too far from that of the original Speed Twin. It combined this with excellent mpg figures, still a serious consideration in the year after Suez, returning at least 75 to the gallon overall, and never dropping below 60, however hard it was thrashed. There may have been some cost-cutting in the design, but this achieved the aim of a competitive price, with a 1959 3TA at £228 being £3 cheaper than a 350 Matchless G3L single, while being for most riders by then a far more desirable machine. In service, the unit machine also proved an exceptionally reliable and tough engine, as emphasized by the expansion with very little change a couple of years later to the 500 capacity. Together with the fact that they shared a common 65.5 mm stroke, today this means good spares availability for both. That unit 500 then became the subject of Doug Hele's wizardry and was the basis of a highly successful road racer — 'Basically a 5TA, which made it pretty amazing', as Harry Woolridge put it — and of the quick, hot Daytona twin-carb roadsters. From 1967 on, handling at speed passed from the barely acceptable to the more than respectable and the T100s with their surviving 350 cousin, the T90, became excellent all-round sports motor cycles, joined at the end in 1973 by a dual-purpose 500 trail bike, the TR5T Adventurer, which briefly revived memories of the original, versatile TR5 Trophy.

This change from the mundane to the desirable is not, however, the only Jekyll and Hyde aspect to the smaller unit twin range. For in contrast with the happy memories of the people who rode them at the time and those who were originally responsible for looking after them, a very second-hand smaller unit twin Triumph represents a step on the biking ladder that many riders would prefer to forget — oily, dodgy handling for a pre-'67 machine (and even for a later one if the swinging-arm was on the way to seizing, as they were prone to do), almost always already butchered mechanically by their several previous owners, and with a punishing schedule of often awkward maintenance. Finally, despite an engine that would keep running when it was knackered, the electrics on a pre-'68 machine could still side-line a rider with sickening regularity. As a *Used Motorcycle Guide* reader put it in 1988, a 3TA could only be recommended to 'to anyone

with a sense of humour'.

In this instance I singularly lacked it, during the brief period in the '70s when I owned a pristine, one-owner, low-mileage 1959 Twenty-One. It was principally the nervous, uncertain feeling to the handling which I hated, and which seemed a feature of the design, since the bike had been ridden mildly and very well looked after — but perhaps this ignored the fact that it was about 15 years old and had covered a bit more than the 20,000 miles at which the factory recommended that the swinging-arm spindle be renewed, which it hadn't been. The small twin also seemed distinctly undergunned, but then I had just stepped off a 650. I got rid of the 3TA as soon as I could to a Triumph fan, actor and playwright Paul Copley, who was well satisfied with the bike and indeed put it on stage as part of an excellent play he wrote called *Pillion*!

My own first motor cycle had been the other British 350 unit twin, Norton's Navigator, so I knew just how suitable the capacity was for a learner, and how much lighter, smoother and more responsive than the 350 AJS single which had provided my only motor cycle experience before that. But in 1957 the appearance of the Navigator was still four years away, and if its handling was a long way better than the 3TA, its reliability was definitely not. The public voted with their cheque-books in showing which 350 was the clear favourite, just as they would do when comparing the T100 with the other British unit 500 twin, BSA's vibratory and uninspiring A50.

It was probably the smaller unit Triumphs' intentional lack of pretension which contributed to their frequent dereliction. Plenty were built, and with the popularity of the 350 and latterly 500 class on the wane during their lifetime, they were never, with the partial exception of the Daytona, perceived as Classic classics, and so have been available cheaply for novices and butchers. Their basic toughness was never in question: they rarely let you down on the road, and it took really relentless sustained hammering to make them throw a rod. But as world traveller Ted Simon said of his 1973 T100P, 'They thrive on attention, like certain people, and repay you for it', and he found that his Triumph's ultimate message to him was 'I'll get you there — but don't rely on it'. Within those limitations, the C-range are still practical machines to be reckoned with.

All this was far in the future early in **1957** when the Twenty-One was launched, 'A new twin with unit construction of engine and gearbox and extensive rear panelling'. Unit construction was familiar from the majority of foreign motor cycles, and conferred compactness, a more modern look, some loss of weight, and lower manufacturing costs, particularly in conjunction with the Lucas RM 13/15 alternator which provided the Twenty-One's electrics. But in the engine, the gearbox, primary chaincase and the engine itself remained separate entities, not sharing their oil as with modern true unit construction. But the sprocket centres at each end of the primary drive were fixed, and all three entities blended together in appearance, with slotted filler caps for chaincase and gearbox oil screwed into the top of the engine casing.

The overall layout of the engine was much as before, with gear-driven camshafts fore and aft of the iron cylinder and alloy head, and with a longitudinally split crankcase. But on the left-hand side of the latter, the crankcase became integral with the inner half of the primary chaincase, and then extended rearwards laterally to cover the gearbox sprocket. Within the cover, access to the sprocket was via a circular plate fastened by six bolts, with an oil seal in its centre. On the right, the shapely form of the timing side cover, with its triangular plate, was still very recognizably Triumph. The crankcase half was cast as one with the gearbox shell, but the shape of the latter was also still clearly discernible from the outside. Covers on both sides were retained by what were then up-to-date Philips cross-head screws.

The four-speed gearbox internal layout differed from the normal Triumph in that the layshaft, running on bronze bushes, was positioned to the rear of the mainshaft rather than below it. This was compact and meant that the gear cluster could be removed or refitted as a single unit without disturbing the adjustment of the gear-change or selector mechanisms, though the clutch had to come off first. At the base of the box was a combined oil drain and oil level plug, one concentric with the other, so that unscrewing the inner bolt told you if there was enough oil within, while unfastening the outer bolt, and hence the whole assembly, drained the box. This fiddly and messy arrangement would also appear on BSA's unit singles, and remain with Triumph 750 twins until the end.

Within the engine the solid heart was the crankshaft, the forged one-piece type with built-in sludge trap and three radial bolts securing a light version of the flywheel, which would not be adopted by the pre-unit machines until 1959. The crankshaft assembly was pressure-fed with lubricating oil on the right side via the timing side plain main bearing bush, with its deep central oil feed groove distributing the oil through matching holes in the crankshaft plain journal diameter to the big-ends. The crankshaft was splined at its left-hand end for the alternator, so there was no engine shaft shock absorber, just the clutch cush-drive. The driveside main bearing was a ball race. Big-end shells as on the previous year's pre-units were fitted, but the con rods showed evidence of cost-cutting, being steel stampings with small end bushes.

On the iron barrels, even the base flange was finned, and they were painted silver to give the illusion of an all-alloy engine like their companion pre-unit 500; but iron they would remain, with the exception of a few works special scramblers. In the alloy head, with integral cooling slots as on the pre-unit's delta head, the separate rocker boxes were redesigned with the famously detachable screw-on slotted inspection caps, plus new exhaust and inlet valves, the latter being larger, and set at a modest 80° angle. Steel inserts screwed in the exhaust ports, sleeve mounts for the $1\frac{1}{2}$-in exhaust pipes. The engine's lubrication was by the familiar, and still vulnerable, double plunger pump, but with the plungers reversed so that the scavenge was now on the left. Lubrication of the rocker gear was helped by an external pipe taken from the scavenge return line, and the familiar oil pressure indicator button was fitted to the front of the crankcase, ahead of the timing chest. Compression was 7.5:1, and a single Type 375 Amal Monobloc carburettor was fitted, at this stage with no air slide.

The primary chaincase was newly designed and compact, just 8 in wide and $6\frac{1}{2}$ in deep. Within it the short primary chain wheel and chain were now duplex, and featured no arrangements for tensioning the chain yet. In another economy, the clutch drum and sprocket were not forged, but of cast iron. The clutch ran on rollers and there was a new design clutch pressure plate, with a central adjusting screw and lock nut, and with adjustment possible via a slotted inspection

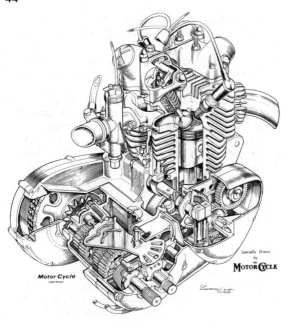

*Motor Cycle*
COPYRIGHT

Specially Drawn
by
MOTOR CYCLE

*The 'Twenty-one' 350 unit engine anatomized.*

cover in the outside of the primary chaincase. There were five steel driven plates, and the four driving plates were located by internal grooves.

The 6-volt electrics had the alternator stator mounted on studs in the crankcase. Ignition was by coil, with a Lucas car-type distributor in a protective rubber sheath mounted upright, unlike the pre-units' less accessible horizontal position, behind the right cylinder. The distributor was skew-driven from the inlet camshaft. A combined ignition and light switch was mounted in the nacelle and featured an emergency start position, and the headlamp was one item that had not been skimped, being a prominent full 7 in, and contributing to the sense of a full-size motor cycle.

The chassis was admitted to be derived from the Tiger Cub, which was not encouraging. Like the other twins at that stage, it was a single downtube frame with a bolted-on rear frame, with the swinging-arm pivoting unsupported from a lug attached to the base of the saddle tube, and controlled by three-position Girling units. Where it most resembled the Cub was in featuring a dropped tank rail which at its front end bent upwards to run parallel with the front downtube, making the petrol tank a partially stressed

member. But unlike the Cub, the rail was then raised into a heavy 'swan-neck' steering head lug, which gave a steeper steering head angle of $66\frac{1}{4}°$, as well as being underbraced. Another innovation was that in place of conventional footrests bolted to additional brackets (or on the left for the pre-units, to the primary chaincase), the 3TAs' rests screwed into lugs in an H-shaped bridge piece at the base of the seat tube. The footrest introduced for the 350 was used on all the smaller unit twins until the end, taking the same 1938-on footrest rubber which was found on all but the TR5 Trophy and the o.i.f. twins.

The front forks introduced the two-way damped type which would be adapted for the larger pre-unit and unit twins. Giving a claimed $4\frac{3}{4}$ in of movement, they were a definite improvement on previous Triumph forks. One drawback was that, as with the bath-tub pre-units, the new 'fireman's helmet' front mudguard, generously flared at the rear, and with ribbed edges, was the sole bracing member between the fork legs. This meant that not only did the legs have to be additionally braced if the guard was changed, but that as we shall see, the standard mudguard was subject to strong stress.

In the quest for a low, rider-friendly profile, wheels and tyres were $17 \times 3.25$ in front and rear, with the front one's spindle carried in split end-clamps. Seat height was just $28\frac{1}{2}$ in, though the rider felt somewhat perched on the machine rather than part of it. Brakes were 7·in front and rear, in a full-width front hub and a single-sided rear one.

The Twenty-One's styling was its single most striking feature, however. The front mudguard mounting, swept-back handlebars and nacelle established continuity with previous Triumphs, as did the Shell Blue Sheen finish — though originaly catalogued in Silver Grey, the 3TA went out in the familiar blue, and only adopted two-tone colours in its last year. In fact, the nacelle was a little different from previous ones, featuring separate grommeted holes for the cables where previously they had risked a distorted run by passing through the handlebar grommets. The petrol tank, with parcel grid and the new-for-'57 grille-type badges, also looked similar to previous ones, though in fact was different; at $3\frac{1}{2}$ gal it gave a good range. But it was the flared front mudguard's companion at the rear which was the real departure — the 'bath-tub' (so called because of its resemblance in profile to an inverted tin hip-bath).

Beneath a twinseat hinged on the left, the enclosure consisted of two 22g panels with ribbed edges, with one panel on each side of the machine. There was a rubber beading strip between their junction, and their flanges at the rear were bolted together, with the flanges themselves turned in to hide the join. The panels were decorated at the front on each side with a chromed 'Twenty-One' metal name badge, in what Meriden wags called 'toothpaste' script. Removing one of the panels, for instance the left one to clean the box-type air filter, involved taking the seat off its hinges, undoing a screw at the front, the upper pillion footrest nut, two screws in the top rear frame tube and a further fixing bolt and nut, as well as disconnecting the rear lamp wires. The right panel did not have to come off to drain the oil, however, as until 1959 the drain plug was in the end of a short tube welded to the 5-pt tank's lower rear corner, and thus accessible.

Raising the hinged seat gave access to the coil, rectifier, battery and oil tank cap. This access was supposed to encourage regular battery maintenance ('Enclosed, yet More Accessible than Ever'), but in practice side-panel battery access is always better, since the length of leads means that an under-seat battery has to be disconnected and lifted out every time you want to have a look at it, and this chore would remain on the unit Triumphs for some time. Also underneath the seat, which came with a support to prop it open, on top of the steel rear mudguard which was out of sight beneath the panels, was a car-style moulded rubber tool tray. This was not universally popular. Theft was not such a concern in those days, and though the seat was not lockable, the seat catch could be removed to provide a measure of security; but the tray tied a rider to the factory tool set, and emphasized the paradox of increased enclosed area but less actual storage space. The tray would be discontinued after 1960.

The Twenty-One was well received, and a genuinely popular model among its intended market of everyday commuters and tourists. It offered reasonably brisk acceleration of 0–60 in about 18 sec, and still in third gear, though from there to its top speed of 82 mph took another 30 sec. But though lacking the bigger twins' low-down torque, it was brisk enough

for most riders' requirements, comparing favourably with most 500s on the road then. It was also acceptably smooth, with vibration never acute enough to inhibit performance and only noticeable in a period from around 55–60 mph.

Due to thorough development, initial service problems were few. There were some instances of oil leaking from the cylinder flange, but this was traced to the fixing studs and cured by the use of Hermetite. The early chaincase was prone to leak oil, and within it the duplex chain, lacking attention, could bang on the casings; Meriden's Service department replaced chains with plenty of life in them because of this omission. The clutch could be less than perfect, prone to dragging and slipping, noisy if there was any wear in the plate gears or if the centre's rollers were worn, and the centre nut sometimes came undone. It should be torqued down to 50 lb/ft. The gearbox was subject to leaks along the gear pedal spindle, and to selector problems, with a tendency to jump out of third gear due to an overstressed selector cam plate, but a stronger later (1971) component is available today and a further improvement will be detailed later. The tappet adjustment was minimal and awkward to achieve accurately, with valve clearances of just 0·010.

On the cycle side, stresses on the petrol tank could cause splits, and the same was true of the big front mudguard. 'They often used to split,' recalled Service man John Nelson, 'and we replaced them, free of charge. One chap had 14, and although we never found out why, it convinced the engineering department that they had to alter the design. They changed the centre fixing to a rubber-mounted type of stirrup, which cured it.' But that would not take place until 1964!

The frame's handling 'felt decidedly odd', as *Classic Bike*'s Peter Watson, who owned a 1964 model, put it: 'till you mastered the cornering technique required', which was getting all gear changing and braking done before a turn, and always powering round, since if you lost your nerve and shut off the bike ran wide, and if the brakes were applied in a fast corner the machine could leap across the road in a heart-stopping manner. But most found the handling acceptable in everyday riding, with the rear end, not aided by the extra weight of the bath-tub, being the first to protest with a slight warning wallow if pushed hard, and the brakes very adequate to the performance. And the engines could go on and on – Watson quotes an owner of a 1959 ex-Police 350 with 215,000 miles on the clock, and still on its original bottom end.

**1958** brought only detail changes for the Twenty-One, with an optional prop stand plus a redesigned centre stand with a small pedal extension. Under the bath-tub there was now a drilled lug on each side of the sub-frame and in the rear suspension unit's upper mounting gussets, to assist in fitting a luggage rack, though drilling the fairings themselves was left up to the owner.

**1959** saw the 3TA joined by the 490 cc 5TA Speed Twin, with continuity emphasized once again by a finish in traditional Amaranth Red. With the same fairing, it was very much a bored-out 350, the bigger, over-square engine giving 27 bhp at 6,500 rpm. The main internal difference was the use of the customary H-section forged alloy con rods in place of the 3TA's steel stampings. Overall gearing was raised with the use of a 20-tooth gearbox sprocket as opposed to the 350's 18-tooth, and a slightly larger bore 376 Monobloc carb was fitted, along with a 3.50 × 17 in rear tyre. At 350 lb dry, the 5TA proved a pleasant enough all-rounder in the 3TA mould, with a top speed of nearly 90 mph and, when new, capable of cruising 'two-up at 70 mph all day, and returning around 70 mpg overall. If increased output made it marginally less long-lived than the 350, once again vibration was at an acceptable level.

Carburettors by now incorporated a sprung plunger cold-start device, though riders again complained that they needed double-jointed hands to use it from the saddle. For that year, both models had their box air filter fitting revised. Previously it had been by nut and bolt, but now the use of a welded-on stud at the base of the filter, passing through a lug on the seat tube, meant that if the battery was removed, the filter could be extracted without having to take off the left-hand bath-tub panel. The oil tank filter's oil pipe union was extended to bring the feed pipe connection lower down for ease of access under the panelling. However, the tank itself, which had previously been unsupported underneath, was redesigned with a base mounting via a bolt which crossed the machine, and this meant that the previous accessible extended drain plug was now deleted.

On the engine, cylinder head finning for both models was revised, and the 3TA's inlet manifold enlarged. In the gearbox, in an unsuccessful attempt to cure the selector problems, the plunger which moved the camplate around was redesigned, and to tackle the oil leak there, an O-ring was added to the gear pedal spindle. The 3TA's exhaust pipes were altered to the 5TA's new type. As on the other models, a different grade of Neolangite was fitted in the clutch friction plates, the front brake's cam lever was revised to give improved leverage, and the chromed covers fitted to the left side of the full-width front hub lost their louvres and became plain.

**1960**, with the demise of the pre-unit T100, brought the first performance unit twin, though it was a slightly bizarre début. The T100A Tiger ran at 9·0:1 compression, had E3325-form camshafts, though with the 3TA's followers, and gave a claimed 32 bhp at 7,000 rpm. It featured Energy Transfer ignition so that it could be quickly converted for running without battery or lights for competition – yet it was offered with the necelle and full bath-tub fairing. 'The T100A retaining the 3TA's styling was strange,' wrote Harry Woolridge. Was this Turner's determination to pursue his unpopular idea, or the need to use up components in the knowledge that, for export models, the bath-tub would start to be phased out the following year? But the contradiction represented by an enclosed sports model was unfortunate, and it was of this model that Mike 'Café Racers' Clay relays the cruel epithet that 'It looked as if it was standing still when it was doing 100' – though the mid-90s was the T100A's actual top speed. Many were cannibalized, with their engines going into scramblers.

As a practical sports roadster the big drawback with a T100A was not the black panelling, with white that year for the lower half of the tank only, but the ET ignition. In this system, the Lucas 18D2 distributor and RM13/15 alternator were retained, and a separate, normal AC circuit for battery charging and lights was provided. However, the alternator stator had five leads, and the rotor was not keyed to the crankshaft but driven by a dowel on the face of the engine sprocket, engaging with either one of two sockets arranged 125° apart on the inboard face of the rotor. A socket 'S' was for road use, the 'R' one for racing. Two of the alternator coils

*A 1960 T100A 'sports' 500, but with full bath-tub—a confused machine.*

were linked directly with the energy transfer ignition coil. The intention of this system was to ensure that for ignition a 'timed' generator pulse created a maximum electrical energy pulse when the distributor contact breaker points opened to start the engine. In practice this system was far too dependent on precise ignition timing, which distributor electrics (see p. 19) had difficulty in providing, and usually resulted in an engine that would either start from cold, or start and run when hot, but not both. Though Triumph's competition department had found a better compromise setting than their BSA rivals, for T100A riders hot-starting was a problem. It was an impractical system for road use, and was soon dropped.

Within its iron barrels, which reverted to a black finish, the T100A's internals were not polished, and it was otherwise all 5TA, but the sports machine's silencers were packed with glass wool with a Triumph mute in the tail which could be detached for racing, while the 3TA/5TAs, in keeping with their civilized aspirations, had baffles and a resonance chamber. For all the small machines, the Triumph splined q.d. rear wheel became available as an option. Within the engine

there was thought for the extra stress which the T100A's performance would place on the timing side main bearing bush. Its housing, previously retained by a peg and cut-out in the housing flange, changed to a housing located by a plate, with a screw fitting in a slot in the timing gear case side. Though it was not much of a problem for road use, even after this the heat of competition could still cause the bush to turn in the cases and cut off oil to the big-ends. For all the C-range, the bath-tubs were modified at the rear, where the bolted-together flanges, previously turned in to hide the bolt, were now turned outwards for ease of access, and the rear number plate modified accordingly. An O-ring seal went on the shaft of the oil pressure indicator button, another leak point both before and after this. A new steering damper knob and damper plate which located to the frame without a bolt were fitted.

Finally, for both 500 machines, in the clutch there was now a fifth driving and sixth driven plate, and this meant a deeper clutch sprocket and housing, clutch centre, longer springs, spring cups and clutch operating rod, as well as a primary chaincase with more clearance and mountings to suit, plus a revised left-hand exhaust pipe retaining bracket. Billed for all the C-range, but in fact not adopted by the 3TA until the following year, the 500's primary chaincases also now fitted a long-overdue chain tensioner. This was a flat spring blade with synthetic rubber facing, in contact with the lower runs of the chain. Adjustment was via a horizontal internally threaded sleeve running upwards at an angle from the bottom rear of the primary chaincase and engaging with a screwed rod, so that turning the rod with a screwdriver tightened the sleeve and, inside the case, bowed the tensioner blade upwards. The trouble was that the access plug to the adjuster doubled as the chaincase oil drain, so that every time you used it the oil had to be messily drained out and renewed; and fairly frequent, accurate tensioning was a necessity, or in the restricted interior of the case, the chain would still rub against the bottom of the inner, while if neglected for too long the tensioner would fragment and foul the chain and alternator. A further drawback was that if the thread into the chaincase became worn, it caused a leak that dropped oil just in front of the rear wheel. The tensioner was to be an unsatisfactory feature from then on.

**1961** saw the T100A modified into a more conventional as well as more powerful sports roadster, wth the Energy Transfer system dropped for it in mid-year at engine no. H22430. The reason was the existence of purpose-built competition models in the shape of the export-only unpanelled TR5AC and TR5AR 500 models. These retained an ET system which at the beginning of the model year had had its alternator and ignition coil matched more closely, with the distributor now operated over a 10° auto advance range for the T100A, and condenser capacity increased. When the change came, the T100A now fitted the 5TA's nacelle with the ignition switch changed from the Lucas 41SA to the 5TA's PRS8, with an emergency start position, though both incorporated switching circuits connected to the alternator's windings, hopefully to provide 'switch control' of the output. With regular coil ignition, the T100A's distributor's auto advance range went back to 15°.

The sports engine's output was boosted to a claimed 34 bhp by an increase in its 376 carburettor's bore size from the 5TA's $\frac{7}{8}$ in to 1 in, and by the adoption of E3134-form camshafts for both inlet and exhaust, which

must have made for a hairy monster. Perhaps in response to these stresses, from engine no. H18641 the gearbox of all the T100A and other sports 500s replaced the 5TA/3TAs' bronze bushes for the left end of the layshaft with needle rollers. Both the T100A and 5TA also had their gearing slightly lowered by a 19-tooth gear sprocket. For the 3TA, the lever and screw on the clutch's quick thread mechanism were modified. Finally the brakes on all models were improved by introducing a self-servo effect to let the shoes float, then moving the friction strips around towards the trailing end of the shoes. The floating effect was achieved by the ends of the shoes which were remote from the cam being made so that they slid off the fulcrum pin, instead of being hollowed to pivot on it. The new shoes could be used on previous models' brakeplates, but not vice versa. Testers noted a marked improvement. There was also new friction material in the clutch plates.

For the whole C-range, the frame too changed, featuring a steering head angle steepend by 2° for better cross-country performance without adversely affecting the handling on the road. On competition versions for America, where they had found out the hard way what punishing use did to the 'swan-neck' steering head lug, to the frame's single upper rail and to the stressed petrol tank, an additional frame stiffening strut, an upper version of what was being done on the 650's frame, was bolted into place under the fuel tank to triangulate the frame's upper section. Rather stingily, this would not be applied to the roadsters until 1965, but since it was bolted on, can be retrofitted with advantage to '61–'64 machines. The new front frame also allowed adjustment to the fork steering-lock stops. The rear silencer support was modified. For the 3TA and 5TA, the styling band around the petrol tank became optional. The unpopular underseat tool tray was replaced by a conventional tool roll, though stuffing the roll into place could have its problems. In mid-year, for the T100A and 5TA, the air filter box was altered to accept a renewable element. And folding kick-starts became standard for all.

**1962** saw the situation on the fast roadster rationalized, with the end of the T100A and the arrival of the T100SS ('Sports Specification'), which introduced new abbreviated 'bikini' or 'skirt' side-panels, as

*1962 T100SS, the first proper sports model in the C-range.*

well as a separate 7-in chromed headlamp shell. This contained the ammeter, with the speedometer now being mounted on a separate bracket. The new model's finish was striking, a pretty two-tone Kingfisher Blue and Silver Sheen, with a light-coloured top and edging strip for the dualseat. 'The T100SS', judged Harry Woolridge, 'was the first true sports unit machine, it put the C-range on the map.' Works prototype versions of the bike had taken three Golds in the 1961 ISDT, and rocker Mike Clay recalled how, unlike the unit 650, the handsome T100SS impressed café society as making a better-looking 500 than the pre-unit, by emphasizing the machine's smoothness and compactness.

The skirt rear fairing in this year's version ran from the rear of the gearbox to the top of the rear suspension units, covering the area beneath the seat and the round, felt-element air cleaner, with a conventional sports rear mudguard taking over the shielding duties at the back. Beneath the seat the oil tank fitted a quick-release cap, and an anti-froth tower was added to its top rear corner. In the left skirt panel was set a combined light and ignition switch. At the front there was also a sports mudguard, but now for the T100SS with the T120-style rubber gaiters, and the guard carried a suitably plain front number plate without the traditional ornate surround. Wheel sizes increased to $19 \times 3.25$ front and $18 \times 4.00$ rear. The sporting look was emphasized by the siamesed exhausts fitted to all the twins except the T120, with the single silencer on the right being a new pattern, with the inlet pipe coaxial with the silencer

barrel rather than offset as previously. The handlebars, unusually for Triumph, were the curly-shaped, conventional $\frac{7}{8}$ in diameter type as found on the other US competition models, with Amal twistgrips and a bar-mounted choke lever. For the T100SS and the whole range of twins, there was a new method of attaching the clutch cable at the gearbox end, with a short arm to take the nipple projecting upwards from the gearbox protected by a rubber shield; the gearbox end cover now no longer had to come off to change a cable.

Inside the T100SS engine the camshafts became the successful mix of form found on some 650s, still with a race E3134 form for the inlet, but with the sports E3325 form for the exhaust. Claimed power output was still an impressive 34 bhp at 7,000 rpm. Electrics, as for the whole C-range, were via Lucas' new RM19 alternator.

The T100SS had been tested by *Motor Cycling* late in 1961. They found it tractable, with a near flat torque curve, and scorching acceleration through the gears. They liked the gearbox ratios and action but found that riders with small feet had to take their foot off the rest to reach the gear pedals, a complaint that would remain for the C-range. The kinked handlebars were sloped slightly downwards, and this threw some weight on the wrists over distance, but otherwise the ride was comfortable. The brakes were a little prone to fade at speed, the underseat tool roll to split and threaten the underseat wiring. Other than remarking that it could cope with rough roads, there was significant silence on

**Left** *1963, and a genuine sports 350 again, the nice-looking Tiger 90 with abbreviated 'skirts'.*

**Right** *A fuller view of the 1963 Tiger 90.*

the subject of how what was essentially the 3TA chassis coped with a machine over 15 mph quicker, for the test bike achieved a best speed of 98 mph.

**1963** brought a companion for the T100SS in the shape of the T90 Tiger 90, a similarly styled and tuned 350 which raised the 3TA's modest 18.5 bhp output to a rather striking 27 bhp at 7,500 rpm. This was a first instance of the free-revving C-range breaching the factory dictum of 'Never Go More Than Seven' (thousand rpm). In a striking all-Alaskan White finish, the Tiger 90 ran a 9:1 compression ratio, via a new head and pistons (only interchangeable with the 3TAs' as a complete unit), higher gearing from a 17-tooth gearbox and 46-tooth rear sprocket, bigger inlet valves, and the same sports cam form mix as the T100SS.

The result was a machine with a top speed of over 90 mph, but also what a later 1967 *Motor Cycle* Reader's Report found to be a narrow power band, with real urge coming in only from around 4,500 to the 7,500 rev limit. Though the T90 could be ridden all right in top gear at 30 mph in town, there was little power at the bottom end and speed fell off quickly on hills or in head winds, so full use had to be made of the gears. Vibration was also noticeably present, particularly between 4,000 and 5,000 rpm, where it was bad enough to help split petrol tanks. Fuel

consumpton averaged around 68 mpg. Handling and braking were considered only average by many, but the overall judgement was favourable, the Tiger 90 with its good acceleration and light weight at around 330 lb dry being judged fast, comfortable and, with one exception, reliable.

The exception was the electrics, and this year's T90 and T100SS heralded the end of the distributor, for they fitted Lucas 4CA twin contact-breakers, mounted behind a plate in a new timing chest cover, and driven by the exhaust camshaft. For points models, the latter was now tapered to accommodate the auto advance, and the inlet cam no longer carried the distributor skew gear. The 3TA and 5TA retained the distributor. On the points models, twin ignition coils on rubber mountings were attached to the frame tank rail. Given the distributor's shortcomings, all this seemed a useful updating, but it ushered in a new period of electrical grief and unreliability.

The problem was the 4CA points design. In this, the points plates seved as a mounting point for both condensers as well as both the two sets of points now required to fire the two separate coils. Being mounted on the same plate, the two points could not be timed individually, and the timing had to be compensated for by varying the points gap. For with the auto-advance unit bolted to the

end of the camshaft, the contacts only opened precisely 180° apart if the camshaft was rotating exactly centrally with the points, which was not usually the case.

This imprecision, in conjunction with the erratic method of voltage control via the lights-switch, could make life very difficult for owners, who did not appreciate it. They found it less than ideal that the coils were mounted on an extension of the head-steady bracket where they were subject to maximum vibration, and the switches and rectifier positioned inaccessibly under the seat, where they got dirty. The answer to the contact problem would come from 1968 on with the 6CA and later 10CA points, which had neither set of points mounted directly on the metal plate, so that each cylinder could be timed independently. The two separate condensers were also moved elsewhere, so there was then more room for manoeuvre beneath the points cover, which previously had a tendency to short out on the condenser terminals. The later systems can be substituted for the earlier if the necessary parts are assembled, the condensers mounted with the coils, an extra spacer put beneath the pillar bolts, and the later deeper points cover is fitted.

Back in '63, the T90 and T100 retained the siamese exhaust system with a new resonator silencer, while the 3TA and 5TA reverted to

separate pipes. The sport skirts were abbreviated from the previous panelling extending past their rear fixing, and then disappearing under the seat, to panels which cut off just behind the upper fixing point, but now included neat valances bolting to them and running round the back of the seat. The body of the panels was also now decorated with a right-angled flash, with the nameplate now positioned in the angle. Beneath the fairing, pancake-type air filters with round perforated chrome casings were fitted. The left panel now carried the separate Lucas 88SA ignition and lighting switches. New 3-gal petrol tanks were fitted for both sports models. The oil tank became rubber-mounted.

In the T100SS engine, a new cylinder head design gave greater depth and allowed the use of a thinner and more flexible copper head gasket. For all the C-range, the rocker box caps now had a knurled edge and were retained by a sprung steel strip, like the top of an Amal Monobloc carburettor. This helped with, but did not entirely cure, the problem of spontaneous detachment. In the gearbox the second pair were made closer, and the camplate incorporated a strengthening bridge piece to prevent it 'opening out' under hard use, by reinforcing the outer track, but once again this was an improvement rather than a cure. The clutch's shock absorber replaced the previous four-vane with a three-vane type,

with clutch ends, springs, cups and three-hole pressure plate to suit. The T100SS rear sprocket, like the T90, went to 46 teeth, and for both this was fitted to a 1952-type combined drum and sprocket with a hub revised to suit. The T100SS' front wheel went down to 18 in, and all but the 3TA now fitted ribbed front tyres. The 5TA's lower fork crown was modified, while the sports model's forks fitted the T120's internal springs.

**1964** brought no new models, but there were improved front forks, and the clutch operating mechanism, off the previous year's new unit 650s. In addition, the Tiger models stripped off completely, and the 3TA/5TA put on their abbreviated skirts — this was the '60s, which meant the end of the 'sensible' bath-tub.

The new clutch mechanism, which replaced the previous diecast scroll-operated one, was a distinctive design, though in fact derived from an early Burman arrangement used by Matchless. It was operated by $\frac{3}{8}$-in ball-bearings in a ramp. There were versions with four balls and springs, plus five friction plates, on the BSA unit twins before 1966, and on the BSA unit singles, but the Triumph version featured three balls and springs with six friction plates from the start.

On the right hand of the clutch thrust rod there was a pair of steel pressings, with one secured to the gearbox cover and the other rotated by operation of the clutch cable. Between these pressings were the three balls, seated in indents. As the inner pressing was rotated by the cable, so the balls rode up beside the seating, imparting a lateral thrust to the clutch pushrod. It was not an outstanding

design, and for the clutch to work well careful assembly and sound springs were needed as well as plates in good condition, undistorted and without burred internal tags. With the new mechanism any trace of pressure plate wobble could cause drag, and today a popular substitute for the standard plate is an alloy pressure plate marketed by SRM, which runs on needle roller bearings and has a larger thrust contact area than the normal one. The new clutch still needed its traditional freeing-off before starting up, and frequently contributed to a crunchy gear change. When properly set up, however, the clutch action was light, and it could be a joy to use.

The new forks were of external spring design, with springs now mounted around the outside of the fork inner tubes instead of within them. The fork crowns were adapted to suit, and for the T100SS/T90 the fork shrouds now had their legs cut off just short of the lower crown. The new fork layout, as well as being much stronger, permitted larger fork oil seals. At the lower end of each spring, within the chrome-plated housing, which was now screwed into the top of the fork slider, was a large-diameter oil seal with two internal lips which bore against the inner tube, with a garter-type spring ring operating on the seal lower lip. The T100SS and T90 continued to fit rubber bellows, and for them steering dampers were fitted with a rubber sleeve to discourage both unwinding and rattles. For the sports models there was a new method of front mudguard attachment, with their hooped stays now three in number, and the front two both fastened on each side to a single lug mounted high on the front of each fork slider.

Early versions of the fork were criticized as far too harshly sprung, which would lead to a 1965 revision. But the new fork was a great improvement, though its final refinement was to come in 1968.

In the engine, in an attempt to cure oil leaks, for all the C-range the pushrod cover tube became a parallel tube with a common seal at each end, with the cylinder head and gasket modified to suit. The tube was now supported at the lower end by a cup under the bottom seal. The T90's head was also modified to accept the smaller $1\frac{1}{4}$ in diameter exhaust pipes it now fitted. The 5TA/3TA abandoned their distributors and changed to points electrics like the others. In the gearboxes for all, the complete gear set was changed, with a strengthened tooth-form. For the T100SS/T90, the conversion to needle roller bearings on the gearbox layshaft was completed at its second end with the change of the previous bronze bush within the kick-start spindle. The 5TA's exhaust camshaft was changed. For all C-range engines, the pair of head-steadies became of 650 type. Also for all, speedometers became of the Smiths Magnetic type, which would prove unsuited to parallel twin vibration, as evidenced by the fact that Police machines retained certified Smiths Chronometric instruments from then on. For the Tigers a matching rev counter was offered, for the first time in the UK, with a drive from the left-hand end of the exhaust camshaft, though its press-in slotted drive thimble would prove wear-prone in service.

On the cycle side, the Tigers were now unpanelled and handsome with it. Their exhausts reverted to twin systems, with the smaller $1\frac{1}{4}$ in bore pipes for the T90, a competition-bred modification to improve low-down punch. Silencers were as previously, except that they now featured triangular mounting plates, with the rear frame adapted to suit. With the Tiger's panels gone, the twin switches were mounted still on the left but in a T120-type side-panel, though lacking the 650's lower rubber-bushed fixing spike. Like the rest of the range, the Tigers fitted the 650's battery and tool tray assembly, new rear chainguards, and new rear number plates enlarged for that year's suffix registrations. The Tigers, in two-tone Hi-Fi Scarlet and Silver for the 500 and Alaskan White and Gold for the 350, had now achieved an appearance of conventional good

THE ZENER-DIODE AS FITTED TO THE 12 VOLT THUNDERBIRD. THIS IS A VOLTAGE REGULATOR CONTROLLING THE RATE OF CHARGING TO THE BATTERIES.

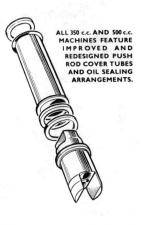

ALL 350 c.c. AND 500 c.c. MACHINES FEATURE IMPROVED AND REDESIGNED PUSH ROD COVER TUBES AND OIL SEALING ARRANGEMENTS.

THE CLUTCH OPERATING MECHANISM ON ALL 350 c.c., 500 c.c. AND 650 c.c. MACHINES HAS BEEN REDESIGNED TO FACILITATE EASY REMOVAL, AND SERVICING.

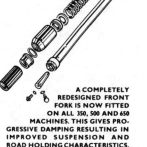

A COMPLETELY REDESIGNED FRONT FORK IS NOW FITTED ON ALL 350, 500 AND 650 MACHINES. THIS GIVES PRO-GRESSIVE DAMPING RESULTING IN IMPROVED SUSPENSION AND ROAD HOLDING CHARACTERISTICS.

**Left** *Getting near its final appearance, the 1964 T100SS 500.*

**Below right** *Smart 350, the 1965 Tiger 90.*

looks which they would largely retain for the rest of their days.

The 5TA/3TA had the skirts of the previous year's Tigers, topped by the T100SS/T90s' 3-gal petrol tank. Their nacelles were adapted for the preferable separate light and ignition switches, with the nacelle legs altered, the shrouds now being separate from the nacelle sections. Beneath the skirts, the rubber-mounted oil tank was fitted, and the air filter body modified. Their rear hubs became the same kind as the Tigers had adopted for 1963. Their front mudguards remained the 'fireman's helmet' but with the previous bridge piece finally changed to the rubber-mounted stirrup, with two pieces of bent strip bolted to the guard, and with their lower ends attached to a T-shaped bracket. Rear mudguards were their own style of blade. As on the whole C-range, these had a redesigned lifting handle, now running straight back and round the outside of the guard.

**1965** was mainly notable for modifications to the chassis, with the frame adopting the top rail bracing strut, and softening measures for the harsh front forks. Triumph twins were being produced and sold as never before, and it was no time for major revisions.

The upper stiffening strut in the C-range frame was bolted on, as it had been previously for some US competition models. The intention was to stop the stressed petrol tanks fracturing, and the tank itself changed

to a $3\frac{1}{2}$-gal item, insulated from the frame rail at its four fixing points by rubber buffers.

The front forks, in response to justified criticism that their harshness attacked the comfort of the ride, had their travel increased by an inch, though Peter Watson wrote that total movement was still not much more than 2 in. This was achieved by using longer, lower-rate springs, with increased length stanchions, bottom outer members, and inner damping sleeves, which gave improved and more progressive damping. The method of constructing the sliders was also revised: previously steel tubes with brazed-on fork ends, the centre members were now extruded from a solid billet of steel. The T100SS/T90s' rubber gaiter and fork top cover were made neater, with a light alloy cover above each gaiter, and the front fork spindle altered to suit the new fork dimensions.

Within the engines, the leak-prone oil pressure indicator button was abandoned, to be replaced by a blind domed cap. The flywheel's three radial bolts dispensed with the washers they had previously fitted, and were now secured by Loctite, an early instance of the benefits this wonderful stuff could bring to parallel twin engines. Also on the flywheel there was now a milled slot in the wheel, so that by removing a threaded plug machined in the crankcase behind the barrels, a service tool could be inserted and TDC located, to help time the engine accurately when a timing disc was used for this purpose. In the gearbox, for this year only, a felt washer was placed outboard of the gearbox output sleeve oil seal, in an attempt to protect the oil seal's edge from grit.

In an ongoing striptease, the 5TA/3TA finally discarded the 'fireman's helmet' front mudguard in favour of a conventional one with twin mudguard stays and a plain number plate without the chromed surround. The 3TA adopted the T90's small-bore exhaust cylinder head with its smaller ports. The T100SS handlebar became slightly flatter and more rear set. On all, the optional q.d. rear wheel now ran on ball journal bearings rather than the previous taper rollers. And there were minor changes to the brakes, with the front brake anchor plate now incorporating an adjustable fulcrum pin and front cable abutment, which replaced the previous abutment in the front fork slider, while the rear brake anchor plate spindle bore increased in diameter, to permit full area contact for the rear brake shoe.

**1966** saw the last panelling go in what would be the cooking 5TA/3TA's final year. The UK 500 Tiger became known for that year only as simply the T100, while the US variants were either the T100R (Road) or T100C (Competition), for this last year still in either East or West Coast versions — for fuller details see the works by Nelson or Bacon.

Confusingly, a few T100C Sports Tigers, with their dual high-level exhausts and silencers and wide gear ratios were released in the UK from 1967 to '71. In the year before the beginning of the second, improved phase of the C-range's career as sports roadsters, there were still substantial new benefits, particularly 12-volt Zener diode-controlled electrics (which today permits the fitting of quartz halogen headlights and electronic ignition), as well as a gradual increase in sports specification. The new sleeker 'eyebrow' tank badges, fitted together with matching stick-on knee grips, exemplified this.

The badges went on new 3-gal fuel tanks, since in addition, the frames for all the C-range had the extra top tube made integral, it

**Left** *1965 5TA with 'skirts' off previous T100.*

**Right** *Now stripped for 1966, its last year, the 5TA kept just its nacelle.*

**Below right** *Also in its final year, the 1966 'Twenty-one' 3TA had come a long way since 1957.*

now being brazed rather than bolted on at both ends. The range also fitted new oil tanks with capacity increased to 6 pints. The anti-froth tower was now fitted in front of the filler cap, and there was a metering screw in the tank's neck to regulate a new facility, an oil supply taken from the return line to lubricate the rear chain.

The early 12-volt system was served at first by twin 6-volt batteries on their own carrier, changing progressively in mid-year to a single 12-volt battery. The latter was rubber-mounted on a revised carrier common to all Triumph twins. It was accompanied by an improved tool tray bolted to the rear mudguard. The Zener diode and heat sink were bolted alongside the batteries on the left. Ostensibly they were there rather than in a better-cooled position under the tank nose to 'permit owners to fit a fairing more easily'. As well as overheating from their position out of the airflow, early examples had the earthing wire mounted between the diode and heat sink, causing what John Nelson called 'epidemic diode failures' until the earth was relocated beneath the diode fixing nut. Another early electrical problem with pre-ignition 'random sparking' led to the quick introduction of a replacement 160° dwell auto-advance cam unit. Still in the electrical department the horn, which had come in for some stick for feebleness, was relocated visibly under the tank nose. For the T100/T90

the ignition key became a less thief-friendly Wilmot–Breeden type. A red ignition warning light went into the headlamp shell, and a cut-out button went on the right of the handlebar.

In the engine, the Tigers adopted Hidural aluminium bronze valve guides, the same material used on the Bonneville. The previous iron guides had been good and hard-wearing for ordinary use, but in competition, or with a worn guide, due to different rates of expansion, sometimes they could not retain their interference fit in the alloy head and worked loose. The intermediate timing wheel became a new harder-wearing type with a bronze bush; the pinion teeth were now cut from the wheel and it was then induction heat-treated. Inner valve springs of increased loading were fitted, and this applied to the 5TA/3TA, with the 5TA also adopting the T100 camshafts and valve clearances. Within the primary chaincase the tensioner blade and its trunnion were altered. In the gearbox the clutch mechanism cable adapter was modified, and the 1965 felt washer on the gearbox sprocket was deleted and a lock washer fitted. A crankcase protector designed to guide a snapped rear chain safely around the gearbox sprocket was fitted. The clutch pressure plate's adjusting screw was enlarged. For the Tigers, wide and close ratio gear sets became available optionally. For both 350s, con-rods changed from steel stampings to forged alloy. On the Tigers, the crankcases

now acquired a hole to take the drive for the optional rev counter, of the 650 type. This featured a right-angled drive gearbox, and the cable was less vulnerable. The drive could be fitted to earlier models, but since it ran at quarter rather than half engine speed, a suitable rev counter head was also necessary.

The 5TA and 3TA retained their nacelles for a last year, but dropped the enclosure, and adopted a plain side-panel on the left as the switches were in the nacelle. They fitted the Tiger's rear mudguard. Their wheels also standardized with the other two, becoming of 18 in diameter. They took the T100/T90 prop and centre stands. For all models, the swinging-arm's width increased to allow fatter knobbly tyres to go on the off-road variants. After over a decade, the standard

(but not the q.d.) rear wheel sprocket reverted to the bolt-on type, for quick and easy gearing changes and also because the cast-iron sprockets were items that could wear out very rapidly, sometimes in as little as 5,000 miles. All 500s fitted the lower fork crown off the T100C, and in the UK models' air cleaners, the US-style paper filter elements became an option.

This was the last year for the soft-tuned 5TA/3TA, and some other things beside states of style and tune were changing, as the range narrowed down to emphasize ease of production and performance. *Motor Cycle* Reader's Reports on the Tiger 90 and 100 in 1966 and 1967 both found detail work and finish on the models only adequate, with chrome liable to rust and the machines needing garaging to be preserved. In the 500 survey they pinpointed 1966 as a bad year for reliability. But the market for a well-finished, reliable commuter machine had virtually gone by the mid-'60s, and the 350 and even 500 cc capacities were already recognized as unfashionable ones, with registration numbers dropping, particularly since the slicker Japanese offerings had eaten up the learner market, and with the 500 Kawasaki triple, were about to blast into the medium capacity speed stakes. All that there remained to do, in the prolonged absence of that troubled project, the 350 Bandit/Fury, was to use the expertise of Doug Hele and the team, and the experience gleaned in the titanic Daytona racing victories of 1966 and '67, to style the C-range for the American and youth markets, jack up the performance, and build in steering and roadholding to match.

This exclusive pursuit of the fast end was a pity in some ways, because, as their many variations suggested, the small pre-units were very versatile. One field where this was demonstrated was their use as military and Police machines. We think of the side-valve TRW twin (see Volume 5) as the military Triumph, and a radically lightened Doug Hele military ohv prototype weighing less than 300 lb came to nothing. The 650 Saint was the better-known Police machine, and reportedly a point of BSA office politics (see Volume 5) again prevented a military 500 Triumph twin rather than the BSA B40 single being adopted by the British Army when they re-equipped in 1967. But though less than 20 of the T50 WD, a military 5TA with nacelle, were made, by 1966 larger orders had been won in Europe for a military 3TA with a single seat, alloy guards, and wheel bearings plus suspension units sealed against water.

Within England, Police specifications varied from force to force, but one interesting Police version of the 3TA from 1961 fitted an electric starter, just as Norton's little unit twin would do on their 400 cc version. The Triumph starter lay ahead of the engine, slotting neatly into holes in the front engine plates, and driving through the timing gears. By 1968 both 350 and 500 Mercury military/Police kick-start variants were selling well abroad, where on the rough roads of underdeveloped countries both a lighter weight than the 650, and their ruggedness, were appreciated. As mentioned, it was a T100P, the Police version of the late single-carb T100, which Ted Simon rode round the world on his 'Jupiter's Travels'.

**1967** saw the start of the T100's refinement, as over the next three years it was brought to a near-final pitch of development, since after that the race effort concentrated on the triples, and the company's struggle to survive precluded any further major work. Meanwhile, the T90 shared many of the benefits.

Doug Hele's influence was directly evident in the 1967 T100, which was now offered as the Tiger T100S (for single carb) and T100T (for twin carb) Daytona, the latter to commemorate victory in the race for which the machine's new cylinder head had been developed. US export versions of the twin-carb machine were the T100R Daytona Super Sports, and T100C Sports Tiger. The main event for the UK, the T100T Daytona, had its power raised to 39 bhp at 7,400 rpm, with a top speed on test of 113 mph.

The principal means by which this was achieved was the new cylinder head. On arrival at Triumph from Norton, Hele had been unimpressed with the Triumph combustion chamber, considering the Norton's 'superior'. When given the job of creating a racer from the existing T100 in six months, he and his team therefore re-formed the existing head to include larger combustion chambers, which in turn allowed larger inlet valves and valve seats. The seats were cut deeper into the head so that the combustion area was not interrupted, and the valves were set at a narrower angle. On the production T100T inlet valves were of $1\frac{17}{32}$ in diameter, against $1\frac{7}{16}$ in for the T100S. Exhaust valves for both remained at $1\frac{5}{16}$ in, but were now made of

*A 1967 production version of the T100T twin-carb cylinder head, directly derived from the Daytona race winner.*

more heat-resistant material. The T100T fitted new valve spring cups.

Induction tracts were now parallel; this allowed a standardized single carburettor manifold for the T100 and T90, the latter adopting its own version of the head. But on the twin-carb 500 versions, the stubs for the pair of $1\frac{1}{16}$ bore 376 Monoblocs could still be splayed, to permit twin perforated 'pancake' air filters to be fitted, and for the T100T these fitted a coarse felt element. T100S carb size remained at 1 in. On the T100T one float chamber on the left of the two Monoblocs was incorporated to serve both, and there was a balance pipe between the induction tracts, another race-bred dodge.

The T100T's head also fitted the T90's smaller $1\frac{1}{4}$-in exhaust pipes, as part of a quest to maintain gas velocity and boost mid-range power as well as top end. The T100T fitted E3134-form cams for both inlet and exhaust, plus suitable tappets with enlarged, shallow $1\frac{1}{8}$ in radius feet. The T100S adopted the E3134 for inlet but stayed with the sports E3325 cam form for exhaust, both with the standard $\frac{3}{4}$ in radius cam followers. The exhaust cam for all now also embodied an internally machined rev counter drive slot. The

T100T's compression went up to 9.75:1, while the T100S stayed at 9:1, both using the Hepolite pistons which the factory had gone over to. These embodied a shorter gudgeon pin and revised gudgeon pin circlip. Recommended piston ring gap was 0.010–0.014 in, but this was later revised to 0.015–0.020 in. T100 pistons from '67 on will not interchange with previous ones.

To improve scavenging, the oil pump scavenge plunger was increased from 0.437 in to 0.487 in. A kick-start oil seal and the housing for it, were added to the gearbox cover. Within the gearbox, an early instance of the move to UNF thread form was encountered, as the gearbox mainshaft adopted this. It became slightly longer and with a suitable nut to hold the kick-start ratchet together. The clutch hub was now more securely mounted on the mainshaft, in view of the previous problem of it working loose. An extended threaded section on the end of the shaft permitted the use of an aircraft-type lock nut to replace the previous plain clutch centre nut and tab washer. The new shaft could be used in earlier gearboxes if the new pinions were also fitted.

The more powerful engine was also

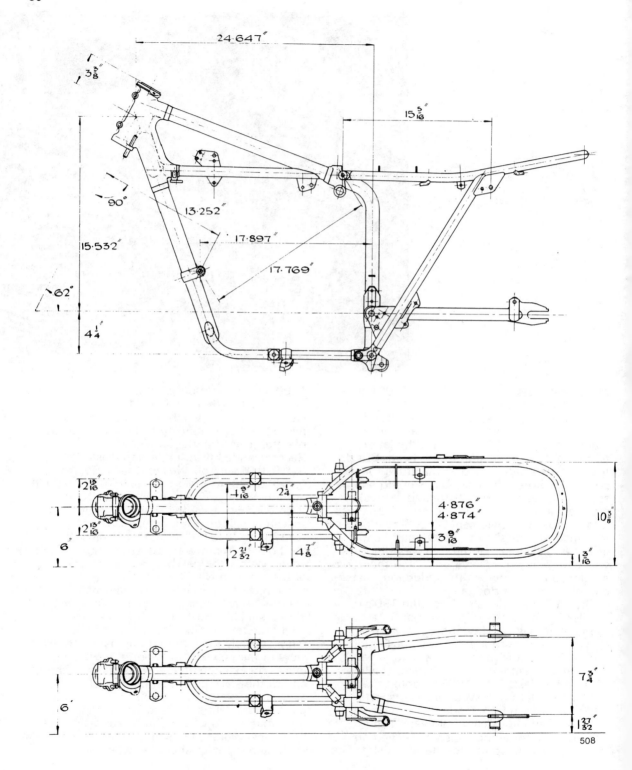

matched by a substantially revised frame.
Since the 1964 fork and '65 tank tube brace,
handling at road speeds had been much
improved, but racing in particular revealed the
continued existence of weaving and a light
front end at speed. Work on the 650 had led
Hele to pinpointing this to steering geometry
and weight distribution, as well as the
unbraced swinging-arm. The C-range front
downtube was therefore increased in
diameter, and the frame top tube strengthened
so that it, rather than the lower one, became
the main top tube. But the top tube was also
shortened, to lower both overall frame height
and the engine height by $\frac{1}{2}$ in, with the front
engine plates modified to suit. This also
helped give a 3° steeper steering head angle
at 62°, with the previous 'swan-neck' steering
head lug giving way to a short, fully
triangulated head lug.

And at the rear, the swinging-arm spindle
was at last anchored, by triangular support
brackets, to the sub-frame rails which
supported the seat. The swinging-arm itself
was redesigned, as well as stiffened and
widened again. It still pivoted on bushes
fitting over the hardened steel spindle, but the
spindle was now only a tight push-in fit, and
held in place by bolts through the rear frame's

side plate into the spindle. This meant that
removal did require swinging the rear frame
assembly clear at the bottom, but could be
done without the need for the previous
threaded special extractor (though still not
without considerable difficulty). The right-
hand bolt was fitted with a grease nipple,
which was a good deal more accessible than
the previous one beneath the swinging-arm
housing. On the left end of the spindle there
was a hole to take a C-spanner for use in
reassembling. During that process, correct
working clearances had to be determined by
shims between the swinging-arm pivot lug
and the frame lugs, and grease then applied
until the frame aperture was completely filled.

The new frame, which was 2 lb lighter than
the old, fitted new versions of the centre and
side stands. The front forks were altered to
suit the frame, with their cup and cone head
races now as on the 650, and a redesigned
top fork lug incorporating on the left a Yale-
type anti-theft steering head lock; the
previous slot in their top stem for a padlock
was deleted. The fork top crowns now
became the same as the 650s, which meant
that the handlebars, which changed to the
previous $\frac{7}{8}$ in 3TA/5TA touring type, were
mounted in eye bolts carried in bonded

**Left** *Doug Hele-developed
1967 frame with strengthened
top and front downtubes,
steeper steering head angle and
stronger head lug.*

**Right** *The new 1967 chassis
also featured a stronger
swinging-arm, properly
anchored at last by these
triangular support brackets.*

rubber bushes pressed into the top crown. The rubber-mounted handlebars were safe enough, but could give a peculiar sensation under heavy braking. Another anti-vibration measure were the new fat 'cushioned' handlebar grips, which not everyone liked. American models continued to fit high-rise bars in rigid mountings, and these mountings could be had as an option in the UK if a bar-mounted windscreen was being fitted.

The C-range's fuel tank was a revised 3-gal model with a three-point fixing system. The dualseat on all was now the 'Quilltop', which was slimmer at the nose, slightly raised at the rear, and distinguished by transverse ribbing on its top, which was grey with white piping, and by a chrome strip running around its base. The crossways ribbing helped keep a rider from sliding rearwards under hard acceleration. In contrast to the new steering head lock, however, on this seat the previous removable seat plunger knob was replaced by a one-piece plastic-headed seat catch plunger, so the tools in the trays bolted to the rear mudguard were at risk from the light-fingered. The left-hand side-panel carried only the Lucas 41SA ignition switch, as the 88SA

rotary light switch was now housed in the headlamp, together with the ignition warning and high beam lights. On the handlebars there was an ignition cut-out button on the right. At the rear, the previously kinked brake-rod became straight, while at the front, the T100T was finally fitted with the T120's 8-in SLS front brake.

This was timely, as the blue and white Daytona was a seriously fast machine, and with realistic top speeds around 105 mph, not much slower at the top end than a Bonneville. Despite Hele's work to produce mid-range power in race terms, the 650 naturally had the bottom end urge, and critics of the 500 with its light flywheel would call it peaky; a friend's T100S had only moderate acceleration up to around 50 mph, after which it took off. A 1968 test found that gear-changing to keep the revs up was necessary if the T100T was to give of its best. Power only began for the road Daytona at around 3,500 rpm, with a noticeable step at 4,000 and another at 6,000. It could be revved safely and quickly to 8,000 rpm, though 7,000 through the gears was enough; taking it all the way produced 44 mph in first,

*A Triumph T100T Daytona for 1967 on test with* Motor Cycle.

66 in second, and 88 in third.

Gearing, which was the same for the T100T and T100S, was on the low side, with the ratios closely spaced for good acceleration, until a big jump between third and top; a five-speed box would have been welcome. The gearing could of course be raised, and the controls racerized, in pursuit of top speed. As it was, when pulling away, the clutch had to be slipped a little for best results, and the 1968 test Daytona was prone to stall when pulling up at low rpm, a trait I also found on my friend's '69 T100S. Overall T100T economy was good at around 55 mpg, and oil consumption at around a pint every 600 miles if the engine (rings, valve guides, etc.) was in good condition. As well as the gearing, the bike's touring handlebars and mid-set footrests were also a compromise between roadster and sportster, and the styling, handsome rather than dazzling, and with the tank-top rack still in place for the UK machines, did little to suggest the speed of which the T100T was capable. This was scarcely a sales aid.

On the move, a T100T could be cruised at 80, with brisk acceleration to the mid-90s in hand, and both the riding position and the new seat were comfortable. At 356 lb kerbside, the bike could be flicked around like a 250, and the steering was now judged reassuringly positive on fast main-road bends, with a low centre of gravity and good ground clearance encouraging hard cornering, wet or dry. In fact, it was stable right up to the ton. A more recent test by Richard Dames-Longworth in *Classic Bike* concurred on the quick steering and rigid-feeling chassis, but added that in fast bends 'you had to have faith' and lean into them slightly more than the machine's angle in order to keep the steering neutral, and also that this Triumph still didn't appreciate throttling back in mid-bend.

Very firm suspension front and rear helped the stable ride but not comfort, and the standard 130-lb springs of the rear units were judged too harsh in 1968. This was no 5TA for smoothness — high-frequency vibration was there at 4,500 rpm and got worse from there on. With its small pistons, the shakes for the rider were not excessive by current standards before about 85 mph, bearing in mind Doug Hele's reflection that 'I suppose people were learning to live with vibration in order to get the power'. (If you want to know

*Dual-purpose version of the unit 500, the mostly-export T100C on test during 1967.*

what 'excessive' is, ride a tuned A65.) However, odd appendages like the gear lever could drop off, and bulbs blow, though not so frequently as on the sports 650. And as Dames-Longworth commented, the Daytona was not a very relaxing ride, since it had to be kept constantly on the boil. With the 1968 8-in SLS front brake for the T100T, even before the ultimate 1969 improvement, the stoppers were powerful yet controllable, giving a 28½-ft stopping distance from 30 mph. *Motor Cycle*'s final judgement was: 'A highly developed, purposeful, practical sportster for the enthusiast'.

The downside for the T100 was never too serious. There were still some transmission problems, with jumping out of third still a feature, as well as periodic failure of the first gear and kick-start pinions at this time. Despite the modification to the oil pump, scavenging remained a potential problem, and again today, fitting the four-plunger 750 pump is a good idea. Even more than the rest of the C-range, routine maintenance had to be observed — if tappet adjustment was neglected, for instance, the tip of the cam follower could snap off, and this should be checked regularly. High oil consumption and a smoky exhaust indicated the perennial valve-guide wear, which could cause valves to stick or the guide to work loose in the head. And on the cycle side, despite the new swinging-arm spindle arrangements, the bushes were still in danger of under-lubrication, meaning premature wear and ultimately seizure. It happened to my friend's T100S.

**1968** saw the front forks reach their final form, and the contact-breakers greatly improve. A number of other detail changes also made the C-range more practical vehicles.

The forks had been developed by Hele and Percy Tait to incorporate floating shuttle valves in the base of the main tubes to provide two-way damping. An earlier form of damper unit had apparently gone on US competition models since 1966, but the new forks gave precise damping control, by a relatively simple device screwed into the bottom of the stanchion tubes. It had required meticulous development, however, as on bump, the holes in the valve cup and the stanchion lined up to provide free passage for the oil, but on recoil the cup dropped, with oil being forced through the small working clearance surrounding it, and everything had to line up just so. The result was stiffened recoil damping and the control of pitching on bends. The forks also changed to UNF threads that year. The fork top covers had headlamp alignment slots, and a hole on the left for the ignition switch. Bottom outer members became extruded.

In the engine, the T100S adopted the T100T's cylinder head with its 39° valve angle and larger $1\frac{17}{32}$-in inlet valve. For the whole C-range, the carburettors changed to Amal Concentrics, in the same sizes, and the inlet manifold was now held in place by cap bolts. The rocker boxes, while the same shape, were cast in a substantially thicker section, and the cylinder barrel base nuts became the 12-point type, giving better accessibility, and being capable for the first time of taking proper tightening up with a ring spanner. The T100T fitted stronger con-rods. For all models the pushrod covers dispensed with the bottom cup. The feed from the lower return pipe to the rocker oil feed pipe was reintroduced. Then in mid-year, the rocker ball pin assembly to the rocker altered, to cut off the oil supply to it while increasing that to other parts.

The primary chaincase now had a detachable circular cover carrying the Triumph logo and giving access to the alternator rotor. This revealed, from very late in the year at engine no. H65011, a fixed pointer to allow stroboscopic ignition timing, and since this more accurate method was favoured, the

*A neat and compact race-bred roadster, the 1967 T100T Daytona.*

engine drive sprocket no longer had a rotor drive peg facility for use with a timing disc. Within the case, the primary chain tensioner trunnion reverted to the pre-'66 design. The clutch nuts were altered. In the gearbox, in an attack on oil leaks, the high gear incorporated a bronze bush extending into the increased bore oil seal in the back of the primary chaincase, with a new gearbox sprocket nut to suit, and the gearbox sprocket cover plate now in common with the 650. An O-ring was also fitted to the gearbox camplate spindle carrying the gear indicator finger. The gear pedal rubber lost its Triumph logo, as did the kick-start pedal.

In a welcome move, the ignition switch went on to the left-hand fork cover, where it could be seen and reached more easily. In the headlamp the light switch became a toggle, which was welcome again because the rotary one had been difficult to operate on the move. In consequence there was a new left-hand side panel which located on two pegs provided on the frame, and had a built-in tool compartment, so the underseat tool tray was eliminated. It also gave access to the clear plastic casing of the battery, which sat on a new carrier and was fastened at the top by a rubber strap and hook in place of the previous wire clamp. All these were rider-friendly touches and were welcome, though the side panel was still not lockable. It lost its 'toothpaste' metal name badge, which was replaced by a transfer. In another improvement, the Zener diode, now in a finned heat sink casting, was moved into the air stream beneath the headlamp. Finally the biggest single uprating for the electrtics was the new 6CA contact-breaker, providing independent adjustment of the points gap and timing for each cylinder. Though harnesses, connectors and the points system would never be perfect, taken in conjunction with the following year's encapsulated alternators, these improvements brought a partial end to the worst period of electrical unreliabiity. 'Clearhooter' horns were also fitted.

New versions of the 6-pt rubber-mounted oil tanks were fitted, and as mentioned, reintroduced the lower return pipe's 'twig' feed to the rocker oil feed pipe. The rear chainguard was revised. The T100T's air filter had cloth and gauze elements. The exhaust pipes were given more rigid location by chromed cross-bracing struts carried to the front engine mounting plate studs, as the previous ones had been fracture-prone. On the petrol tanks, thicker stick-on kneegrips

*A welcome improvement for 1968, 6CA contact-breakers with independent adjustment for each cylinder.*

*The 350 Tiger 90 for 1968 had very much the looks of the T100.*

were fitted. The dualseat's cushioning was thickened, and its hinges changed to pressings hinged on pins welded to the frame. The rear mudguards became rectangular, and now with three holes for the light fixing. Finally, the T100T Daytona was fitted with an 8-in SLS front brake in a new hub, with a fluted cover plate. It was the previous one for the 650, and even if it was offered to use up stocks, it was still welcome, and also meant that the 500 avoided teething troubles that year with the 650's new 2LS brake's cable run.

**1969** saw the T100's peak, with a strengthened bottom end, longer-wearing nitrided cams, the best front brake, and a number of useful items as standard which had previously been optional. The situation was complicated by a BSA Group rationalization, the changeover to UNF threads. These were the same as American National size. A nightmare for the storemen then, and tedious to detail now, wherever possible these have, however, been mentioned, to indicate where '69-on and pre-'69 parts are not compatible.

Keeping the 5TA's plain bush timing side main bearing, through which the big-ends were fed, on the very rapid T100T, had already been revealed as unwise at Daytona. Though perfectly adequate for most use, at really high speeds, due to different rates of expansion with the surrounding alloy, the bush could turn in the crankcase, cutting off the oil supply to the big ends. It was now replaced on the timing side by a ball journal bearing, with oil to the big-ends being fed

through a redesigned timing cover. Lubricant then went via an oil seal, directly into the end of a new crank, with UNF threads at each end and for the flywheel bolts, and with an extended shaft. A new adapter was fitted to the top end of the scavenge pipe, and there was a revised oil pressure relief valve. This ball journal was a superior arrangement for high-speed use, as the oil did not now reach the big-ends, having been pre-heated by travelling through a bush whose accurate fit was necessary to maintain good oil pressure. A ball-bearing also positively located the end float of the crankshaft, which was important because the drive side main bearing also changed, from a ball-race to a roller bearing. If end float had been present, it would have thrown an excessive load on the lip of the outer race of this drive side roller. The external clues to the presence of the new bearings were two bumps at the front and rear of the timing chest. With the new arrangements, the T100 could be thrashed with confidence.

The crankcase on its left side had a raised pad for the engine number, on which a multiple Triumph logo was embossed to discourage thieves from re-stamping. A new cylinder barrel with increased wall thickness was fitted, part of the general policy of increasing joint face thickness to combat oil leaks. An oil pressure warning light was fitted in the headlamp shell in place of the ignition warning light, and to operate this, the new timing cover incorporated an oil pressure indicator switch in a hole already capped to take a gauge, with also a new, relocated, oil pressure release valve, also with UNF threads.

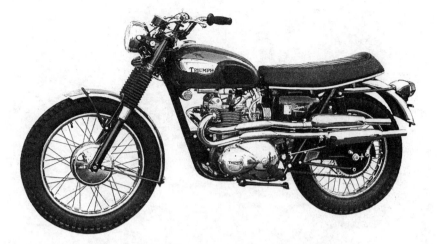

*A T100C adapted for European enduro use by main dealers Comerfords in 1968.*

The warning light was usually more trouble than it was worth, scaring owners when it malfunctioned, which it was prone to do in hot weather, or even when it accurately indicated that pressure had dropped below 7 psi, as Triumph engines would operate quite happily on 5 psi when hot. As Titch Allen once put it about oil pressure gauges, 'If you had no gauge, you would not worry about oil pressure as long as the engine kept going'.

The timing cover, too, was altered at the points plate to add a second oil seal, and the points plate mounting was revised. The spindle of the advance—retard mechanism was now pre-lubricated, and had to be left alone, as if wet lubrication was added thereafter, it caused a glutinous paste and a seized spindle. From late in the previous model year, at engine no. H63307, the T100T's con-rods were strengthened again, now being of thicker .536 in H-section and without a small end bush. In mid-'69, the centre-punching of con-rods ceased, and nuts were now to be tightened to torque settings or bolt stretch figures provided by the factory.

The camshafts became of superior heat-treated steel, and nitrided, finally ending the problem of rapid camshaft wear. The plates and fixing screws which located the right end of the camshafts directly in the crankcase were altered, and the cam gear crankshaft nut became of Unified Thread. The pushrod covers changed yet again: though of similar appearance, within them the tappet guide blocks were modified to allow the fitting of an O-ring, and the top end of the tubes became 'castellated', with top locating fingers.

From mid-year came news of 'a simple but effective "Service Fix"', which could be applied to C- or B-range machines with the new pushrod covers, namely the addition of Viton black rubber oil seal O-rings, part no. E11283, to back up the white rubber seals in the recesses at the top and bottom of the pushrod cover tube. Assembled with suitable care, this was said finally to cure the leak-prone tubes. The cylinder head was revised to suit these castellations, as well as adopting UNF threads. In it the T100S adopted the previous year's T100T valve spring cups. The left-hand crankcase was machined with a left-hand thread for the rev counter drive, as the previous right-hand thread had used to come undone. The primary chaincase too acquired UNF threads, as did the cap of the sump oil filter assembly.

So too did the gearbox inner and outer cover, as well as the clutch mechanism cable abutment and the kick-start lever. Within the gearbox a new camplate plunger and spring were fitted to try to combat the selection problems. The combined clutch housing and chainwheel no longer had cast-in pockets, but were individually balanced. From engine no. CC187734, the location tabs were deleted from the clutch thrust washer and thus the holes deleted from the clutch hub. Finally, the electrics benefited enormously from the adoption of the RM21 alternator with two leads and fully encapsulated stator windings, which was immune to the primary chaincase's oil and more resistant to vibration.

On the cycle side, the trend was to commonality of components where possible.

**Left** *Practically perfected, the 1969 T100, here in T100T Daytona form, with timing side ball journal bearing, 8-in TLS front brake, etc.*

**Below** *During 1969, the best solution yet to pushrod oil leaks.*

**Below right** *A 1970 T100T with revised engine breathing. A good view of the excellent TLS front brake.*

The parcel rack, a last vestige of Triumph's individual style of the '50s, was finally dropped from UK models. There was a new square 'picture frame' tank badge, with the Triumph name in relief against a white painted panel. The tops of dualseats became aerated, and tops plus their piping became black. A new, wider version of the front fork was fitted, with the width of fork stanchion centres increased from $6\frac{1}{2}$ to $6\frac{3}{4}$ in to allow for wider tyres. This meant a new wheel spindle, fork crown, stem and top lug, with the top crown adopting Unified Threads. In January, from frame no. AC10464, two additional holes were drilled in the fork stanchion and improved their action, something that could be done to any existing '68-on fork. After a first year in service, the steering head lug's anti-thief steering lock plunger platform was extended to avoid accidental misuse of the lock. The forks fitted clipless gaiters, and the front mudguard's rear stay adopted a one-bolt fixing. The front guard itself became a wider one off the 1966 US competition models, and there was a new front number plate with cut-out and holes moved. The rear chainguard was revised again, with the inner part now extended down to the lower chain run.

Finally, for both the T100T and T100S there were new and powerful twin leading shoe front brakes, in 8 in size for the Daytona and 7 in for the T100 and T90. Both had air scoops behind wire mesh covers. Universally acknowledged as among the best drum

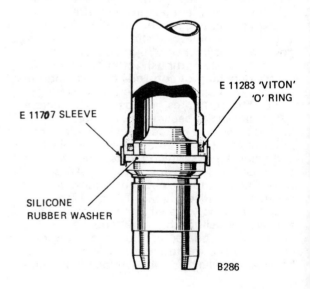

E 11283 'VITON' 'O' RING

E 11707 SLEEVE

SILICONE RUBBER WASHER

B286

brakes available, they will be found more fully described in the unit 650 section (see p. 95). For 1969 the brakes had a modified bell-crank lever, which allowed a safer and tidier cable run, parallel to the fork leg. The brakes' chromed cover plate also changed its pattern from flutes to concentric ribs, and internally, new grease retainers were fitted. The front brake cable now operated a stoplight switch. Either of the brakes can be retrofitted in a suitable wheel hub to any C-range machine, though care should be taken in the fit of the protruding slot on the brake anchor plate with the lug on the forks; the lug can be built up with weld where necessary.

Elsewhere on the machine, the oil tank now fitted a dipstick attached to its filler cap, with the distances between the high and low markings representing a pint of oil. A modified wiring harness allowed the fitting of winkers if desired. At the rear, the chromed springs of the Girling units were exposed, which may have worn quicker, but was what all we young riders wanted. For the UK, the springs were now 145 lb/in rate.

The exhaust system also changed, the pipes now being coupled by a link pipe very close to the cylinder head. Originally this had been part of Hele's brilliance in improving gas flow, with the cross-pipes being set as close as possible to the ports, and each pipe reduced

in diameter just downstream of the balance pipe junction. However, on production machines the constrictions were omitted, and the effect was simply to reduce noise; which at least allowed the same not-very-restrictive baffled silencers with their wonderful throaty note still to be fitted despite oncoming noise legislation. Ball-ended control levers were fitted as standard.

The centres stand for the whole C-range became the one on the 650s, with its revised geometry for that year, and the prop-stand became thicker and with a curved end that allowed its previous 'flip-up foot' to be deleted. Both gave better ground clearance. It was also announced that the prop stand, along with other previously optional items such as the q.d. rear wheel and the rev counter, would now be standard through all, though whether this policy was implemented is not clear.

This was the last year for the Tiger 90 350, though there had been some confusion on this too, as it had seemed to be dropped at the end of 1968. The '67-on improvements had made it into a genuine 90 mph machine. Even if it featured even more of the 500's peakiness, it accelerated impressively in mid-range, and now, as then, being undervalued, can sometimes be overlooked.

**1970** saw one last significant modification to the engine, with a revised breathing

system, but essentially development on the 500s had ended, and it was detail modifications only from now on. This stagnation was noted and, in view of the Japanese competition, deplored at the time, since while the road 500s remained at 39 bhp, the race engines had been tuned to give 54 bhp with a fair degree of reliability. Future incarnations might have involved fitting a hot 500 Daytona motor in the 350 Bandit/Fury's frame, which in any case had been developed from a chassis produced by Ken Sprayson at Reynolds for Tait's 500 racer. People who have subsequently tried this mix with frames left over after the Bandit fiasco report a delightful cross-breed. But at the time the company's fortunes did not allow it, and from today's perspective what was left was still a fast and sturdy motor cycle.

The new breathing arrangements, adopted in different versions by all Triumph multis, gave improved crankcase oil tightness, and an end to some loss of power at high rpm. The inlet camshaft's previous breather disc, drive slots, and centre bore with breather vent, were blanked off, and the left-side crankcase modified accordingly. The exhaust camshaft also changed, now incorporating a solid, screwed-in, rev counter drive plug, a more reliable arrangement than the previous push-fit pressing. The camshaft bushes were altered to suit. The former drive sprocket oil seal was deleted, and the engine now breathed directly, via holes in the left crankcase, into the primary chaincase. An elbow-shaped vent was plumbed into the top rear end of the chaincase. The vent took a big-bore plastic tube to the tail of the rear mudguard, and thence the atmosphere, though thanks to a baffle plate within the chaincase, most of the oil content of the vented mist settled in the chaincase.

A new oil tank was also fitted, of a similar appearance to and interchangeable with the previous one, but with a greater capacity, although the same $5\frac{1}{2}$-pt fill was recommended. The lead to lubricate the rear chain was discontinued, and the oil tank's froth tower breather outlet was linked to the new breather outlet through the primary chaincase, joining a silver D-shaped breather pipe attached to the left side of the rear mudguard.

There were other internal changes. The valves' split cotters were altered. The right-hand crankcase half was machined to delete the previous year's timing side ball main bearing's abutment ring, as in December, from engine no. XCO6297, a clamping washer was fitted between the timing pinion and the inner spool of the timing side main bearing, to retain the crankshaft and limit end-float. The tappet guides became as on the 1969 T90. The cam gear wheel nut became Unified Thread. In the clutch, the three-ball thrust plate was modified. A new set of gears were used, but with the same ratios, the gear teeth being improved by shaving and gas-carburizing for a better surface finish.

On the single-carb T100, the Concentric was now semi-rubber mounted, as on the 650 twin-carb models for the previous year, with rubber washers under the retaining nuts, and flange O-rings. This was not the O-ring supplied in the Amal sets, but a thicker one, Triumph part no. E9711. The distinction was important, as the wrong O-ring negated the anti-vibration effect and distorted the carburettor flange. A single air filter with a common cloth and gauze body was standardized, with the carburettors rejetted accordingly.

On the front forks, the length of stanchion on which the sliders bore was hard-chrome plated and ground to a micro finish to prolong oil seal life. The front brake anchor became larger and longer, and the previous tapped hole for the mudguard bridge was replaced by a welded-on lug carrying a separate square nut. A new front mudguard was fitted, and it had no holes for a front number plate, which from now on was often mounted across the forks either above or below the headlight, until front plates were deleted for 1974. The steering damper was dropped on all C-range variants, replaced by a chrome fork stem top sleeve nut. The prop stand acquired a stop bolt to allow its position to be adjusted. The exposed spring rear dampers now fitted a castellated collar to protect the adjuster cams from grit. A new chromed grab-rail was fitted, which incorporated the new rear mudguard stay/lifting handle. The rear number plate was modified again to suit. In the rear wheel, internal and external threads changed to UNF. The T100T's 1970 purple and silver colour scheme was entirely in keeping with the spirit of those flamboyant times.

The end of the year marked a break-boundary in T100 production, as during the 'long wait' at Meriden for the oil-in-frame

650, all 500 components were used up early. When the model resurfaced in the chaotic year of 1971, it was principally in twin-carb versions, one exception being a single-carb version of the T100C street scrambler. This was a pity, as for all but complete speed freaks, the 1967-on T100S was the best option. With a less volatile but still lively cam mix, less rapid wear from the lower state of tune and compression, and less fiddly carburettor balancing, this is the one to look out for. However, though officially there would be no more single-carb roadster 500s offered in the UK, in fact a few new Police T100P models, converted with a dualseat to civilian use, came up for sale in the disorganization of the intervening years, and it is also not difficult to convert a Daytona to a single carburettor. Today this is unlikely to happen, as the Daytona is beginning to be something of a cult bike, with prices adjusted accordingly.

**1971** confusingly saw the former T100T now offered in the UK as the T100R Daytona, the former nomenclature for the American version, and accompanied by the T100C Trophy which had resolved itself into a high-level exhaust American street scrambler, in either twin- or single-carb form. Theoretically

now available in the UK, in fact few were sold.

Within the engine, even thicker section con-rods were fitted, with for the first time the cap nuts and bolts also altered. The new-type pushrod covers reverted to oil drain holes at the top end rather than the castellated 'fingers', and the top O-ring was modified to suit. There was a new feature on the rocker boxes to overcome the awkwardness of using a feeler gauge while setting the C-range's minimal tappet clearance. The boxes were fitted with screwed-in side-plugs, sealed with O-rings, which when removed allowed a gauge to be slipped in from the side. Early in the year a new, one-piece oil pressure relief valve was introduced. And the Concentrics replaced their gauze internal strainer with a cast-in weir and and a useful float bowl drain plug. Attached to them for the UK, there was a redesigned air filter to suppress induction noise, still with a pancake-type filter, but within an integral plenum chamber and fed via a horseshoe-shaped induction pipe.

In the gearbox, the inner cover was modified to accommodate a circlip change. More significantly, the gearbox camplate finally became a stronger type with a brace across it (Triumph part no. T4218), which

*1971, and Daytona, now T100R, sported winkers.*

went some way to curing the selection problem, and can be substituted for the previous one. In some cases the camplate may then jam against the index plunger spring boss, and should be ground away to give about 30 thou clearance, though any more will weaken the boss.

The T100C in single-carb form had a 36 bhp engine, as like the T100R compression had dropped to 9:1. Weight for both models had also crept up to 356 lb. As previously for export, the T100C engine fitted iron valve guides, and either one or two $1\frac{1}{8}$ in Concentrics. The T100C had a small chrome headlamp, speedometer only, a bash-plate under the sump, an optional steering damper, folding footrests, stainless steel mudguards, no centre stand and a shapely, unlinked separate pipe and coupled twin silencer exhaust system carried at crankcase level on the left, with the rider's and passenger's legs protected from the hot pipes by a curved wire mesh screen known at Meriden as 'the chip basket'. As sold in these years, it was more 'street' than 'scrambler', with gearing and tyres like the T100R.

Both models fitted Lucas direction

indicators. Like the headlamp, which was carried in new brackets, the winkers were rubber-mounted, though this failed to stop them frequently malfunctioning. The indicators meant new and soon unpopular Lucas switch gear in alloy housing, for the winker switch and cut-out button on the right, and for dipswitch, horn, and headlamp flasher on the left. The housings went on new higher-rise export handlebars, still rubber-mounted and good-looking but limiting at speeds above 70 mph, and so inappropriate for the Daytona's potential performance. The ignition switch was relocated slightly to the left side of the front fork cover. Fork crowns and shrouds were modified to suit all this, the fork crown top being fitted with caps for handlebar attachment and the new shrouds being of built-up construction. The instruments had new dials.

The tail light changed to the pointed Lucas 679 'teat' type in an alloy housing, which sat on a new and rather unsightly extended bracket, with the rear number plate now side-plate mounted. The q.d. rear wheel was no longer available. A third oil tank, still interchangeable with the previous, and bigger again but with the same recommended $5\frac{1}{2}$-pt fill, was fitted. The rear chainguard went back to the 1968 type. All models carried the front and rear orange side reflectors on each side required by US law. The T100R fitted a new exhaust system, and in mid-year, for the UK, this was fitted with the 650's long tapering cone-shaped silencers in an effort to keep noise levels down.

**1972** saw little change. The exhaust pipes on both low- and high-level systems became of the 'push-in' type, deleting the previous screwed-in stub mounting, though dummy finned exhaust pipe clips were still fitted. The push-in exhausts were not to be popular, as they could work loose and distort the exhaust ports. The T100R's exhaust pipes, still coupled close to the ports, changed again, becoming shorter.

The clutch mechanism ramp lever was altered to improve clutch action, and in mid-year, the clutch shock absorber front and rear plates changed in line with the 650s, going to a through-bolt design.

**1973** found the T100C dropped, and in its place for off-road use, though in a very different way, came the soft-tuned TR5T Trophy Trail Adventurer. This was a production version of what scramblers in particular had been doing for years—putting a Triumph engine in a purpose-built oil-bearing frame. The result, originally for export only but available in the UK from November 1972, was an on/off road machine of great charm, and not a little effectiveness. In America that year, contestants on Adventurers won more medals than any other team in the ISDT qualifying contests, and in the event itself, the British team on TR5Ts and Triumph-engined Rickmans came second.

The TR5T's Meriden-built frame was derived from that of the world-beating BSA Victor unit singles, but differed from it dimensionally. This means that home-brewed examples cannot be put together by dropping a Triumph engine into the versions of the oil-bearing frames used for the 1971-on BSA B25SS/B50SS unit singles or their Triumph T25/TR5MX equivalents, at least not without resort to a hacksaw and a welding torch. Triumph (and Adventurer)) specialists Roebuck can supply details. As it was, the TR5T's engine featured alternative central cylinder head studs, and modified rocker boxes on extended cylinder head mounts, to help shoe-horn the engine in and out of the frame.

The TR5T's engine was a standard T100 running at 9:1 compression, but with a 1 in diameter carb, soft cams, and a close ratio gear set with a special high gear pair, giving a lowish 6.57:1 top ratio, in combination with a 53- as opposed to 46-tooth rear sprocket. This produced a very flexible engine. The frame, like the other o.i.f. machines, carried its four pints of oil in thick top and seat tubes. Rear chain adjustment, as on the T25SS etc., was by snail cam. The excellent forks were naked alloy Ceriani-type, running on taper roller head races, and giving 6 in of smooth movement. Footrests were folding. Small chromed mudguards gave minimal protection, particularly the high fixed front one.

The 5½ in chrome headlight was effective, however, and the twinned instruments, their cases chromed on later models, looked smart, as did the polished alloy tank with its shapely red or yellow panels. The wide, 22 in long seat was more comfortable than the contemporary roadster one and could handle a small pillion passenger. The Adventurer was

**Left** *Earls Court, November 1972, and though not perhaps dressed for the trail, this showgoer seems to appreciate the 1973 TR5T Adventurer. As does the Pearly King.*

**Right** *Also known as the Trophy Trail, the oil-in-frame 500 TR5T road/trail bike was a neat package.*

prettier in the metal than in photographs, the only false note in terms of appearance being the matt black silencer (the Y-junction exhausts were chrome), which though unobtrusive was an unattractive design with a horizontal seam, and vulnerable off-road. The high bars were cross-braced, and a compromise, not being wide enough for serious off-road work, but with down-turned ends which became uncomfortable after a while on the road. Indicators were provided, mounted on the bars and by the end of the seat.

The pretty 2.2-gal polished alloy petrol tank, and $3.00 \times 21$ front and $4.00 \times 18$ rear Trials Universal tyres, demonstrated that the Adventurer was better thought out and more serious about its off-road capabilities than a street scrambler; and if its 322-lb weight kerbside, $7\frac{1}{2}$-in ground clearance, vulnerable low-slung silencer, and wet-prone electrics in standard form made it more of a trail bike than a serious competitor, big road/trail machines have since proved themselves a popular format. For walking pace speeds the engine was set too far up in the frame for perfect stability on poor surfaces, but otherwise the Adventurer steered well, except over slippery ruts — it had, after all, been designed for the hard dry dirt of America. It handled as well with a rider in the seat as standing, was comfortable, and provided a responsive ride, with power available below 2,000 rpm and easy, flowing torque, but with enough pulling power on tap to transform it into a bucking bronco on rough, steep grades, which with a determined rider in control it could rocket up with gusto.

On the road too it was fun and stable to ride at moderate speeds, with a chuffing exhaust note, reasonable acceleration and good cornering, with no problem from the

## The 1973 Trophy Trail 500 (TR5T).

1. Chrome front fender mounted high for off-road riding.
2. Small teardrop headlamp, chrome finish—quickly removable.
3. Enduro-type speedometer, adjustable trip odometer to 1/10 mile.
4. Quick removable turn signals mounted on handlebars.
5. Steel ball-ended clutch and brake levers.

6. Enduro-type handlebars.
7. Small switch console incorporates thumb-operated high/low beam lever and turn lever.
8. 2½ gallon polished alloy tank.
9. ¾-length competition saddle.
10. Tucked-in rear turn signals—quickly removable.

11. Class A tail light to meet 1973 federal specifications—polished alloy mounting bracket.
12. Newly-styled rear fender finished in bright chrome.
13. 53-tooth rear sprocket, 6.57:1 overall gear ratio.
14. 4.00x18 Trials tire—polished alloy conical rear hub.
15. 500cc vertical twin engine—one carburetor. Four-speed gearbox incorporates special internal ratios for trail and enduro riding.

16. Skid plate for engine protection.
17. Dual downswept exhaust fits into cannister-type silencer under gearbox. Also fitted with USDA-approved spark arrester. Low exhaust noise of 84.5 dbA.
18. 6¾" fork travel—polished hard-chrome finish on stanchions.
19. Lightweight 6" front brake—conical design—finished in polished alloy.
20. 3.00x21 Dunlop Trials front tire.

**Left** *The TR5T's good points anatomized. The less said about the 6-in front brake the better.*

**Right** *An early 1974 spec T100R released by the workers' blockade in 1975 and out on test. Note the cigar silencers.*

dual-purpose tyres. Maximum speed was around 80 mph. Rattling engine noise and vibration were there, but not bad for the rider. The really bad bit, on or off road, were the brakes, for while the conical 7-in rear was merely vulnerable to water, the tiny 6-in front, designed by the Rickman brothers for use on their two-strokes, was ineffective off-road and dangerously so on tarmac. Riders who used their Adventurers mostly on the road tended to substitute the 8-in conical hub brake from the other o.i.f. models. But overall the Adventurer was a fine package, sadly condemned to a premature end.

For the T100R that year there were only a few detail changes, with the wheels and tyres going to 3.25 × 19 front and 4.00 × 18 rear, the front brake anchor plate being painted black and the mudguards being shorter, chromed and with chromed stays, while at the rear the rear stay/lifting handle was modified to provide mountings for the relocated direction indicators, and the rear light was now a Lucas 917, on which the polished aluminium case had built-in side reflectors, to replace the previous circular bolt-on type. The forks fitted new left- and right-hand top covers with reinforcement of the headlamp mounting slots, and the bottom members also

changed slightly. The petrol tanks no longer had a top weld seam and hence no decorative chrome strip. On the handlebar controls the thumb levers were now longer and the kill button was wisely moved to the left, away from the indicator lever. Drive for the rev counter came via a new one-piece right-angled gearbox, which was interchangeable with its predecessor.

And that was really that for the T100, although in line with Hopwood and Hele policy of providing improved interim models until their modular range came on stream, after a few 1974 Series I T100Rs with torpedo-type silencers had been built at the beginning of the model year, a pre-production batch of about 10 Series II T100D machines was partially completed when Meriden shut down in September 1974. These included adaptations of the bigger twins' silencers and front ends, with alloy forks and disc brake, as well as what John Nelson calls 'major engine improvements'. A couple of hundred Daytonas in varying specifications were among the bikes refurbished and sold off when the blockade lifted in 1974/75.

This section will conclude with a few thoughts and tips on the C-range. Machines before 1965 can provide reliable, general purpose hacks, while after that, still for medium-range use, and particularly after 1967, performance and handling can be more impressive. If '67-on handling at the front makes you think that the head-race bearings are on the way out, it's worth checking the middle fork sleeve nut, which requires little pressure to tighten, and consequently is prone to vibrate loose. Of the performance, as Royce Creasey put it, 'Total maniacs ... will find the Triumph 500 twin ideal ...'. It should be remembered that a 39 bhp output, very similar to a Gold Star, Venom, or indeed most Manx Nortons, in conjunction with a 338-lb dry weight, made the T100T Daytona just about the fastest production British 500. That light weight, plus a low build, have in the past also made the smaller unit twins favourite with girl rockers.

In the engine, much of the advice for the pre-unit (see p. 36–40) also applies. As mentioned, 500 barrels are in short supply, and if a C-range engine is rebored, piston ring condition is vital. Some advise running a rebored engine in for 750 miles and then changing the rings. Piston ring and bore wear generally can be cut by the use of more effective K and N air filters, with suitable rejetting. In additon, the pre-'69 plain bush timing side main bearing is tough enough for normal use, and a groove worn in it is acceptable and does not indicate that it should be changed, as it floats on oil. But if replacement does become necessary, the bushes, in either steel-backed or solid bronze, can present a problem of alignment, because the original line-reamers, which used the opposite drive side bearing as a guide while they reamed the bush to size in situ, are no longer available. A steel-backed bush is preferable, but depends on the original dimensions of the case being correct. Too tight a fit can cause seizure, spinning, and possibly a mangled timing side crankcase, while too much clearance between bearing and shaft can cut off the supply of oil to the big-ends for which the bush is responsible. Approach with care.

Wear points generally were the primary chain and its tensioner, exhaust valves, tappets and the clutch, especially pre-1962. There is a possible solution on the primary chain tensioner, which is to fit the tensioner off the later duplex-chain unit BSA/Triumph singles, the B25/B44/TR25W. This tensioner,

available from unit BSA specialist OTJ in Edenbridge, was fastened under the studs of the alternators which both ranges shared, and only some small spacers are needed to fit it on the Triumphs. While on the subject of alternators and electrics generally, aside from their shortcomings, the '57–'62 distributor parts are now in short supply, and many do and did convert earlier machines to points, though this means locating a new timing cover and all the associated parts, tapered exhaust camshaft with points drive, wiring, retiming, etc. Conversely, if the distributor is retained and a new inlet camshaft is being fitted, it must be the kind with distributor drive gear machined on it.

An aid for the tricky chore of accurate tappet adjustment on the 500s is to substitute the existing adjusting screws and nuts for a kit of lightweight screws, counter-bored for Allen keys, and fitted with alloy nuts. In the clutches, on versions with lock washers, these can be exchanged with advantage for a suitable heavy duty spring washer. In the three-ball clutch, problems in operation may be helped by grinding the ramps to stop the balls skidding. Noise may be caused by wear in the 'ears' of the plates which should be replaced, or in the rollers of the clutch centre; if replacing the latter, the correct $\frac{1}{4} \times .236$ rollers, not $\frac{1}{4} \times \frac{1}{4}$, must be fitted.

In the gearbox, replacing the early plain bushes with the later needle rollers has been mentioned, and with selector problems, substitution of the '71-on camplate (and some even welded on an extra stiffening plate to that). In addition to this, the pointed plunger can be ground to round off its tip, and the spring pre-loaded to fit a $\frac{5}{16}$ in ball-bearing between it and the plunger, or between the spring and the gearcase, though it is important to get the plunger exactly in line with the camplate. Finally, a Daytona can be converted to single-carb spec using the appropriate manifold and one of its own $1\frac{1}{16}$ carburettors, but the main jet has to be changed to 170 and the throttle slide to a No. 4.

C-range interchanges with other Triumphs are limited, as the 650/750 engine was taller, longer and wider, and will not fit in 350/500 frames. Bath-tubs on the 650 were $\frac{1}{2}$ in longer and had different fixing points. Both bath-tubs and skirts today are in short supply. Ironically, after years of dumping, they are now rather sought after, and some replicas in

*This was to have been the main 1974 500, the T100D, with disc front brake. But only a handful were made.*

glass fibre are available. 650 gearbox internals, shaft, gears, selectors, camplate, etc., were also totally different from the C-range. Within the range, converting a 350 to 500 means new pistons, barrels, cylinder head, and con-rods, as well as gearing up, and is not worth it. But since the same stroke was used on all versions, any crankshaft up to the end of 1968, suitably balanced, will fit any C-range machine. After that, as well as the change in mains came the Unified Threads. If in doubt about a component, UNF bolts had a circular recess in their heads, studs a circular groove in the end, and nuts had interlocking circles on the side.

In conclusion, most of the C-range had their points, but it's hard to quarrel with the notion that a '69–'70 T100S was one of the two or three best all-round roadsters that Triumph ever produced.

## Triumph: The unit 350 and 500 twins — production dates and specifications

### Production dates
Twenty-one/3TA — 1957–66
5TA Speed Twin — 1959–66
T100A Tiger 100 — 1960–61
T100SS Tiger 100 — 1962–65
T90 Tiger 90 — 1963–69
T100 Tiger 100 — 1966
T100S Tiger 100 — 1967–70
T100T Daytona — 1967–70
T100C Trophy 500 — 1971–72
T100R Daytona — 1971–74
TR5T Trophy Trail/Adventurer — 1973–74
T100D Daytona Series 2 — 1974

### Specifications
**3TA, T90**
Capacity, bore and stroke — 348 cc
(58.25 × 65.55 mm)
Type — ohv twin
Ignition — Coil
Weight — 3TA (1959) 345 lb; T90 (1962) 336 lb

**5TA. T100, TR5T**
Capacity, bore and stroke — 490 cc
(69 × 65.5 mm)
Type — ohv twin
Ignition — coil
Weight — 5TA (1959) 350 lb; T100A (1960) 350 lbs; T100T (1969) 337 lb; TR5T (1973) 322 lb

### Triumph 650 unit twins, pre oil-in-frame (1963–1970): 6T Thunderbird, TR6 Trophy, T120 Bonneville

The unit 650 Triumphs of the '60s were probably the ones most people owned, since by 1972 it was reckoned that around 250,000 Bonnevilles had been built — at least three times as many as any comparable Norton or BSA range of twins. At first they were not rated as highly as their unit predecessors. But the knowledge of regular improvements, endorsed by production race victories, meant that Triumph enthusiast Derek Gedling spoke for many when he characterized the unit bikes as charismatic rather than classy, but added, 'Having said that, the 1969 Trophy was arguably the pinnacle of all that Triumph learned over many years. That was as good as they got.'

During the period the Bonnie and its single-carb cohorts were pre-eminent, partly through their own attractiveness, performance and price, but also because of a certain lack of opposition. The main 650 rival was BSA's own unit, the A65, which was simultaneously launched; it was decidedly uncharismatic, rarely a hit on the street, and in tuned form revealed itself as vibratory and rather unreliable. The same could be said of both remaining pre-unit offerings, the AJS/ Matchless twins and Royal Enfield's 750

Constellation, though each had its merits. Norton's Featherbed-framed 650 SS was the real contender — the 750 Atlas and its AMC hybrids once again shook too much — but due to company upheavals, Norton's 650 was built in relatively miniscule numbers compared to the Triumph. Only towards the end of the decade would a second generation, of Royal Enfield's 750 Interceptors, especially in Mk2 form, and above all Norton's 750 Commando, see the Bonnie begin to be superseded as the top twin.

The background to the unit 650's introduction will be found in Volume 5. Here it can be said that in tune with the progressive nature of the Bonneville's development, in these first unit machines there were some steps forward and some steps back. Broadly there were gains in the frame and, soon, the forks, but losses in smoothness and electrical reliability. For **1963** the B-group consisted of the same T120 Bonneville sports twin-carb flagship; the TR6 Trophy, which despite its competition-bred name was now, in the UK, primarily a roadster and virtually a single-carb Bonnie; and the partially enclosed 6T Thunderbird, the single-carb cooking version.

On all the 650s the new unit construction engine went into a frame which reverted, after the last big pre-units' duplex downtube, to a classically Triumph single downtube, but now in a thicker $1\frac{5}{8}$ in diameter 12-gauge tubing. The most significant development was at the rear, where the brazed-in forged lug carrying the rear fork pivot, which was new, had its ends secured to the rear engine mounting plates, and these in their turn were bolted to struts on the rear sub-frame. There was a definite, noticeable improvement in rigidity on the previous unbraced 'torsion bar' arrangement, though until the introduction of an O-ring the new set-up was still prone to rapid wear, particularly on the inner faces of the end plates which controlled swinging-arm float, and this could then lead to renewed poor handling. But the increased lateral rigidity created an assembly stiff enough to eliminate most of what had led the T110 frames to be known as 'instant whip', though a further and final development in that direction would not come until 1968.

The unit engine, like the C-range, reassuringly retained the shape of the gearbox and timing chest, clearly discernible on the timing side crankcase cover, emphasizing how, despite the unified overall construction, internally these two areas, as well as the primary chaincase, remained separate, with their own supply of lubricant at this time. The engine exhibited a new compactness and sleekness of line, one reason being that the previous magneto ignition was gone, with sparks as well as lights now deriving from the 6-volt, crankshaft-mounted alternator, via two MA6 coils, rubber-mounted on the frame beneath the tank. As on the C-range, the points were now fitted accessibly behind a chromed circular cover at the front of the timing chest. Drive for them, as for the rev counter, was taken off the exhaust camshaft. Since the points were the same 4CA type as used for the C-range, and the system employed the same 'switch-controlled' voltage regulation, they hence lacked individual timing adjustment for each cylinder. For details of the system's problems, please see p. 50–51.

One area of engine redesign which particularly interested enthusiasts was the top end, where, though the barrels remained of cast iron, the previous problems of cylinder head cracking and gas sealing were tackled with a new light alloy, nine-stud head. Still with splayed ports on the twin-carb T120, the latter's inlet manifold was now not of alloy as on the others, but featured steel screw-in adapters. The nine-stud head featured increased finning of the head itself, as well as now on the rocker boxes. The caps on the latter changed from the previous hexagon-headed type to ones bearing cruciform slots, which, though their edges were serrated for a securing spring, with vibration still proved prone to unscrew themselves and fall off. On the unit 650s, access for adjusting the tappet clearance was not good, and a 'cranked' feeler gauge had to be used.

On the head itself, the 'ninth', centre, stud required a socket to remove it, and was difficult to get at with the exhaust rocker covers still in place. But its presence did help gas sealing between the cylinders. The other 8 bolts had their centres increased diametrically outward, which as well as countering cracking left room for future increases in inlet port dimensions.

At present, the valve sizes were the same as previous, though the new valve springs were shorter, and the 6T fitted new valve spring cups. Also different was a hollow dowel fitted in the joint faces between the head and barrel, for oil feed to the tappets. Failing to replace this at rebuild time would lead to bad oil leaks. It can be mentioned here that the camshafts, unlike the C-range's which ran directly in the cases, for the 650s ran on Oilite bushes. The heads and barrels would go (and were often fitted) on pre-unit eight-stud machines.

Further down, the new, still one-piece but lighter, crankshaft with its less substantial

**Left** *The unit 650 newcomer — the TR6 Trophy single-carb sportster for 1963.*

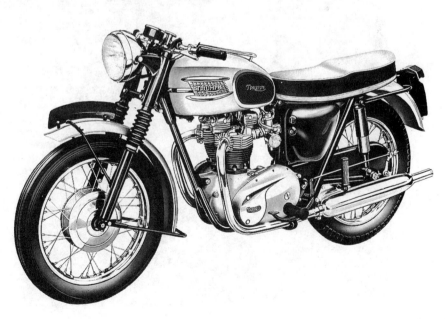

**Right** *The first unit Bonneville, T120 for 1963.*

flywheel and 85 per cent balance factor, shared its essential dimensions with previous ones, and with appropriate balancing, exchanges were possible. The same polished alloy con-rods were fitted, with pistons giving 8.5:l c.r. for the T120 and TR6. The new shaft did, however, have an extended right end ground surface journal replacing the previous oil control bush in the timing cover, for the shaft married with a new and effective timing side oil seal in the timing side cover. This was a welcome move as it ensured constant lubrication under pressure to the big-ends. The crankshaft timing gear changed from the previous one, due to variations in the timing side shaft clamping, with the intermediate cam gear wheel revised. The crankcase itself had the oil pressure indicator button moved round to its front, and the oil pump's scavenge plunger was now on the left, as with the C-range.

Another major change was the move to $\frac{3}{8}$ in duplex primary chain, running between fixed centres, so the tensioning was now by a rubber-faced blade like the C-range's. This was operated by a combined drain plug in the base of the chaincase and was subject to the same inconvenience as on the smaller units. Transmission changes included a new three-spring clutch, clutch shock absorber, and operating machanism. The clutch, in a new housing, featured an extra pair of plates, making six pairs in all, as well as fitting a revised centre, secured by Woodruff key, with a copper thrust washer located inboard of the clutch sprocket in an attempt to reduce rattles, so that the load was taken directly on the sprocket face. The shock absorber became a three-vane rather than the previous four-vane type, though according to John Nelson, the early rubbers on the first examples were prone to breaking up until replaced by new ones of a softer mix and with chamfered edges. The new clutch-operating mechanism, located in the gearbox outer cover, was the three-ball type as described for the C-range on p. 52. Though the design was similar to that of the C-range, the only parts in common were the pivot, springs and balls. The gearbox internals were largely unchanged. The layshaft

*Compact, and not looking too different, a unit single-carb 650 engine in 1963.*

*The gleaming 1963 TR6 Trophy. Many would prefer this single-carb sportster.*

was still below the mainshaft, with the layshaft running in needle rollers and driving the speedometer cable, and the same kick-start quadrant, oil seal and sprockets were used, though there was an initial problem with top gear selection from slight fouling of the quadrant.

The new engine was compact and good-looking, especially with the Bonnie's splayed head, and with a neat decorative flute embossed with the Triumph name on the primary chaincase, to distinguish it from the C-range. The chaincase, incidentally, no longer supported the left-hand footrest. For the factory, the 650 unit construction's benefits were that it was cheaper and easier to produce, just as alternators were cheaper than magnetos, and yet enough of the old was retained to ensure minimum disruption of production. For the owner, its virtues were rigidity and lightness, and low engine weight contributed to the lowest dry weight for the machines as a whole of all British 650 twins: at 363 lb, a 1963 Bonneville was nearly 30 lb lighter than both the last pre-unit T120 and BSA's new A65 Star unit twin, all of which helped produce sparkling performance. The down side, as well as electrical unreliability, was vibration, which, though probably not greatly increased from the previous high-performance 650s, coupled with transmission harshness to give a rather less comfortable ride. In addition, initially there were a few instances of main bearing failure because the new crankshaft was sufficiently stiffer than the previous one to pressure the bearings diametrically. Overall some charm was traded for some stomp.

On the cycle side, as well as the rear end revision, the fork crowns were new, and incorporated a steering head lock as well as eye-bolt mountings for the handlebars, which were carried from now on in bonded rubber bushes. The handlebars, for the Bonnie and TR6 at least, had become a conventional $\frac{7}{8}$ in diameter. The 6T's lower fork crown was modified. The T120 fitted a front mudguard with the same shape as previously, but with different rear and bridge stays, and beneath it the front wheel dropped from the previous $3.25 \times 19$ to $3.25 \times 18$ in dimensions, while its rear tyre contracted from $4.00 \times 18$ to $3.50 \times 18$ in. All the 650s now fitted the same blade-type rear mudguard; and for those with q.d. rear wheels, the attachment altered.

The 6T Thunderbird's bath-tub panelling now shrank to abbreviated 'skirts' similar to those featured on the T100SS and the new Tiger 90 (see p. 49). The 6T's version, however, lacked the C-range's machines pair of switches on the left-hand side panel, as these were carried in the nacelle, which to accommodate them carried a smaller ammeter now placed centrally between the speedometer and the steering damper. By contrast, the T120 and TR6 adopted a new left-hand side panel with the separate lights and ignition switches mounted on it (somewhat inconveniently for the rider). The two-level dualseats with grey tops and lower trim band on all were now, like the C-range, hinged, from the left. The T120 and TR6 had a new 4-gal petrol tank, with a 3-gal option also available, now fastened by two rubber-mounted bolts in the base at the front and one through a flange at the rear. Badges and trim were as previously, but the knee-grips became the stick-on type and there were larger tank indents at the rear to accommodate them. 'Easy-lift' centre stands developed for Police models were fitted to all. The Thunderbird's exhaust system reverted from single to twin silencers. The TR6 exhaust system remained siamesed, but with a revised right-side section, and both it and the 6T now fitted a circular air filter with coarse paper internals on their carburettors, much more accessible than the previous D-shaped type, while the Bonnie's twin $1\frac{1}{16}$-in Monoblocs remained unprotected, and also without air slides. The twin-carb flagship was striking in two-tone Ivory and Gold colours, a sporty finish first seen on the Ariel Golden Arrow as well as on that year's Tiger 90.

In addition to the three home-market 650s, there were also USA T120R and T120C variants in both East and West Coast versions, soon to be joined by the T120 TT dirt racer. But though their production came to dominate Meriden's output in the '60s' domestic market slump, export models are not covered in this book. Details and illustrations of them can be found in John Nelson's definitive *Bonnie*, to which this section is much indebted. The unit engine, however, was also the basis of the Police model which came to be known by Neale Shilton's acronym, 'Saint', for Stop/Scoop Anything In No Time. Since many of these found their way on to the UK market at the end of their official duties, some details may be in order, though exact specifications often varied

between different regional forces.

In 1963 the basic model was distinguished by its lack of rear enclosure, and by a pull-up knob on the headlamp shell which gave a boosted output from the high output alternator for when the radio was in use. Like other Police models it fitted a single seat, and in place of the customary tank-top rack there was a recess for the radio equipment. In addition, both the engine and gearing had been specially set up to the required type of power. It retained the Thunderbird's 7.5:l c.r., but used the Bonneville's E3134-form inlet camshaft, while breathing through a special Monobloc, not interchangeable with the standard instrument, and with its own appropriate air cleaner. Small-bore exhausts were fitted, which comp. shop experience knew could help provide a worthwhile increase in bottom-end torque. In addition, gearing entailed a wide-ratio box but with overall lowering of the ratios to give superlative acceleration. The result, in conjunction with special large Resonator-type silencers and police riding skills, was a machine powerful enough to offer a 102 mph top end, and that was despite the extra weight of its equipment plus leg shields and a windscreen, which normally scrubbed at least 10 mph off a machine's speed. It also provided a combination of smooth, quiet power delivery (they always seemed to appear out of nowhere) with rapid acceleration where necessary, with 11.8 seconds being recorded from 30 to 80 mph. Assembled and tested by a special team, even well used,

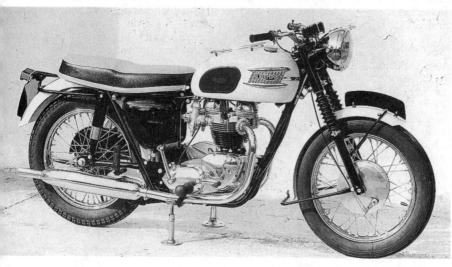

*650 flagship, the black and ivory-finished T120 for 1963.*

*The 6T Thunderbird stayed with the nacelle. The 1964 version features separate holes for cables.*

these could be desirable machines, and as one West Midlands Chief Driving Instructor put it, 'The SAINT always produced the goods'.

**1964**, with the B-range handling improved, saw the steering addressed by the fitting of new forks, common, with a few minor variations, to the whole range. Identifiable by their larger diameter shrouds, these were the 'external spring' forks with the spring going round the outside of the fork inner tubes instead of inside them. Though more substantial than previously, and taking slightly more damping oil at $\frac{1}{3}$ pt per leg, the only real design differences from the previous ones were damping and springs, as well as the fact that the external springs allowed an improved oil seal arrangement, as the previous forks had been prone to leakage. At the lower end of each spring, within the chrome-plated housing screwed to the top of the fork slider, was a large-diameter oil seal with two internal lips against the inner tube, and a garter-type spring ring operated on the seal's lower lip. At the top end, a rubber seal was added to the steering damper to stop it unwinding. In practice, as on the C-range, the new fork would be found unacceptably harsh in operation, and was retuned for the following

year.

On the T120 and TR6 the rubber bellows stayed in place, while on the 6T the nacelle was changed to accommodate the new fork. Its 'legs' were altered, with the shroud now separate from the nacelle sections. On top, the actual nacelle, though still featuring separate switches, changed to the same type as the C-range. The Thunderbird's front mudguard had its bridge piece changed for two pieces of bent strip bolted to the guard and with their lower ends attached to a T-shaped bracket. Its rear blade mudguard now differed from the other two, though like them it fitted a common redesigned lifting handle, now running straight back and round the outside of the guard. In addition, another piece of production streamlining was that all now fitted a new number plate common to the whole range.

The Thunderbird also took the lead in adopting 12-volt electrics, with twin 6-volt batteries mounted under the seat and fed through a rectifier, and with — a welcome touch — charge governed by a Zener diode with a push-in connection, mounted on a light alloy plate under the tank nose. However, this early alloy-plate heat sink was not very satisfactory, and could cause electrical failures.

In the engine and gearbox for all there were some major revisions in the light of the first year's unit experience. The crankcase was redesigned in the region of the sump filter, with the aim of improving the oil pump's scavenging. A greater gauze area was provided for the filter, as well as a larger drain plug. The timing of the engine breathing was modified, with the breather disc located in the left bush housing of the inlet camshaft and the breather tube connected via a connector piece with the oil tank froth tower and run to the rear of the machine. The oil tanks themselves now fitted separate drain plugs, as well as changing their lower fixing from a bolt

*Modified T120/TR6 mudguard mountings for 1964.*

to a rubber-isolated spigot.

In the gearbox, as a measure to ease production problems, the sprocket splines were strengthened and had two tapped holes added to them, and the high gear splines altered. Neither sort were interchangeable with the previous ones. The new high gear required a gearbox sprocket cover plate with a larger centre hole and oil seal to suit. To help oil tightness, the kick-start lever was modified, with its previous sealing ring changed to an oil seal fitted into the outer cover inner housing. The gearbox quadrant spindle deleted a groove and its threaded end. The clutch shock absorber rubbers were altered as mentioned.

The previous year's main bearing failures led to the use of 'three-spot' bearings which gave greater clearance and hence coped better with increased pre-loading of the bearing. But unfortunately, drive side bearing failures were to persist. This did not discourage Meriden from pumping up the sports model's power a little. The T120's inlet valve became of Nimonic material, and its diameter was enlarged to 'Thruxton' $1\frac{19}{32}$ in size, with the exhaust at $1\frac{7}{16}$ in, and the choke of the carburettors on both T120 at TR6 was increased to $1\frac{1}{8}$ in. This produced a claimed extra horse for the T120 and 47 bhp at 6,700 rpm. The Bonnie's twin carbs became 'handed' left and right, and a balance pipe was fitted between the two induction stubs to help achieve even tickover. The TR6 adopted its own round air filter with coarse felt element.

On the cycle side, to help counter the effects of vibration on the rider, the 650s, which already employed two head steadies, now had their rear engine mounting plates modified. The footrests were now mounted directly onto these rear plates, which increased ground clearance but meant that the footbrake pedal had to be redesigned, and the rear brake rod was re-routed to the inside of the left suspension unit. The resulting kinked brake rod was rapidly found unacceptable and it would be changed the following year. The centre stand was given a brazed-in operating arm in place of the previous cottered one which had caused problems. A deeper and wider rear chainguard was fitted, with a new 'pull-on' stoplight switch mounted on it. At the sharp end, the speedometer and optional rev counter changed from Smiths Chronometric to the inferior Magnetic instruments, whose anti-vibration claims were soon found to be highly optimistic. Finally, the T120 and TR6's front mudguard's tubular stay and strip bridge were modified so that both ran to a point ahead of the fork leg, where they were bolted to a flat plate on each side, which in turn was bolted to the fork leg.

As a *Motor Cycle* T120 test put it, 'The amount of enjoyment [the Bonneville] provided is something which can never be listed in a mere performance summary', let alone in a catalogue of modifications. A combination of lightness and around-town docility with incredible acceleration, particularly from 65 to 85, and a 14.6-sec standing quarter plus a top speed of 112 mph (on that test, but 108 was more usual) added up to a rider's machine which the coil ignition, for all its faults, made easy to start and to get the best from. It was also economical: a 1965 Rider's Report on the Bonnie found average petrol consumption to be around 60 mpg, while a Thunderbird test in 1963 gave 69 mpg at 60 mph. Many seasoned riders still favoured the single-carb, 7.5:1 c.r. Thunderbird with its 37 bhp output as the best all-rounder. With its looks restored by the 'skirts', mechanically noisy as they all were, but with a quieter Resonator silencer, the Thunderbird offered better acceleration lower down the rev band than the T120, and was no slouch either, with a top speed of just over the ton.

The handling on all had improved, though the new forks' damping, despite that year's revision, was still only just adequately comfortable, and a light front end and the weave that it could cause remained, revealed for instance while running at high speeds downhill, or by hard acceleration which had the front wheel skimming the tarmac. The Rider's Report owners agreed that though the 'Rattle Snake' (as the previous flex-prone frame with its rear end wallow and weave had been known) 'had curled up and gone to sleep' on long fast bends, particularly the bumpy ones, it was still best to keep the power on. Detail niggles included the Bonnie/TR6 mudguarding, skimpy for English weather, as well as its lighting and horn. They also noted the Bonnie's frequent electrical problems, and at factory level, John Nelson could confirm that the most important development of them all in terms of service problems would be the switch to the 12-volt,

Zener-diode control system in 1966, plus further progressive electrical improvements.

The gearbox remained notchy but acceptable, and the clutch when in good adjustment very light and pleasant to use. Rider comfort was good, with the new tank an ideal size between the knees, and the Bonnie's bars, swept-back but flat, gave a wind-cheating forward lean, though the unit machines and their 31-in seat height provided a slightly taller ride than previously and were a 'little high for short-legged riders'. The compensation for 1964 was improved ground clearance. The SLS brakes, 8 in front and 7 in rear, were good enough for low and medium speeds, but not really up to the high-speed

*Bob Currie powers a 1964 Bonnie out of a bend.*

potential. The free-revving T120 could cruise anywhere between 45 and 85 mph; it could be held above that too — *Motor Cycle*'s Bob Currie held 108 for 15 miles — but as the Riders reported, at 90 you had to watch for bits falling off if you held it too long. The engine, though, proved itself tough, and would 'take a belting' and stay in tune, and oil leaks were conspicuously absent from most test reports, emphasizing that less-than-perfect owner rebuilds may well be the main cause of the big Triumph's reputation for oiliness. At this time, however, the gearbox was a prime source. But much, including the 650's undeniable high-speed vibration, could be forgiven while you were experiencing the Bonnie's power, which came in a steady surging tide rather than a power band's kick in the pants. Unquestionable sales success in 1964/65 showed that Triumph were providing what big bike riders wanted, if speed was their game.

At the factory, worries persisted about the drive side mains and about piston skirt seizure, often from contact-breaker problems, leading to over-retarded ignition at high rpm. While the 1964 piston skirt troubles probably related specifically to electrical deficiencies causing high piston crown temperatures, interestingly, on the twin-carb models, piston trouble would most often come on the drive side (left) cylinder. Production race wizard Syd Lawton had a theory on this puzzling phenomenon. On his endurance race Triumphs he always fitted a richer main jet on the left-hand carburettor. His reasoning was that because oil was fed into the crank on the right-hand side, more lubricant reached that side's big-end, which ultimately cooled the piston crown. So the left-hand piston had it harder, and a one-size richer main jet helped it run cooler. The 1964 Thunderbird in fact fitted a new piston with a slotted oil control ring groove and closer running clearance, aiming at improved quietness. Meanwhile, the contact-breakers going out of adjustment also contributed to vibration, which was splitting mudguards and oil tanks in some cases.

The other persistent problem in the engine was rapid wear of the under-lubricated exhaust camshaft, resulting in 'threepenny bit' flats on the lobes. Exhaust cam followers also wore, despite the dowel hole allowing pressure-fed oil to pass to them, because they lacked the inlet follower's splash feed from the crank. Solutions for this would consist of a combination of lubrication and metallurgy. In the meantime, Triumph specialist Brian Bennett estimates Bonneville valve guide life at between 12,000 and 18,000 miles. Ignoring maintenance would aggravate the problem, as incorrect valve clearances led to valves 'hammering' their seat, which also deteriorated fast. The reduced tension on the springs then caused valve bounce and further hammering, as well as letting the cam followers and the camshaft hammer against each other and wear the camshafts.

In the transmission, the duplex primary chains still wore quite quickly, and the clutch could present problems. The unit clutch's copper thrust washer between the clutch hub and basket, when worn, allowed the clutch body to oscillate when the clutch was engaged. In addition, the three clutch-securing nuts were of brass at this time, and the small protrusions on their inner face were likely to become worn down, causing the springs to remain up and the clutch to drag. Later steel screws plus stronger T140 springs can be the answer. In mid-1964, from DU66246, the clutch-operating mechanism was modified, with an operating spoke for the cable nipple deleted and the cable now slotting directly into the three-ball spider.

**1965**, which saw the Bonnie in a beautiful Pacific Blue and Silver finish, brought one major internal revision to the 650 engine, as well as a number of detail changes. To try and counter the continuing occasional drive side main bearing failure, for this year only the crankshaft was now postively located on its drive rather than its timing side. This was achieved by fitting a new crankshaft timing pinion which butted up to the outer face of the main bearing journal instead of the inner spool of the bearing itself. The new pinion also provided the necessary clearance on the opposite bearing side. The engine drive sprocket was also altered so that it now butted up to the inner spool of the driveside bearing rather than the end of the crankshaft splines. It was hoped that this reverse arrangement would also lead to more positive alignment of the quick-wear primary chain. In practice, a change of bearing the following year would be needed to do the trick as far as the bearing failures were concerned.

The problem of wandering ignition timing due to the near impossibility of resetting both cylinders correctly with the 4CA points had

*Thruxton Bonneville production racer at the 1964 Show, and available for that year only — and not to very many riders.*

made it imperative to use an accurate method of finding TDC, which meant provision for stroboscopic timing. So for this year, in the top face of the crankcase behind the cylinder block, a tapped hole was provided, closed off with a plug. When the plug was replaced with an adapter carrying a headed plain pin, the engine shaft could be rotated until the pin engaged with a notch in the flywheel and hence locked the engine at TDC. In practice, it was found at the factory that for strobing up it was more important to be able to set the engine fully advanced (38° BTDC) electronically, and the notch position would be altered accordingly.

On the cycle side, the external-spring forks had their damping made more progressive and revised to give an inch more movement, with longer, lower-rate springs being fitted plus longer stanchions, bottom outer members and inner damping sleeves. Until 1971, however, the 650's suspension would remain on the hard side, both at the front and with the 145-lb rear unit springs fitted as standard to the Home models. The method of front fork construction changed also, with the fork's sliding members no longer steel tubes with brazed-on fork ends, but the entire lower member now being extruded from a solid billet of steel, with the shrouds adapted to suit on the Thunderbird's nacelle forks as well as the other two.

Externally also the T120 and TR6 fitted a light alloy collar above neater rubber fork gaiters. The steering damper became a stepped design, and had to be fitted with the thick end downwards. The front wheel spindle was adapted to suit the fork changes, and all wheels now incorporated new bearing grease retainer discs and felt sealing washers, not terribly effective solutions to the problem of rapid wear; today sealed bearings are the answer. The 6T's voluminous front mudguard changed to a conventional design, with bolted-on front stays attached to clips round the fork legs just above the wheel spindle. It also severed a link with the past in discarding the old front number plate with its shapely surround in favour of a plain one; the TR6 and T120's front plate now had a stay cut-out. In the optional q.d. rear wheel, ball races were substituted for the previous taper roller bearings, which had been prone to wear.

The swinging-arm pivot bolt was moved from the left to the more accessible right side. The angle of the prop stand lug was modified to stop bikes falling over on a rising camber. The previous year's kinked brake rod became a straight pull job, mounted on the cam spindle so that it could pass inboard of the

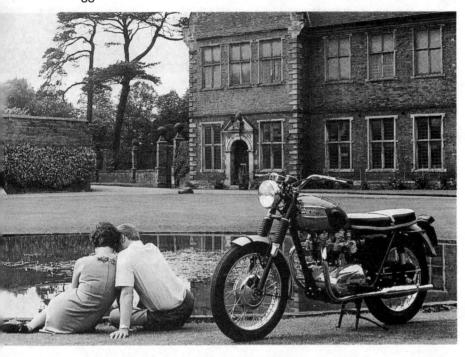

*The stuff that dreams are made of. A fine day, a bird, a stately home and a 1965 TR6 Trophy.*

rear sub-frame tube via a short tube welded to the outer face of the left-hand rear engine mounting plate. The brake pedal was formed with the spindle, so that it operated in a bush in the frame. The horns were now mounted beneath the tank nose rather than under the seat as previously. The exhaust system, as vulnerable to cracking as on other Triumphs, was altered and strengthened, with the pipes becoming more swept back, as well as being joined by an extra stay across the front of the engine. For the UK sports models, T120 included, the longer Resonator silencers were fitted, and the silencers' clips were also linked, though the silencers themselves still remained prone to cracking circumferentially behind their mountings. The wider of two optional centre stands (to allow for fat rear tyres) was now fitted as standard.

In the engine the oil pressure relief valve finally deleted the leak-prone, impractical indicator button with its two springs, and became a single spring type behind a plain dome nut. Within the primary chaincase, a longer alternator cable nut was fitted to help prevent one of the hazards of alternator electrics, the alternator wires fouling the primary chain. In mid-year, at DU22682, the cylinder head fitted alloy exhaust pipe adapters in place of the previous steel adapter stubs. These had tended to chatter and wear their threads away, and when that happened, air could be taken in by the exhaust valves, causing a weak-running engine. But the alloy adapters would soon prove unsuitable too, due to loosening off, and the steel stubs were back by mid-1966. Pegging them with self-tapping screws is a stopgap measure; helicoiling, or a shrunk-on alloy collar welded into place, are more permanent solutions.

In the gearbox, oil tightness was pursued, and for this year only a felt washer was fitted next to the sprocket nut, outboard of the output sleeve oil seal, in the hope of protecting the seal's edge from damage by grit. The kick-start's ratchet spring and sleeve reverted to a shorter, pre-1955 design, but with new parts, including a thrust washer, to prevent some previous burring-up, which could stop the kick-start returning all the way. A permanent welch washer now replaced the previous bolt used to seal the drilling/boring access hole in the rear of the box.

**1966** was a major change year, the first of four years of ongoing improvement. The 650's frame geometry adopted a race-bred steering head angle; all adopted stronger mains, positive lube for the cams, 12-volt electrics and a bigger oil tank; and there was a first braking improvement. At the same time, however, the Bonneville's state of tune was increased to the point where, as John Nelson put it, 'Many at Meriden felt [that they were] transforming a high-speed tourer into a disguised production racer, which unless all the high performance parts were used, caused premature fatigue and failure'. The situation developed where Service was surreptitiously curing customers' 'rough' T120s by quietly substituting E3325-form inlet camshafts, 8:1 c.r. pistons and lower gearing.

Although this was the 6T Thunderbird's last year, its place was very much to be taken by the single-carb TR6 Trophy, and it will be remembered that for a road bike, it was the less temperamental 1969 Trophy rather than the T120 with its difficult-to-synchronize twin carbs which was judged to be 'as good as they got'. Until around 1968, though upgraded in line with the T120 on principal engine and frame modifications, the TR6 always retained the basic reliable cooking model specs, i.e. valve guides, tappets (as 6T) etc., despite using Bonnie pistons and cams. 1967 would bring tappets commonized with the T120, and 1968 commonized valves.

Doug Hele's development work and racing experience with the 500 twins for Daytona, with the hands-on element provided by Percy Tait, led directly to the frame change for the 650s which tackled the previous front end lightness and high-speed steering weave. Hele isolated the problem as largely one of weight distribution. A prototype machine's centre of gravity was lowered and more trail achieved by cutting more than an inch from the frame top tube, so that the engine was lowered half an inch, with half an inch added

to the trail, and the head angle (in the 650 production version) was reduced to 62°. With Hele back from Daytona, improvement was incorporated in early 1966 at engine no. 25277, with a new front frame (interchangeable with the old) incorporating a new head lug casting. The revised frames can also be easily identified because for the first time they fitted lugs for attaching a fairing, though the Thunderbird's nacelle had to come off for one to be used on that model.

The swinging-arm also had its right side leg moved out by $\frac{1}{4}$ in to take larger section rear tyres, and the rear frame was modified to incorporate two round pegs on the right side to accept a new rubber-mounted battery platform. A little later, at DU27672, a new bottom fork lug gave the 650s a slightly tighter turning circle.

Into the modified chassis of the T120 and TR6 went an engine whose performance was increased as a direct result of Hele's work in establishing Bonneville supremacy in production racing over the next four years. The BSA unit twins could be discounted and, as on the street, the struggle that mattered was with what were largely, ironically, also Hele's own creations, the 650SS Nortons, which had dominated the endurance race scene from 1961-64. Hele's experiments in increasing the Triumph's power had centred on camshafts and exhaust systems. It was discovered that valve springs designed for use with the Dowson cam, a mild camshaft with quietening ramps, when used in conjunction with 'R'-type exhaust cam followers, with their base radius of $1\frac{1}{2}$ in compared with the $\frac{3}{4}$ in standard, gave both quick valve lift and a

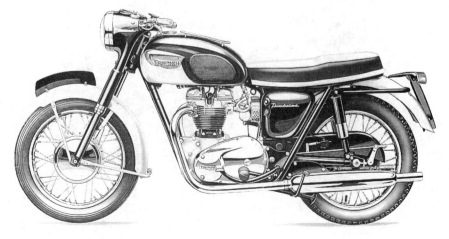

*1966 6T Thunderbird in its last year retained its solid good looks.*

longer period of opening. The torque curve was fattened between 5,500 and 6,000 rpm which, with a 7,000 red line, was more relevant to racers than road riders, but it did provide greater flexibility in the gears. This arrangement, together with a compression rise to 9:1, went on the 1966 Bonneville. This raised its claimed output to 48 bhp at 6,700 rpm. All the 650s adopted the 6T's shorter valve springs, with valve spring cups shortened to allow for this.

With the high-performance cam followers, the lubrication problem for the exhaust cam and follower became even more crucial, so for all the 650s the timing side crankcase now incorporated a positive oil supply to the followers. Additional drillways carried a pressure-fed oil supply for a metering dowel in the timing cover to the cylinder base flange joint, from where oil was taken through the tappet pads to further drillways in the exhaust cam follower guide block, both on the standard and the T120's 'R' tappets. Cam followers with oilways have a milled flap on the outside to suit the supply to the guide. Despite the new arrangements, camshaft wear would continue to be a problem. At DU42399 an additional dowel was added to the crankcase/cylinder base joint, to prevent oil pressure loss in case an oil leak developed at the cylinder base. The new cam followers were designed for use with the new pushrod cover tubes, always difficult areas to keep oiltight. The new ones, like those on the C-range, were flanged and had straight walls, and they seated in a silicone rubber washer, retained in a cup washer or collar, top and bottom, with the bottom one located over the

tappet guide block at the base flange.

The crankshaft played its part in the engine's uprating. For all the 650s, as well as reverting to drive side location it shed 2½ lb while maintaining the previous 85 per cent balance factor. This was done by changing the periphery to a stepped cross-section, and it also fitted longer flywheel bolts. Improved acceleration and a livelier feel were the stated aims. The drive side location was done by keeping the primary chain drive sprocket and matching timing pinion introduced for 1965, but inserting the previous clamped washer between the new pinion and the inner spool of the new timing side bearing, to clamp the crankshaft on that side. At the same time a new induction heat-treated intermediate cam gear wheel was fitted. Meanwhile, the bearing on the drive side was changed from the previous form to a heavier duty single-lipped roller. The new arrangements evidently cured the bearing failures, and the lighter crankshaft was as strong as the old, with breakages not occurring until three years later on the ultimate, highly-tuned works production race version. But with the lighter flywheel, vibration 'peaks' from 5,000 rpm increased in intensity.

The 12-volt electrics for the T120 and TR6 still had the tricky 4CA points and, for this year, like the Thunderbird, at first featured two 6-volt batteries in series, until DU32994, when they changed to a single battery with appropriate battery carrier, carrier lining and cross-struts. From the start there was also a new tool tray behind the battery, common to all models. Unlike the Thunderbird's Zener diode, which was carried under the nose

*1966 T120 Bonneville.*

of the tank, the sports 650's was mounted on the inside of the left side panel, ostensibly to leave the nose uncluttered so that a fairing could be fitted if desired. As well as being out of the cooling wind in this location, the earthing tag had to be moved from under the contact face of the diode to the rear of its heat sink at DU30800, and a new right-angled heat sink plate had to be fitted after DU32898 due to failures from 'heat soak' in sunny California. The rectifier was mounted on an improved bracket from DU27007. The ignition switch was changed to a Yale-type one, but it was still carried, for the T120/TR6, along with the light switch, in the left-hand side panel, whose top fixing changed from vertical to horizontal lugs. At DU31565 ignition warning and main beam warning lights were incorporated in the T120/TR6's chrome headlamp shell, along with the ammeter.

On the cycle side, the larger 6-pt oil tank was fitted, and on more flexible rubber mountings. In its neck was an oil bleed adjusting screw controlling the flow of lubricant taken from the return line to the rear chain. The front brake, while remaining a full width hub 8-in SLS type, fitted a new drum with shoes which provided a 44 per cent increase in braking area. This was done by mounting a vertical spoke flange on the right, so allowing the drum surface to extend to the outside of the hub at the same time as making the drum more rigid. At the rear, too, for the standard but not the q.d. wheels, there was a new cast-iron 7-in brake drum, now once again with a bolt-on sprocket, which not only provided sporting riders with an easy way to change gearing, but also meant that a worn sprocket could be renewed without replacing the whole brake drum. A 1967 Bonneville test would describe the new brake as 'extremely powerful', with a stopping figure of 29 ft from 30 mph, while the 1966 Thunderbird test mentioned below achieved 27 ft, though for powerful braking from higher speeds the best was yet to come.

Both standard and q.d. rear wheels altered in another respect, their right-side hub spoke flange being modified to accept the slotted drive sleeve for a speedometer drive gearbox, since speedometer drive moved from the gearbox layshaft, which deleted its drive pinion and the cable take-off point in the inner cover (as well as the previous year's felt washer on the gearbox sprocket, a locking washer taking its place). The new conventional speedometer drive box on the rear hub, though not particularly reliable, was not only easier to replace, but also meant it was no longer necessary, as previously, to substitute a different drive ratio if the gearbox final drive sprocket had been altered. The drive to the rev counter also changed, from the previous simple spade and abutment type to a right-angled drive. It could be substituted for the previous one if a later rev counter head and cable were used.

The Bonneville celebrated its additional performance with a Grenadier Red and White finish with, for this year only, white handlebar grips. With the new 650 frame, as well as a modified dualseat, a new narrower 4- or 3-gal petrol tank was fitted, which severed another link with the '50s in fitting the first 'eyebrow' tank badges. Unfortunately, this petrol tank (F7004) proved itself extremely vulnerable to the hotter twin's increased vibration period, and from then until the end of 1968 a great many of them would split and be returned under warranty.

Further miscellaneous 1966 changes included a longer kick-start shank to cope with the higher compression, modified prop stands and a new primary chain tensioner blade and its trunnion. In the clutch, larger adjusting screws were fitted on the clutch pressure plate. From DU31119 the steering dampers fitted new plastic damping sleeves, and from DU39464, as mentioned, the previous year's alloy exhaust port sleeves reverted to steel ones. Finally, the 6T adopted the sports model's lower fork crown, as well as front mudguard stays now extended and bent to run under the spindle caps where they were retained by the pairs of spindle bolts, while at the back the sports model's blade rear mudguard was fitted.

This was the Thunderbird's last year, the tourer having run out of road in an increasingly youth- and performance-dominated market. It was a pity, since a 1966 *MCM* test characterized it as 'A big-hearted bike with built-in "niceness" that no amount of brutal testing could eradicate'. Still with 7.5:1 compression and its milder cams, available acceleration was spread through the power band with better torque at the lower end; top gear could take you from 20–100 mph. Suspension was found to be on the hard side, though this inspired confidence while cornering, during which the big centre stand was found very ready to ground, and got worn severely during the test. (A *Motor Cycle* 6T test the same year confirmed the absence of back end whip, though reported that on 70-mph bends, if the throttle was eased or the brakes applied, the back end would still wobble.) The new front brake worked well, though it needed a good pull on the lever which, as always on the full Triumph swept-back bars fitted with the nacelle, seemed to be designed for a man with a 12-in handspan. The light clutch action, easy starting and good lights from the 12-volt system were all praised, but the one exception was the noisy gearbox, which with slight clutch drag went 'into the pig category'. Other tests that year also commented on the current Triumph 'box, which made deliberate changes a must. But otherwise to the end the Thunderbird was still 'a thoroughly pleasant motor cycle'.

**1967** saw the Bonneville's performance escalation continue, while both it and the TR6 adopted a number of practical improvements. The Trophy now dispensed with any previous off-road pretensions and took over the 6T's role while increasing its own state of tune. In mid-year came early moves to UNF threads, and a useful uprating with the encapsulated alternator stator.

In the engine, the T120's inlet cam now

adopted the same E3134 form as its exhaust, though with the previous $\frac{3}{4}$-in radius cam follower. The camshafts themselves became copper-plated. The Monobloc carburettor's main jets went up to 240, and late in the year, from DU59320, 30 mm Concentrics were fitted for both 650s, located by high-tensile bolts and locknuts.

The TR6 cylinder head now fitted the Bonnie's larger ($1\frac{7}{16}$ in) exhaust valve, E3134 exhaust camshaft, (R) exhaust cam follower with $1\frac{1}{8}$ in radius feet, and an inlet valve size increased to $1\frac{19}{32}$ in. Compression was raised to the T120's 9:1. But the Trophy's inlet camshaft retained the softer form, while its inlet manifold was adapted to take the Saint's slightly larger $1\frac{3}{16}$-in 389 Monobloc carburettor. The intention was to provide the Saint's combination of smooth low speed and high acceleration. Exhaust camshaft wear had remained a problem in the 650s, and in addition to the copper-plating, the pressure oil feed to the cam followers at first received a new version of the metering dowel in the timing case, which incorporated a filter gauze and a 'jiggle pin' in the metering jet to clear blockages. Then from engine no. DU63043 these were again abandoned in favour of timed tappets, which were designed to open the feed ports in the tappet guide block as the cam rotated off its base circle. Soon

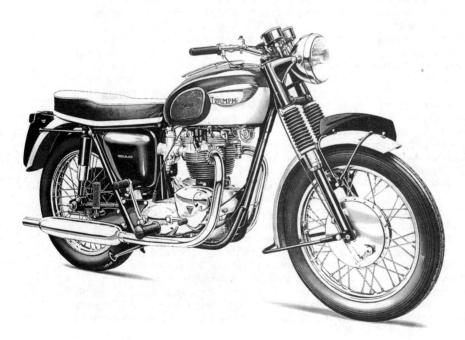

*1967 T120 Bonneville, with many detail improvements.*

afterwards, from DU63241, rubber O-rings were fitted at the base of the tappet guide blocks. The pushrod cover seals had also been modified once again.

In addition, a new oil pump with a scavenge plunger size increased from $\frac{7}{16}$ in to 0.487 in was fitted. It was done to counter wet sumping, which could happen if the engine was run flat out for prolonged periods. This was because the previous pump had found it difficult to return oil from the crankcase to the tank rapidly enough to prevent smoking exhaust pipes. The 650's new pump would lead to a lowering of the oil level in the crankcase – not good for camshaft lubrication. According to John Nelson, the scavenging problem, like the alterations to the exhaust cam follower lubrication, was also affected by the newly available multi-grade high-detergent oils. 650 twins were to run happily on 20/50.

Stronger con-rods, still of polished alloy but with an increased cross-section, were fitted. On top of these went Hepolite pistons (previously Meriden had made their own), and there would be initial problems with piston crown distortion (see Volume 5).

In the gearbox and transmission, sharp corners on the layshaft spines were eased off to help stop occasional competition fractures, and plastic gasket used to seal the high gear splines against oil seeping past the gearbox sprocket. Then from DU48114, in what was also an early example of the changeover to UNF threads, the previous clutch nut tap washer was replaced by a self-locking nut and plain washer, something that in a suitable size can be retrofitted with advantage, as before that the clutch nut had sometimes worked loose. From DU48145 the gearbox mainshaft itself was lengthened from 10.984 in to 11.297 in, and featured Unified Threads, with a suitable nut to hold the kick-start ratchet together.

On the electrical side, the light switch moved off the leftside panel and onto the headlamp, being the same circular type with a chrome centre. It was rather awkwardly positioned for accessibility behind the ammeter and beyond the twinned instruments. The speedometer became a 150 mph type. The ignition switch stayed on the left-hand side panel, on which the previous bolted-on strip at the front became welded on. Louder Lucas 6H horns were fitted.

Of the cycle parts, the Bonnie's front wheel and tyre went from $3.25 \times 18$ to $3.00 \times 19$ in, which one test confirmed gave more precise steering. The dualseat changed to a type that was slimmer at the nose, and featured what would become characteristically Triumph crossways ribbing, though for this year the top stayed light-coloured with white piping, and the grey rim-trim strip also remained. The ribbing helped keep rider and pillion from sliding back under hard acceleration, and to aid the passenger the rear end was slightly raised, and a slight hump added between rider and passenger.

The exhaust pipes were now attached to the crankcase nose by two short brackets rather than to each other by the previous cross-strip. A steering head lock was fitted with the previous lock slot in the top stem deleted, and a new fork top crown employed, now common to all models. In an extra groove in the threads of the dust excluder sleeve nuts, an oil-excluding O-ring was fitted. Threaded steering stops were featured, as well as a plate at the top of the headstock drilled to take the steering lock's pin. Thick plastic handlebar grips were introduced. A new propstand pivot bolt was fitted. The rev counter drive box was given an oil-excluding washer. The rear brake torque stay was redesigned and the rear brake adjuster nut altered, with the threads on the rear frame going UNF, as did those of the tank mounting lug and bottom lug also. During the year, from DU55772, the rocker spindle oil feed pipe reverted from the tank to a take-off pipe below the oil tank return line.

In February *Motor Cycle* tested one of the new Bonnevilles in depth, and provided an interesting insight into its strengths and weaknesses. Performance was highly impressive, with maximum upward changes at 44 mph in first, 63 in second, 88 in third, and a best one-way top speed of 110 mph. Yet the T120 was still tractable, and with the UK market Resonator silencer the exhaust note was acceptable around town. There was, however, an irritating carburation flat-spot just off the pilot jet, which could cause stalling at the low speeds necessary for noiseless changes down into bottom on what was evidently a crunchy gearbox. Gearing was judged to be on the lowish side, which meant that the engine was really over-buzzing at high speed in top gear. On the related problem of vibration, which the rubber-mounted handlebars tacitly acknowledged, this T120 was judged to be the smoothest so far, the worst periods being between 4,000 and 5,000 rpm through the bars, and above 5,000 rpm through the seat. The very fact that it was mentioned was significant: what had previously been acceptable ('people were learning to live with vibration in order to get the power', said Hele of the mid-'60s) was beginning to become more noticeable as average traffic speeds rose, and the Japanese middleweights provided standards for comparison.

The recent frame improvements, plus the 19-in front wheel, had put steering and handling on a par with anything comparable, but the steering was still found light, especially at 100 mph, and above that there was a suspicion of high-speed weave. The suspension, front and rear, was excellent, and the brakes smooth and very powerful. The high footrests and relatively low seat gave an unusual riding position ('jockey-like' was not invoked, though perhaps could have been), but one that was comfortable when you got used to it, particularly since the footrests were set far enough to the rear to relieve tension at

high speed. There were a few niggles—the usual excessive-reach control levers aggravated by the new fat handlebar grips; a headlamp giving a wide pool rather than a long beam of light, which restricted speeds to 55–60 mph after dark; the ammeter partially and the warning lights completely obscured by the instruments; and a bleed to the rear chain where setting was critical if the chain was not to be starved or swamped.

But overwhelming impressions were favourable: not for nothing did John Nelson call 1966–69 the years of 'peak performance in sales and customer satisfaction'. In April Bob Currie tested a TR6 and found it a worthy heir to the Thunderbird, with the Saint-type inlet cam making it tractable in traffic and a smooth cruiser at 70 mph. The Trophy had kept the 18-in front wheel, and this contributed to a slight steering roll at very low speeds. There was not much in performance against the Bonnie, with the single-carb machine returning a 15-sec standing quarter against the T120's 14.3, and a strong following wind pushing this one-way top speed up to 113 mph! Once again

*Bob Currie again, sampling a Bonnie for 1968, one of its top years.*

the gearbox was notchy, with deliberate changes of the 'one-pause-two' variety being necessary to avoid a crunch, but the 'box itself was judged solid and reliable.

With **1968** came one of the Bonnie's two or three top years. With a new 8-in TLS brake, floating shuttle valves in the front fork giving true two-way damping, and 6CA points bringing independent timing of each cylinder, the 650s approached full maturity, and, with the final rear frame change later in the year, reached it.

The 8-in twin leading shoe front brake was also adopted by the Trident, the BSA twins and triples, and the T100T Daytona 500, as well as in a 7-in version by the T100S, the Tiger 90 350 twin, and the TR25W 250 single. The fruit of Meriden's Development Department's racing activities, the shoe plate incorporated an air scoop with a mesh covering, while on the left side of the full-width hub was a chromed cover plate with, for this year, a series of rectangular depressions with air slots around its circumference, and held in place by three screws. Internally the front brake hub was modified to permit the use of the larger back plate, but the 8-in brake can be retrofitted to previous models with 8-in SLS brakes. The brakes' cam levers were joined by an adjustable rod, and the brake cable ran in a sweep from a clip halfway down the right side of the front mudguard, down the guard itself for a while, before looping in from the rear to a stop cast in the backplate, and then on to the extended front lever. From DU70083 the front cable abutment gained a split pin, to stop a poorly adjusted cable jumping out of it. The two brake shoes were the same, to suit the cams. An exceptionally powerful brake and superior to both Norton's similar offering on the Commando and the BSA/Triumph conical hub which would follow it, for 1968 the only flaw associated with the new brake would be occasional troubles stemming from the cable run.

The front forks had also been redesigned by Hele in the light of racing experience (see Volume 5 and p. 64). They were now fitted with a shuttle valve damper attached to the lower end of the fork stanchions. The shuttle valve was retained by a sleeve nut, which also held the bottom bearing of the fork leg. In front of this nut, a circlip prevented the valve from passing into the stanchion, and identifying features for this type of fork were

the eight bleed holes above the bottom bearing location. Early 1968 forks fitted sintered iron stanchion bushes, but these were discontinued in favour of the original sintered bronze bushes. The first batch of forks featured the old CEI threads, but a changeover to UNF followed shortly. The amount of damping oil in each leg remained unchanged from the previous year's forks. These forks provided precise control of their two-way damping, hence stiffening recoil damping and controlling pitching in bends. They were also adopted by the 1968–70 BSA twins and, as this suggests, were fine performers.

At the rear end, also race-bred, came a new swinging-arm, mounted on a new lug, and with heavier corner fillets for additional stiffness. Keeping the swinging-arm lubricated was still a problem, so a $1\frac{1}{16}$-in breathing hole was put in the cover plate to counter airlocks while greasing. A swinging-arm spindle O-ring was fitted for sealing purposes. The swinging-arm itself became longer, to the extent that the rear chain went up a link to 104 pitches, and in mid-year, from DU81196, it also became of thicker section tube, going from 14 SWG to 12 SWG. The new swinging-arms were identifiable by an 'X' stamp on the pivot tube, and could be substituted for the previous ones. In total, this represented another substantial improvement in high-speed handling.

On the engine, a long-standing point of maintenance difficulty was cleared up by the provision at the cylinder base of bi-hexagonal, 12-point high-tensile nuts which finally provided adequate spanner clearance. In view of the previous year's problems, the Hepolite pistons had reinforced crowns. New higher lift 'green spot' outer valve springs were fitted, which gave a 10 per cent increase in fitted load with the valve fully open, but maintained the original loading when closed. Inlet valve stems were now Stellite-tipped. From DU78400 the previous oil feed down drillways in the rocker arm to the rocker arm ball pins, which located in the pushrod caps, was cut off. This was done by rotating the rocker arm ball pins through 180°, and the reason was to increase the feed to the still wear-prone exhaust camshaft. Soon after, at DU79965, the T120's rocker arms were simply left undrilled, which strengthened them.

In the gearbox for 1968, the layshaft lost its

speedometer pinion hole. There was a new mainshaft, with an extended nose enveloping the previous longer bronze bush, which was now cut off flush at the gear. This meant a new primary inner cover plate and an oil seal which now operated on the shaft itself rather than on the bush as previously. Since the bush had tended to wear badly and permit oil leaks, previous gearboxes could easily adopt the new arrangement, and by doing so, also prevent oil from the gearbox working its way into the chaincase. The gearbox outer cover now fitted a filler cap in its side.

In an effort to improve selection, there was a new gearbox camplate plunger, spring and holder, with the latter machined so that the hexagon portion on it to take a spanner was no longer machined for much of its length. In a piece of BSA standardization, the gear pedal rubber lost its 'Triumph' logo. The kick-start pedal rubber hole now went all the way through it, and the kick-start mainshaft nut and lock washer changed to UNF.

Several changes were introduced to facilitate strobing up the engine timing. Since 1965 the existing crankcase hole behind the cylinder and the TDC hole in the flywheel had been used by Meriden's production department to set the ignition timing with a stroboscope after the rolling road test. But they then adopted more sophisticated methods — a plug-in transducer into the crankcase TDC location hole, wired to an electronic ignition timing degree indicator. It worked from a 38° BTDC slot machined in the flywheel. To avoid confusion, for 1968 this slot was machined well away from the

existing TDC hole, which resulted in the location hole in the crankcase being moved from the top rear to just below the forward engine mounting. But this proved impractical in use — when the front plug was removed, oil gushed out! — so from DU74052 the hole was moved back to its previous position behind the cylinder, the front hole deleted and the flywheel slot amended. This meant that from the commencement of '68 at DU66246, to DU74052, there are three variations of crankcase and four of flywheel to be contended with. Details can be found in the excellent factory workshop manual.

From a user's point of view, 1968 brought a circular inspection plate in the primary chaincase, attached by three screws. Behind this the alternator rotor now bore a mark, aligning in most cases with a pointer on the chaincase. For those without a static pointer, a timing plate (D02014) could be fitted in place of the inspection plate. The marked pointer permitted stroboscopic retiming and eliminated the need for a timing disc. At the same time, the catalogued ignition timing changed from 29° BTDC static to 14°, and from 39° fully advanced to 38°.

The major electrical change was the introduction, behind a new deeper timing cover, of 6CA points with their two separate back plates, so that finally the timing of each cylinder could be set independently. With this system the condensers were moved off the points plate, larger ones now being rubber-mounted independently beneath the petrol tank front fixing. Another change was to UNF thread on the new contact-breakers, and this

1968 Bonneville, a purposeful-looking, practical motor cycle (it still fitted a tyre pump), with the first version of the TLS front brake.

meant that a UNF-threaded extractor bolt was needed to remove them. At DU82146, felt lubricating wicks were added. The 6CA points were certainly an improvement, but they did not end problems in this area. For instance, the nylon contact-breaker cams could still wear rapidly and throw timing out, and if left standing for long periods, the auto advance mechanism could stick open, with interesting results when the engine was started. The cure would be electronic ignition.

The new points were accompanied by a redistribution of the electrical equipment. The Zener diode at last emerged from its position behind the left side panel, being bolted in a better-cooled position under the headlamp, and now seated in a finned heat sink. The horns too moved to a prominent position below the front of the petrol tank. A new chrome headlamp shell was fitted. It incorporated a new silicone-damped ammeter, as one of the twins' perennial electrical problems had been the ammeter going open-circuit and disintegrating. The headlamp also carried an easier-to-use toggle switch for the lights, while the ignition switch was now more accessibly mounted in a new housing in the left-hand fork cover. The fork shroud was modified to suit, and it also featured headlamp slots rather than the previous holes, so that the headlamp could be adjusted sideways as well as up and down. The fork lower crown adopted UNF threads. After some problems with owners riding away with the lock peg still engaged, the steering head lock was also revised by means of a new head lug with an extended lock shelf. The steering dampers were deleted from the UK models.

Removing the ignition switch and Zener diode to their new positions also meant that the side panel and underseat area could be tidied up. A new left-hand side panel, now common to all models, and carrying transfers in place of the previous 'toothpaste' name badges, was fitted. It was fastened at the front by a single screw, and pivoted on pegs on the rear frame, which unfortunately did not cure the problem of spontaneous detachment; and soon after its introduction the front fastener, a threaded plastic knob, acquired a click-spring retainer to try and combat this. The panel was enlarged to include a tool compartment, though unfortunately the side panel was not lockable. This meant that the previous underseat tool tray could be

eliminated, and the side panel also gave access to the clear plastic battery for level checking. The battery was carried on a new mounting platform and fastened by an elastic strap and buckle rather than the previous hinged bent wire clamp.

Further changes for 1968 included a chrome trim band around the base of the dualseat in place of the previous grey strip. The seat itself provided a thicker cushioned effect, and its previous internal forged steel hinged brackets were replaced by external hinges made from pressings. From DU81709 a longer front mudguard was fitted, and the rear mudguard had also been revised, with the lifting handles modified. On it the rear number plate shape was altered to rectangular, and the rear light fixing to three holes. The prop stand lost its separate foot in favour of a curved extension, now part of the stamping itself. The silencer internals featured redesigned baffles, to counter the previous problem of their loosening off. The petrol tank was standardized at the 4-gal one, and it carried thicker knee grips in common with the C-range, as well as altering its previous pair of front bolts to studs and nuts after DU77670. Finally, the T120's twin carburettors which, as mentioned, were now 30 mm Concentrics, were fitted as standard with pancake air filters with gauze and cloth internals, unlike the TR6's paper innards. The petrol taps now fitted petrol-tight washers.

A new version of the Police 650, dubbed the 'Super Saint', also became available for 1968. Side-car springs front and rear helped cope with the weight of equipment and with the full fairing, which most fitted, in conjunction with an exceptionally swept-back handlebar to suit. It fitted a Bonneville-ported head, but still with a single carb, as well as Bonneville camshafts and 9:1 compression against the previous 7.5:1. The engine set-up produced faster acceleration and a top speed raised to 109 mph, but as one Police rider observed, 'Vibration problems ... were beginning to manifest themselves', though he added that 'I could forgive this machine a lot' due to its handling and manoeuvrability.

The improved handling from now on was what struck riders most. In 1981 *MCN*'s Jim Reynolds rode a nice 1968 T120, and after mentioning that motorway work on the 650 was boring, made the comment that this Bonnie 'needed bends to bring it alive'. That remark would have been unthinkable in the

'50s, and gives the measure of Hele's progressive improvements. Reynolds found that the motor pulled strongly from as low as 2,000 rpm, with peak power from 3,000 to 6,000 rpm, and gave the option of using the box hard and feeling the power to the full, or of lazy cruising in built-up areas in third. Petrol consumption averaged 55 mpg, and while the rear brake was found to be not very sensitive, the 8-in TLS front was superb. Not unexpectedly, he found the damping very hard, but recognized the contribution this made to the Bonnie being in its element on the bends, where it proved a taut handler, including over some patchy wet surfaces. The bike could be laid over and driven round bends, or even taken round on a trailing throttle if the line had been a mistake, and still deliver the same rock-steady handling.

Ironically, though the 650 Bonnies continued to sell well, just how good they now were was somewhat obscured by the launch in April 1968 of Norton's 750 Commando and the imminence of the 750 Trident, on which Meriden's efforts would be concentrated from then on.

**1969** saw the Bonnie riding high with its improved frame, fork and brakes. Internally there was one major change, together with a host of minor ones, often related either to the changeover to UNF thread or to the move of production of gearbox internals to Small Heath (see Volume 5). Together these mean a '69 owner should exercise extreme caution over interchangeability and the replacement of engine/gearbox components.

The big change in the engine was a crankshaft with a heavier flywheel, actually introduced in October 1968 at NC02256 (this model year saw the end of the DU engine/frame numbers, and the beginning of the year/month codes [see p. 182]). While now featuring UNF threads but retaining the previous shaft's 85 per cent balance factor, as

*'As good as they got' — close-up on a 1969 TR6 Trophy, very much a single-carb Bonnie by then.*

John Nelson wrote, the heavier flywheel applied 'a "smoothing" of inertia to the crankshaft assembly ... reducing the "peakiness" of the engine vibration'. It was fitted in conjunction with new con-rods, UNF thread nuts and self-locking bolts and amended torque settings, as well as Hepolite pistons with crown thickness increased once again, and shorter, heavier-section gudgeon pins.

The breathing area also came in for some attention, as for this year on UK and General Export T120 models, for the first time threaded carburettor inlet adapters were fitted. These were UNF for this year, as was the exhaust port adapter. The inlet adapter had a $1\frac{3}{16}$ in diameter inlet that tapered to $1\frac{1}{8}$ in diameter at the throat into the head, a go-faster trick discovered in American competition. The 30-mm carburettors themselves altered slightly, with their previous replaceable pilot jets being changed to fixed internal calibrated drillings. Washers incorporating O-rings were fitted under the carburettor flange units of the T120. The T120 main jets dropped from 210 to 190, needle jets from 0.107 to 0.106 and the elements in the T120 pillbox air cleaner changed to crinkled paper, while the TR6 adopted a new filter body but with the same paper internals as previously. The cumulative result was noticeable. A 1968 T120 test had found power delivery rather lumpy at the bottom end, whereas on the 1969 Bonneville, specific mention was made of 'impeccable carburation' which gave power that came in at tickover and went smoothly up to the maximum.

A change to UNF meant new timing and primary covers (which also featured wider joint faces), as well as gearbox inner and outer covers, sump oil filter bolt, footrests, and most (but not all) studs, plugs, screws and nuts, including the clamp bolt for the long folding kick-start pedal, going to UNF. In the cylinder head, steel sleeves were pressed into the inner holding-down stud holes so that during the machining and polishing of the new inlet port they would be less likely to be broken into. The rev counter drive from the crankcase adopted a left-hand (UNF) thread for its gearbox, and overcame previous problems of loosening off and subsequent breakage. And at the left-hand base of the cylinder, where the engine number was to be found, throughout the whole group a raised pad embossed with multiple small Triumph logos was incorporated, so that any restamped engine from now on would be detectable.

In the lubrication department, the oil pump's feed capacity was increased by a larger diameter feed plunger in a suitable new oil pump body. Early in the year, from DU88714, a further modification involved the lubrication system. The scavenge pipe was made slightly longer (by $\frac{5}{8}$ in), which had the effect of raising the oil level in the crankcase. This can be adopted with advantage on all 1967-on engines (i.e. from DU44394) with the increased scavenge pump, by fitting a pipe increased by the appropriate length. A new, UNF thread oil pressure release valve, as well as an electrically operated oil pressure switch, was fitted in the timing cover, and connected to a warning light in the headlamp shell. For general remarks on this system, see p. 66–67.

But one of the great objects of better lubrication over the previous years, the exhaust camshaft, finally had its problems solved from DU87105 by now being nitrided, as was the inlet cam, a surface treatment process which 'put a complete and permanent end to camshaft wear problems'. Do not be surprised to find earlier models benefiting from nitrided cams, as the process was applied retrospectively to batches of replacement cams for products up to 10 years old which the law required Meriden to carry spares for. In addition in 1969, from JD25965, cam wheels with revised timing marks were fitted.

Oil tightness was also assaulted in another familiar trouble-spot, the pushrod tubes. A new design of tube was fitted, with serrated 'castellated' top ends, which fitted Viton O-rings top and bottom. At PD32574 an additional rubber washer had to be reinstated at the bottom at the tappet guide block, with a pressed-on sleeve on the lower end of the tube to keep the washer in place. As with all the tube-sealing systems, the important thing was to treat each example as a unified system, including the tubes themselves, the tappet guide blocks, and the cylinder heads, and carefully fit everything as appropriate to that particular system.

In the gearbox, third gear was lowered slightly, with the form of both gears in the pair being amended and thus not individually interchangeable. A new, UNF hexagonal threaded camplate plunger spring housing nut was fitted. Then the gears benefited from the industrial production process known as 'shaving', aimed at reducing surface wear and noise; their tooth form was identical to, but their parts numbers different from, their predecessors. Next, from DU88630 a modified camplate pressing, and hence lengthened selector forks, were adopted. And finally, to complete the storeman's nightmare, from CC15546 gearbox shafts with altered running diameters, and gear pinions with different bore diameters, were introduced, none interchangeable with previous ones. Even then gear selection problems remained and would soon lead to an ill-conceived attempt to remedy them. Meanwhile, to combat transmission vibration, the clutch, from DU88333, was given a statically balanced housing, recognizable by the absence of the previous cast pockets.

In the electrical sphere, the increased output RM21 alternator, also with encapsulated stator windings, was a welcome addition. The mounting for the 6CA points plate was revised, with the timing cover also being altered to allow the fitting of a second oil seal as well as the oil switch. With the points themselves, the spindle of the advance–retard mechanism was now pre-lubricated, and if wet-lubricated afterwards, a glutinous paste would be formed that would ultimately seize the spindle. The front brake cable now incorporated a rear light switch. Twin Windtone horns were fitted, relocated on the front downtube, and with mounting brackets lengthened from DU89530, though still fracture-prone. The wiring harness was modified to permit the fitting of direction indicators if desired.

Of the cycle parts, the front forks were altered to allow bigger section front tyres to be fitted. The fork top crown adopted UNF threads and the fork crown was modified so that the stanchion tube centres were increased from $6\frac{1}{2}$ to $6\frac{3}{4}$ in, the top and bottom fork lugs changed, and a suitable longer spindle fitted. Clipless gaiters were now used, and from AC10464 the stanchions received two extra $\frac{5}{16}$-in holes to improve rebound damping control further; these could be added to previous '68-on forks. A suitable new front mudguard was fitted, in fact off some of the 1966-on export models, with its rear stay reverting to a single bolt fixing.

Between the forks, the 8-in TLS front brake was modified. There had been occasional trouble with the looping cable snagging underneath the rear of the mudguard when the forks were fully compressed, so now the brake's operation was modified by the use of a bell-crank forward lever, and this permitted the cable run to lie parallel with the fork leg vertically down to the new operating linkage. Indeed, to keep cables tidy a grommet in the headlamp mounting brackets, and plastic clips, were now fitted. The cover plate on the front brake's left-hand side also became neater, losing 1968's slots and the three fastening screws, and now being simply embellished with circumferential ribs.

Miscellaneous changes included several omissions. There was no more parcel grid for the UK models (see Volume 5 for the grisly reasons). The rear units lost their shrouds and displayed naked chromed springs in late '60s style. The tank badges, with the tank modified accordingly, became the simpler 'picture frame' type. The dualseat, interchangeable with the previous, now featured an aerated top, and its base was drilled with threaded holes to take that year's bolted-on passenger grab-rail, though this was not a standard fitting on UK models. The oil tank gained a dipstick integral with the filler cap, so the old '$1\frac{1}{2}$ in below the cap' rule of thumb for the level could be dispensed with. Finally, the exhaust system now featured the link pipe, for details of which see Volume 5 also. Its result was quieter running, so that despite upcoming noise legislation, the 650s were now able to boost performance a little by fitting a shorter, more cigar-shaped, straight-through absorption-type silencer as previously found on some 1966-on export machines. Early versions of the balance pipe were held by split clamps with two bolts at either end, but mid-year changed to single bolt clips. The geometry of the centre stand was also altered.

This was the pinnacle of the 650s, with little development following due to the presence of the Trident and the imminence of Umberslade Hall's oil-bearing P39 frame. A *Motor Cycle* test described the TR6 Trophy for 1969 as 'A superb maid of all work', with its single carburettor in particular bringing the revs flooding in at a tweak of the grip.

**1970** saw the successful 650 little changed, except for the engine breathing system, which underwent a major revision, and a step backwards which was taken in the gearbox. The new breathing arrangements had already been introduced in a slightly different form on the Trident, though they were said to have had their origin with the twins in Stan Shenton's Triumph racing *équipe*. Basically, the timed breather was dispensed with, and the crankcase breathed directly into the primary chaincase; from there, a large bore pipe, exiting at a junction with a new breather elbow bolted on externally to the rear of the case, carried the air away. In combination with a breather cover plate within the chaincase, the rise of the pipe to its own exit point at the top left of the rear mudguard was sufficient to prevent excess oil being carried away to the atmosphere. There also proved to be enough heat in the chaincase so that any cold, wet air that might have been sucked back through the hole due to the piston's upstroke was pre-heated there sufficiently to prevent it causing the kind of oily sludge that could block oilways or start corrosion.

The initial breathing from crankcase to chaincase was via three holes drilled in the crankcase wall below the drive side main bearing housing, assisted by the fact that an oil seal was no longer fitted on the main bearing. This simple system had the neat side-effect of maintaining a constant oil level in the primary chaincase for the still wear-prone duplex chain, so that from now on, separate topping-up of the case was not required. This system entailed a new pair of (nitrided) camshafts, both now UNF, as were the camshaft nuts, and with the inlet ones lacking the previous breather tube and slotted breather disc drive; at the same time the cam gears, previously screw cut for a puller, now had two tapped holes to take a standard-type puller. In turn, the new camshafts meant a new pair of crankcase halves, the drive side one incorporating the latest pre-sized camshaft bushes. The system would only work satisfactorily if the primary chaincase was reasonably oil-tight, and this the new cases, incorporating the previous year's improvements and benefiting from the pressure relief of the new system, proved themselves to be. One more blow for oil-tightness was also struck with the O-rings in the top of the pushrod cover being modified.

The gearbox inner cover was also modified in the interests of oil-tightness so that a shorter, less leak-prone selector rod could be fitted. From AD37473 a heavier section main bearing circlip was fitted. From ED51080, aluminium bronze selector forks with integral

*Detail on a 1970 export T120 clearly shows the large-bore breather tube exiting from the rear of the primary chaincase.*

rollers were fitted. Then from ED52044 came the retrograde move, with the cam plate changing to a precision pressing operated by a leaf indexing spring. This would prove to be extremely difficult to replace during a rebuild and remained unsatisfactory in service from now until mid-1973 when it was replaced. The clutch hub was also slightly revised, due to the deletion of the previous tabs on the clutch thrust washer, which had sometimes fractured.

On the cycle side, at the base of the front downtube the engine was now clamped by small bolted-on plates rather than by a lug

Detail changes included larger Windtone horns, and from ED44339 their mountings were fitted with two extra sliding brackets to help secure them. A new oil tank was fitted, catalogued at 5½ imperial pints and hence theoretically smaller than its 6-pt predecessor, but claimed to be larger. A combined chromed grab-rail/lifting handle was fitted, which would survive far into the future. Where a rev counter was fitted, the drive was now by a solid, screwed-in plug in the exhaust camshaft rather than the earlier push-fit pressing. New Lucas 17/H12 ignition coils, smaller and lighter, were fitted. The centre stand was modified yet again, and the prop stand now included a welded-on threaded boss, into which was fitted an adjustable stop-screw so that the foldaway position could be varied. A new dualseat pan lowered the seat a little. On the styling front, for the UK models there was a less attractive shape to the petrol tank's gold-lined coloured panel (this year for the Bonnie in silver with the main colour Astral Red). Previously a scallop, it was now a less imaginative oval, which simply surrounded the tank badge rather than using its shape as part of the design.

Finally, there were some further modifications to the carburettors. The Concentrics now fitted a useful plastic drain plug to their float bowls. At the same time the air filter elements of both the T120 and TR6 became filter cloth and gauze. Also, the TR6's single carburettor was now rubber-mounted by means of double O-rings in the same way as the T120's instruments had been the previous year.

That was the last year for the Triumph 650s, as they had been known up until then, and it is an appropriate place to consider a few of the practical mods that experience has taught can be useful in keeping a 650 reasonably reliable on the road. Much of the pre-unit and C-range comments also apply. For a start, tuning with high-performance parts should probably be kept to a minimum. Dave Degens, the well-known Triton builder, won the 24-hour race at Montjuich in 1970 with a comparatively mildly tuned engine — a single 32-mm carburettor, 9:1 pistons, E3134 camshafts rather than the hotter Thruxton or Somerton profiles, and polished ports. In the camshaft area, Triumph cam parts numbers can be very confusing. The best mix for the street seems to be E3134 inlet with E3325 exhaust,

welded into the tube, which helped the assembly process, and with the plates being detachable, also made the engine easier to remove. As with the C-range, the lengths of the front fork stanchions on which the sliders bore were now hard-chrome plated and ground to a micro-finish to prolong seal life. The previous front mudguard mounting lugs were replaced by welded-on steel pressings attached by square nuts to the sliding bottom outer members, and the lower stay was attached to the mudguard by two bolts, again instead of one, as the front guard was now common to all the twins; as was the rear one, which fitted another revised number plate. At the rear, new Girling damper units now embodied a castellated collar to protect the adjusters from road dirt and water. The rear brake backplate and hub adopted UNF threads.

**Left** *Rear unit springs were exposed from 1969 on.*

**Right** *New and not very attractive oval-shaped tank panels, with the plainer 'picture frame' badges for 1970.*

**Below** *1970 T120 Bonnie, the last before the oil-in-frame drama.*

and you can check if an E3134 form is fitted by measuring the lift, which should be 1.126 in, with the others between .020 and .030 less. Meriden cams carried a range of symbols. A star meant provision for contact-breaker drive, a cross meant rev counter drive,

an 'X' a breather tube, and an 'N' signified that a cam was nitrided.

Several of the reliability points to watch for have been mentioned in the text, but it should be added that cylinder head and rocker box gaskets can fail regularly, and care should be

*A last excellent year for the TR6P Saint Police 650 variant in 1970.*

taken to replace them with gaskets to the original specification, i.e. ones which included wires in their composition and were so less likely to collapse. Some favour plumbing in a breather on the rocker boxes, as Meriden were to do later, to help relieve pressure. Of the main bearings, the drive side is the one to watch and listen for. In the gearbox it may be useful to know that the RLS9 $1\frac{1}{4}$-in high gear bearing is dimensionally the same as on the AMC/Norton gearbox, though on the latter lacking the pukkah but not essential Triumph chip guard. Gearbox leaks often stem from the kick-start and gear pedals which operate in rapid-wear steel bushes, points to watch. Keeping the gearbox in reasonable order on a 650 is important, as if a gear was missed at speed, a bent valve could often be the consequence.

While the 1968–70 machines are the acknowledged stars, it should be noted that many of their desirable features can be retrofitted to earlier and perhaps less keenly sought after (and expensive) unit 650s. The 8-in TLS brake, the shuttle valves (to '64-on forks), uprated electrics and the 1970-on breathing arrangements are some of the things that can be added. In addition, modern rear suspension units, particularly Konis, are a useful aid for handling, and the 650 swinging-arm needs just as much attention as the one on the C-range. Check all brackets (silencers, Zener diode, horns, etc.) regularly for cracking, as well as mudguards and in particular the left-hand side panel in the area around the recess for the seat hinge.

Remember that one Triumph dealer in Canada advised his staff that Triumphs needed maintenance approximately twice as often as other British makes, though if they receive it, they can be very durable, as evidenced by the 100,000 miles covered by many Police twins. The probable life of the cam followers has been mentioned, and while the bottom end and gearbox can be long-lasting, 40,000–50,000 miles seems the outside life for bores and pistons. A lot of engine noise emanating from the top end stems from the rocker arms, whose end float was determined by Thackeray spring washers. When the rocker arms became worn, the springs dug into them, causing a clicking noise. To stop this and prolong valve gear life, special hardened steel spacers, available from Triumph specialists, can be substituted. A final point for modern times: Triumph expert Brian Bennett believes that if the use of lead-free petrol is contemplated, the stock austenitic valve seat material should present no problems, but the phosphor-bronze valve guides should be changed for high Duralumin guides.

So we leave the 650s, with the music about to stop for Meriden as in some monstrous game of musical chairs, and something very different on the move when it started again. The factory men's indignation at this is understandable because, perhaps more than any other Triumph, the 650s of the '60s really were the Legends, where the street could meet the élite — reasonably priced bikes that at their best combine the speed and tautness of race breeding with a reasonably practical tractability for everyday use.

## Triumph: The unit 650 twins, pre-oil-in-frame (1963-70) — production dates and specifications

### Production dates
Unit 6T Thunderbird — 1963-66
Unit TR6 SS Trophy — 1963-70
Unit T120 Bonneville — 1963-70

### Specifications
Capacity, bore and stroke — 649 cc
(71 × 82 mm)
Type — ohv twin
Ignition — coil
Weight — 6T (1963) 369 lb; T120 (1963) 363 lb; TR6 (1968) 365 lb

### Triumph 250 singles: TR25W Trophy, T25SS Blazer and T25T Trail Blazer

The classic Triumph post-war singles were the Tiger Cubs, but their 200 cc capacity puts them outside the scope of this work. In 1968 when the Cubs, with sales on the wane, had been moved to Small Heath and were in their final year, the market gap this represented was partly filled with the new TR25W 250 Trophy.

This was a frankly badge-engineered version of the BSA B25 247 cc single (which incidentally was mistakenly described by the company until its final year as 249 cc). It was built at Small Heath with sometimes unhappy results (see Volume 5). However, the TR25W's attractive styling gave it a recognizable marque identity as a Triumph and as a street-trail hybrid. It was principally targeted at the American market, where this style was appreciated, and where BSA and Triumph dealers had not amalgamated, so that a Triumph version was required.

The **1968** TR25W fitted a long, red, angular $3\frac{1}{4}$-gal steel petrol tank bearing Triumph 'eyebrow' badges and echoing the Trident style. The Triumph name was cast on the primary chaincase and on the rocker inspection plate, against black or red paint background. The triangular black fibreglass side panels were also distinct in shape and colour from the B25s', and the mudguards painted, not chromed like the BSA. The red colour for tank and guards again was distinct from the B25's blue. The headlamp was a small $5\frac{1}{2}$-in q.d. competition one. The short seat, with its ribbed top, lacked the B25's rear hump, and the exhaust system was mounted above the crankcase on the right, with the exhaust pipe curling inside the frame over the fork pivot before connecting with a small shortie 'shotgun' silencer with a 'chevron' heat-shield plate attached. The front fork was the gaitered one off the Tiger 90 350 twin. With the exception of the fork, which the BSA would adopt for 1969, these were not major variations, but they added up to a distinctively Triumph machine.

There was something apt about that, for the unit single-cylinder engine, in its original C15 form, had been derived from the Triumph Tiger Cub. It had changed considerably since then, however, particularly in the 1967 revamp to C25/B25 form, which was easily identifiable by its square finned, alloy barrel with iron liner and cast-in pushrod tunnel. Group policy had dictated extracting the maximum power from an engine which was already none too reliable, with claimed output for the BSA being 25 bhp at 8,000 rpm, though by the following year with the TR25W this had been amended to 24. Both were really paper figures, as vibration made it virtually impossible to approach the rev limit. The high output was achieved by the use of 9.6:1 pistons (though usually claimed as 10:1), a larger diameter inlet valve, and camshafts derived from the BSA Victor scramblers, which Triumph's Henry Vale found absurdly fierce for a road bike, and which he said led to snapped pushrods.

The all-alloy engine housed a forged one-

*Bob Currie tests the 1968 TR25W. He found the noise from the shortie 'shotgun' silencer embarrassing. The number plate was last seen on a Merc driven by DJ Pete Murray.*

piece crankshaft with a pair of pressed-on flywheels, each secured by four radial bolts and running on ball journal main bearings for both drive and timing side. The alloy con-rods, after the later C15's roller big-end, unfortunately reverted to Triumph-style plain big-ends with thin-walled shells. The fierce camshaft was gear-driven, and in turn drove the ignition cam and auto advance unit for the 6CA points mounted behind a chromed plate in the timing chest. The camshaft was hollow and incorporated a timed engine breather operating via a port in the inner timing case. The pushrods were unusual, as the inlet and exhaust differed from one another. The kidney-shaped cylinder head fitted hexagonal inspection caps and an oval side-plate on the right to allow valve clearance adjustment, which was done by turning eccentric rocker spindles. For 1968, the oil supply feed to the valve mechanism was taken from the oil union beneath the crankcase rather than from the return line as on the C25 previously. Lubrication for the engine was by the excellent BSA gear-type oil pump, mounted within the timing chest and driven by skew gear from behind the crankshaft timing side pinion. The electrics were 12-volt and ignition was by coil, with a Lucas RM19 alternator mounted on the

crankshaft. The carburettor was a 928 Concentric, mounted at a steep downdraught angle and fitting a pillbox air cleaner in a circular perforated chrome housing.

The four-speed gearbox was mounted in unit behind the engine in the right side crankcase half. For the TR25W, though the first few went out with B25 ratios, overall gearing was then lowered by replacing the BSA's 49-tooth rear sprocket with a 52-tooth item, and the previous 16-tooth gearbox sprocket with a 15-tooth one; from then on only the West Coast export versions retained the 49-tooth rear sprocket. Both first and top gear were lower than the B25s, and in John Nelson's opinion, lowering the TR25W gearing would have a lot to do with its troubles, as it tended to make riders over-rev the engine. The four-spring clutch was operated by rack and pinion mechanism, and embodied a spider-type shock absorber. A lip at the back of the clutch centre meant that only four friction plates could be fitted. Primary drive was by duplex chain with an effective slipper tensioner, while the rear chain was $\frac{5}{8} \times \frac{1}{4}$ in.

This engine was mounted in a competition-derived frame which many rated highly. An all-welded chassis, unlike the C15 with its bolted-on rear end, it had a single downtube and top tube but twin tubes sweeping rearwards from the back of the latter, as well as a duplex cradle beneath the engine. The swinging-arm pivoted on Silentbloc rubber-bonded bushes which, when the time came, were difficult to remove. For the TR25W, with off-road in mind, the frame fitted a bash plate at the front, and gave 8 in of ground clearance, with a tall seat height of 32 in; also to help clearance, no centre stand was fitted. A high and wide handlebar gave a comfortable riding position, with a $3.25 \times 19$ in wheel and tyre at the front and an $18 \times 4.00$ at the rear, where the wheel was quickly detachable. The rear suspension units had partially exposed chromed springs and a chromed top dust-cover. The rear lamp was the 'teat' type, in an aluminium housing with side reflectors, and circular reflectors were also fitted under the tank. The quickly detachable $5\frac{1}{2}$-in headlamp carried a toggle on/off switch as well as push–pull dip-switch. This left the handlebars distinctly uncluttered, as the carburettor fitted no air slide, so there was no choke lever.

Bob Currie tested a TR25W for *Motor Cycle* in 1968 and liked it, finding it a bike you could 'swing about between your knees'. He found the riding position and ribbed dualseat comfortable, and the lowered gearing made for a responsive, free-revving ride in town and around, with good acceleration and apparently not much lowering of the top speed, as 81 mph was recorded at MIRA. He liked the smooth and controlled front end, but found that the rear springing was on the harsh side, and that the good-looking little silencer produced an embarrassingly loud bark. If the dipping button on the headlamp was not ideal, at least the main beam was good, as was economy, with average consumption at around 70 mpg. The SLS 7-in brakes, the front one in a full-width hub, stopped the little Triumph in 30 ft from 30 mph.

The TR25W did have several points going for it, the principal one being that it was a well-equipped machine, benefiting from BSA's development of the model over the years. The 12-volt electrics, with 6CA points, independent coil, Zener diode under the tank nose, and from 1969 the encapsulated-winding RM21 alternator, were all desirable features, as was the steel petrol tank in contrast to the BSA's, which was fibreglass until 1969. At 320 lb dry, this was a genuine medium-weight machine, and the high-level exhaust, folding footrests and tall, competition-bred chassis gave this Trophy real trail potential.

There the positive ended, for the unit 250 engine developed a reputation for unreliability and mechanical trouble which both Meriden and Small Heath factory service personnel confirm. Built as a 'consumer durable', it seemed to embody a throwaway philosophy, and the engine lacked staying power. By tuning up to take on the Japanese without having to retool for a new model, several flaws in the design were rapidly exposed.

The principal one was the alloy con-rod and its plain-shell big-end, which self-destructed rapidly if performance was exploited as the styling and state of tune encouraged. By contrast, the most prominent problem was the tendency, encouraged by less than efficient engine breathing, to leak oil from the comparatively thin joint faces at the head and crankcase joints, the primary chaincase and the sump filter. The engine also leaked from the rocker box's hexagonal inspection caps, but this can be cured with O-rings off a late B50.

Hammering vibration set in at speeds above the mid-50s, and this could loosen the alternator, thence destroying the rotor keyway and, eventually, the crankshaft. The drive side ball main bearings were other potential weak points, but a deep knocking like a main on the way out would sometimes be the cast-iron cylinder liner, which could work loose as the alloy barrel got hot and expanded, and due to a gap of 0.015 in between the top of the liner and the lower surface of the cylinder head, would then begin to move up and down with a hammering motion. The gearbox, while pleasant to operate when in good condition, was another rapid-wear system, with worn selectors and dogs leading to a clonky change and false neutrals, while the clutch and transmission were harsh in operation at the best of times, with clutch pushrods being particularly at risk. Other negative points included cam and cam follower wear, and brittle piston rings. The oil filtration system was crude, and particles could unseat the ball valves in the oil circulation system, as well as making the alloy pistons prone to 'picking up' and consequent rapid bore wear.

For the rider, vibration, and a rattling engine which leaked oil, were compounded by the fact that starting could be difficult. Despite the high compression, kicking the engine over was not a problem so no valve-lifter was fitted or necessary. But the downdraught carb made the motor very easy to flood, and only the lightest of tickling was advisable for firing up. Once the engine was hot, restarting could be a problem. To aggravate this, vibration caused all the usual electrical bothers to the ignition.

There was a military/Police version of the TR25W, the equivalent of the B25 Fleetstar, fitted with fully valanced mudguards, shrouded rear suspension units and 8:1 compression pistons, which are a good detuning idea for a reasonable life expectancy. These versions were also the first to offer a full-flow filter on the oil return line, which would only reach the civilian 250s in 1971.

**1969** saw several of the engine problems tackled. The top of the cylinder barrel was fitted with a corrugated spacer ring, available in three thicknesses, to prevent movement between the top of the liner and the cylinder head. To counter wear, the valve split collets and valve collars differed in length from the previous ones, with the collet faces now tapering at 20° compared to 50° before; these could replace the previous, but only as a complete set. The outer valve springs were also altered.

The width of the crankcase and primary chaincase joints was increased by 15 per cent, and this was a part of the Group changeover, unfortunately never completed, to Unified Threads; some components which did change were the nuts for the sump plate and

the fasteners for the outer and inner timing covers. The crankcase acquired a timing plug in the front of the left-hand case, as well as an aperture in the right-hand timing chest, giving acess to worm drive for the optional rev counter. Other benefits affecting the whole Group range were the RM21 encapsulated alternator, and a new wiring harness with provision for battery-less capacitor ignition, which was a genuine boon for off-road work. The front brake cable fitted a stop-light switch, and the clutch cable a grease nipple and an adjuster. In the headlamp shell, the main beam warning light, previously red, became either green or blue. The con-rods remained as previous, but lost their little end bush. The Concentric carb dispensed with its previous pilot jet, the slide changing from a 3 to a $3\frac{1}{2}$, and the main jet from 160 to 200.

For the cycle parts, the principal change was the front brake which became a 7-in 2LS design, a smaller version of the excellent 8-in one on the BSA and Triumph twins and triples. This went into revised forks with Unified Threads for the cap threads and new internals, shrouds, shafts and seals. At the rear, the suspension unit's chromed springs became fully exposed. The silencer became much bigger and was now fitted with a chromed wire mesh heat-shield, while the exhaust pipe was no longer tucked into the frame but ran back nearly straight from the top of the timing case. Though an improvement, the 250's exhaust note remained a noisy bark. On the petrol tank there was that year's new 'picture frame' tank

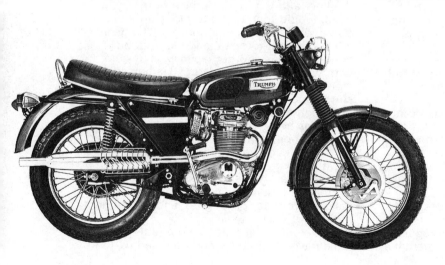

*1969 TR25W Trophy 250—different tank badges, 2LS front brake, and a more substantial silencer.*

badge. A different, hooped-style grab-rail was fitted, no longer attached to the rear lifting handle. Above the engine the head steady lug was revised, with a further lug welded to it. The 19-in front wheel continued to be supplied on some machines, but an 18-in on others.

Finally, and importantly, from early in 1969, at engine no. 12468, a roller main bearing on the same dimensions as the previous tall journal one was fitted on the drive side, with the crankshaft assembly modified to suit. The new crankshaft was interchangeable with the previous if the spacer (part no. E11031) was fitted to the timing side crankshaft. Or the previous flywheel assembly could be converted for use with the roller bearing, by machining the timing side shaft.

The **1970** model year saw an attack on the 250's oil leaks, which had become proverbial. From engine no. JD00388 (actually August 1969) the camshaft engine breather was modified to improve the crankcase breathing. This involved a new camshaft assembly, including the camshaft gear, and it necessitated new timing marks. The previous marking was 'I', the 1970 mark 'V', and both were included on the new wheel until mid-year. This year also saw the contact-breaker bolt, which was part of the assembly, being modified to Unified Threads. So, confusingly, there was an interim camshaft assembly (part no. E11124) with the improved breathing and altered marking but without the Unified Thread bolt, though this could be added to it later. The final assembly was no. E11276. Care should be taken, if assembling a 1970

season engine, not to time it to the 'I' marks, as this can cause damage from the inlet valve striking the piston crown.

The corrugated rings below the cylinder head were no longer fitted, and the con-rod, its bolt and nut plus the gudgeon pin and circlip were altered. The top piston ring changed from a plain compression type to a tapered ring like the middle one. As with other models, the oil pressure release valve became an assembled unit, and an oil pressure switch was now mounted in the headlamp. Finally, the oil pump itself, while the same type, altered to the superior cast-iron pump also being fitted to the BSA twins, with several major components differing from previously.

There was an improved method of locating the spring-cups in the clutch pressure plate, which was modified to suit. The sump filter became detachable from the sump filter plate. A smaller ignition coil was fitted. The carburettor was now rubber-mounted, with the flange altered accordingly, and within the Concentric the needle and needle-jet holder were redesigned. Externally there was now another exhaust system, the third in three years. This one resembled the previous year's but ran to the left instead of the right of the machine, with the pipe and large silencer now heat-shielded by an unsightly moulded cover. The left-hand side panel became steel, and reduced in size to match the oil tank. This became a new component, with a filler cap redesigned to avoid the rider's leg. It was now the same as the other units in this, and discarded its side panel altogether.

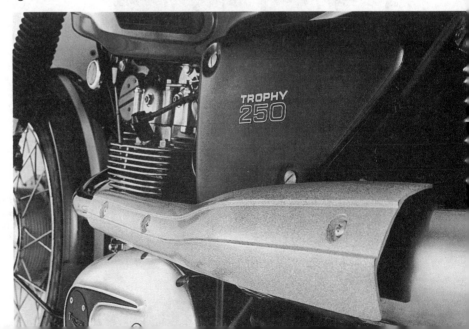

*1970, and the TR25W's silencer changes sides and gains a fibreglass heat shield.*

*The 1970 TR25W—folding footpegs, no centre stand.*

In mid-year the valve split collets and valve collars altered again, the new ones being in common with the up-coming 500 cc B50. And in July, as a matter of urgency, the previous bent wire guide clip for the front brake cable, at the rear of the right-hand fork leg, was replaced by a plastic guide. This was to prevent the cable bend, which formed when the fork went to full compression, snagging on the front mudguard bridge stay lug bolt.

**1971** saw the game change completely when, as part of the new range whose failure was to doom the BSA Triumph Group, the 250 emerged as the T25SS and T25T, with alloy forks and oil-bearing frames. The frames were versions of the Mk IV BSA works' motocross chassis. They carried 4 pt of lubricant in their large top and single downtube, which fitted a filter at its base. Another full-flow filter unit went in the return line, which ran up to a point just under the steering head, where the filler cap for the frame was located. This new filter went some

**Left** *The square-finned 250 engine shown to good advantage.*

**Right** *1971, and all change—strengthened 250 engine in oil-bearing frame with alloy forks and funny silencer. This is the T25T Trail Blazer version.*

way to remedying the previous problems of grit getting in the system.

The new frame, black-painted to distinguish it from its Dove Grey BSA equivalents that year, featured two Timken taper roller steering head bearings, and the swinging-arm pivoted on new rollers. Ground clearance for the SS was down an inch at 7 in, but the seat height was the same tall 32 in. Rear chain adjustment was by snail cam. The supple forks, with their alloy sliders and exposed, ungaitered precision-ground hard-chromed stanchions, gave $6\frac{3}{4}$ in of movement. Damping was by shuttle valve rather than clack valve as previously, and one minus point was the absence of bushes, as well as a lack of gaiters, meaning fork seals wearing rapidly and then leaking oil. The chromed headlamp, a new flat pattern with an unpopular twist action main beam switch mounted in it, was supported on shaped brackets of chromed steel rod, rubber-mounted from the upper and lower fork yokes. A single stay for the minimal front mudguard was supported in rubber mountings attached to the fork sliders. On an equally skimpy rear guard, the tail light was carried on an unsubtly extended pressed tin mounting block, which was also found on the twins.

Between the front forks for the T25SS (for Street Scrambler) went a new conical 8-in 2LS brake. This will be found discussed in the o.i.f. twins section (see p. 148), but here it can be said that though subject to the same problems, the brake generally worked well for the 250, which at a remarkable 290 lb was some 100 lb lighter than an oil-in-frame 650 T120R twin. The rear hub too was conical and contained a 7-in SLS brake which also worked well, and together on test they gave a stopping distance of 28 ft from 30 mph. But the rear wheel was no longer q.d., and with several spacers, it was awkward to change.

Both versions of the T25 carried direction indicators (just as the SS fitted a bash plate and folding footrests), and these were operated by new Lucas switchgear in alloy casings on the high and wide handlebars. But the thumb switches were of awkwardly short reach and the right-hand one for the winkers was sited just above the engine-kill button. Much of the electrical equipment itself was grouped beneath the front of the tank in a 'black box' (which was actually light alloy, and carried square reflectors on its side). This contained the coil, Zener diode, rectifier and the capacitor which was now fitted as standard. A plug and socket connection at the rear of the box let the headlamp, winkers and oil pressure warning light circuits be instantly detached. The box carried the four-position ignition key on its left side.

The engine had been modified internally, with claimed output now down to 22.5 bph at 8,250 rpm, probably due to a camshaft assembly which was changed once again. One important improvement was the con-rod, which though retaining plain split bearings, changed again to become significantly stronger, with the gudgeon pin and the crankshaft altered to suit. This SS con-rod can (and should) be fitted to the TR25W, though doing so involves some machining of the crankshaft. The clutch hub was also redesigned, losing its previous lip at the back, so that an extra pair of plates was now fitted. The clutch chain wheel also altered. The rocker box too was different, which meant new head, base and side cover gaskets, and the take-off for rocker box lubrication returned to a position early on the oil return line, rather than the oil pipe block as previously. Within the head, the valve guides were altered, new outer valve springs again were fitted, and the tappets too changed. The oil pressure relief valve was also modified.

Styling of the T25s was again distinctively Triumph, though it was only the 2-gal tank, red painted with a gold-lined black flash and Triumph transfers, the black-painted side panels, again with large transfers, and the red mudguards, which were different from the BSA B25 versions. A remarkable feature on all was the matt black exhaust systems, with the pipe once again snaking inside the frame tubes before emerging to marry with a large lozenge-shaped silencer, set diagonally across the rear right side of the bike and particularly prominent due to the perforated stainless steel leg-guard which covered it. At the rear a tail-pipe emerged, also covered by a curved and perforated black-painted heat shield. The silencer gave a woffling but healthy exhaust note.

Differences between the T25SS Blazer and the T25T Trail Blazer, which cost about £20 more, began with wheel and tyre size at $3.25 \times 18$ in front and $3.50 \times 18$ in rear for the SS, and $3.00 \times 20$ in front, $4 \times 18$ in rear for the Trail version. The latter fitted a 6-in SLS front brake, more suitable for the dirt. The gearing was lowered: all models fitted a 52-tooth rear sprocket, so for the T25T this lowering was done with a 16-tooth gearbox sprocket against the SS's 17-tooth. The T25T's frame was $\frac{1}{2}$ in taller, and the rev counter supplied with some T25SS models with absent. The front mudguard was mounted higher between the forks, but otherwise the two were identical.

Though the engine with its new rod was a little more reliable, it still clattered chronically and if anything vibrated worse than previously, with the Trail version's gearing making cruising above 55 mph uncomfortable; on both versions on standard gearing, top speeds were down in the mid-'70s. The new models had been launched before Japanese machines had made street/trail bikes familiar, and at the time they looked odd and rather clumsy. As the price of fashion, the mudguards were inadequate and the tanks impractically small.

But the T25s did include one major bonus, and that was the competition-bred frame, which was both strong and offered a better road/trail compromise than the Yamaha XT singles would soon provide. They held the road well and could be swung around the tarmac once a riding style to suit the tall built and wide bars had been adopted. Off-road, their low-speed stability was exceptional, as was a wonderfully small turning circle – also a boon on the road in town – and on the dirt they handled excellently, with very good traction in mud, predictable behaviour in slime and enough poke to climb well on stony hills. Both on- and off-road they were comfortable, the plain black seat well padded, the suspension soaking up bumps, and the riding position well matched to the high bars and forward-tilted folding footrests. Probably the single most irritating feature of the T25s was that they could still be difficult to start when hot.

T25s were built, though in some numbers, for 1971 only, after which the BSA collapse halted production. The only coda was to be the Triumph-badged BSA B50 500 single, the TR5MX Avenger, for 1973 which, since it was purely a scrambles machine and for US export only, is beyond the scope of this book. Today, either the TR25W or T25 offer very respectable chassis for a likeable fun-bike with quite slick acceleration, but basically they are let down by a potentially highly unreliable engine. The engine spares situation at least is good, thanks to the commonality with BSA, and around 20,000 of the 250 Triumph versions seem to have been made. Replica TR25W side panels are available from Lucas Motorcycles, and the 'lozenge' silencers are now obtainable again. The pretty but noisy 1968 small silencer is available from

*The 1971 T25T Trail Blazer's competition-bred frame made it more than just a pose, off-road.*

Armours. Low compression (8:1) pistons can be had, but in standard sizes only; a Rocket III or Trident piston will also reportedly fit, though it is not known what compression this gives. Solutions to many of the mechanical problems can be obtained from unit singles specialists OTJ, including Cord piston rings, polished SS con-rods, decent after-market oil filters, and electronic ignition which can help improve the starting problems dramatically. With money and care, a reasonably reliable, quite stylish and recognizably Triumph motor cycle can be contrived, even if the 250s will always lack real stamina.

## Triumph: The 250 singles — production dates and specifications

### Production dates
TR25W Trophy — 1968–70
T25SS Blazer — 1971
T25T Trail Blazer — 1971

### Specifications
Capacity, bore and stroke — 247 cc
(67 × 70 mm)
Type — ohv single
Ignition — coil
Weight — TR25W (1968) 320 lb, T25SS
(1971) 290 lb

## Triumph Trident: T150, T150V, X75 Hurricane, T160

The Triumph Trident, wrote Mike Nicks in a 1978 *Bike* magazine, was the 'best British motorcycle ever made'. This echoed a judgement made some 10 years previously by Gavin Trippe, the *MCN* journalist who first road tested a Trident. Trippe called it 'the greatest bike I have ever had an opportunity to ride' — and he had owned a Vincent twin. Today, even *UMG*'s cynical Johnny Molloy, while recognizing the Triumph triple as 'overweight, unreliable and heavy on fuel', admitted that 'at times, it is really quite a wonderful bike to ride'. I would second that.

With all that praise, the question that then remains is why the Trident was not more of a success, either in the market place or in popular estimation.

There are several answers, and the first of them goes right back to the roots of the project. It will be noted that the three-cylinder engine's capacity is 740 cc (though originally it was described in error as 753 cc). This capacity was achieved by cylinder dimensions of 67 × 70 mm. The engine was often called 'a-Tiger-and-a-half', due to obvious similarities in layout with the 500 cc Tiger 100, especially at the top end, but the longer-

*Aquamarine Trident triple hits the streets for 1969.*

stroke pre-unit Tiger 100's dimensions had been different at 63 × 80 mm, while the unit T100s were different again at 69 × 65.5 mm. The official explanation for not going with the unit T100 size was that the wider bores would have created problems with keeping the width of the engine to a minimum, while the previous longer stroke was out because the American market required a shorter stroke for potential competition use, particularly on the flat-tracks.

But the triple-cylinder dimensions *were* identical to another model in the range, namely the 250 TR25W/B25, and indeed pistons from the latter can be used in the triple, though the compression they provide is uncertain. This gives the clue to the fact that, in addition to the original 1963 PI triple prototype with its 63 × 80 Turner twin dimensions, the triple was later envisaged as part of a modular range, a concept much loved by designers Hele and Hopwood. Doug Hele has recently confirmed to Mike Nicks in *Classic Bike* that in 1965 work had already begun on both the 67 × 70 mm triple and the key link model, a new 500 twin also with the 67 × 70 mm cylinders and what Hele regretfully described as 'all the good things'.

These included a more efficient combustion chamber plus a stronger crank, con-rods and main bearings than those on the T100.

At this point, however, a deputation from the States headed by Pete Colman persuaded the BSA management to contest Daytona for 1966 with the Group's existing 500 twins. The story of Hele's success with the T100 is a glorious chapter of Triumph history (see Volume 5), but it did mean that the projected new twin was dropped, and the triple, which had already been given some exposure in prototype form, was put on the back burner as the group experimented fitfully in other directions (ohc versions of existing twins) while concentrating on increased production. The Americans, and Colman in particular, remained opposed to the triple, overtly because its weight and power characteristics made it unsuitable for the flat-tracks, and covertly because whereas the US often provided the lead in twin tuning development, the triple was a Meriden initiative on which the knowledge and control were likely to be in the hands of the Midlands men.

As mentioned in Volume 5, Colman was empire-building by making common cause with the new BSA management, who resented Triumph's technical and sales supremacy over BSA at the time. So it was from the States that strong demands came that the triple should be produced in BSA as well as Triumph form, and not just by sticking different badges on two versions. There were also American recommendations about the styling, namely that the style of each version should be both distinctive, and different from the twins. But when the Group turned the job over to Ogle, the stylist responsible for the Reliant Robin, the Americans were far from happy with the result, and after Umberslade Hall had altered the triple's looks once more, retaining only the slab-sided tank and ray-gun silencers from Ogle's work, the Yanks continued their complaints — though these were now because the triples didn't look *enough* like the twins. There they had a point, because the appearance of what emerged meant that it was not considered a true Triumph by many, including some at Meriden (see Volume 5 again).

What all this meant for the Trident was delay and expense. On the latter score, with both BSA and Trident versions of the engines being built at Small Heath, BSA Works Director Al Cave confirms how initial production was confined to just 50 units a week, and 'an incredible amount of time was wasted changing machines over from producing one version to the other and back again'. Meanwhile, years had passed between a road-going prototype being demonstrated to the Police late in 1965, and the announcement of the production triples in September 1968 (and even after that machines were not to become available in the UK until March 1969). As BSA expert 'Polly' Palmer wrote, the publicity slogan 'The One You've Been Waiting For' was all too apt, as the triple's existence had been an open secret among enthusiasts and referred to often in the press over the preceding two years. This long and public incubation period, a sharp contrast to the previous 650 Thunderbird launch, probably meant that the new Triumph was taken less seriously than it might have been, and clearly detracted from sales impact, which both a high price and an initial production ran confined to around 2.500 a year would in any event limit definitively.

As is well known, the other thing the delays did was lead to a practically simultaneous launch with the revolutionary Honda CB750-4. The Honda's sophistication (ohc engine/

disc brake/electric start/five gears) tended to obscure the fact that the early triples actually had a higher top speed than the Hondas, at around 125 mph or more, though it is now acknowledged that those test bikes which nudged 130 had been breathed on by the factory. The triples' sure-footed handling also meant that they were able to blow off the Oriental Four on the bends of fast A-roads. But the Honda quickly developed a well-earned reputation for reliability, whereas the triple's, as we shall see, was patchy at first — though its race record would prove its basic strength, and service personnel today confirm that it was far more reliable than contemporary Triumph or BSA twins.

The clincher was price: by 1971 in America the T150 Trident cost $1,765, while both the Honda and the Trident's domestic rival, Norton's Commando, went out at around $1,490. In the UK the big differential between the 1970 Bonneville at £420 and a Trident at £614 combined with the model's unfamiliar look and layout to mean that many never made the transition from two to three cylinders. The triple's lifetime hit a period of intense inflation, so that the price kept on rising, and by the sell-off of the last reimported T160C Cardinal machines in 1977, it had reached over £1,400. Today the difference in price between twins and triples has shrunk a little, but the triples remain the more expensive machines to run.

One reason why the triples were dear was the way their engines were made. Due to the fact that the pushrod triple was at first conceived as a five-year stopgap model, retooling was kept to a minimum, with the manufacturing process using as much twin-cylinder tooling and technique as possible and consequently being labour-intensive. Initially, the heart of the engine, the one-piece 120°-throw crankshaft, was a masterpiece from the BSA forge, being first made with the three crank throws all lying in the same plane; then the forging was reheated and twisted until the throws were set at 120°. When BSA's troubles forced the forge to close, the crank was produced by conventional means by outside contractors, but putting a T160 engine together still involved 56 stages and 48 jigs and fixtures just to machine the centre section of the crankcase.

The engine's bottom end, with leak-prone vertical splits like a twin, consisted of seven different castings, and making it oil-tight was

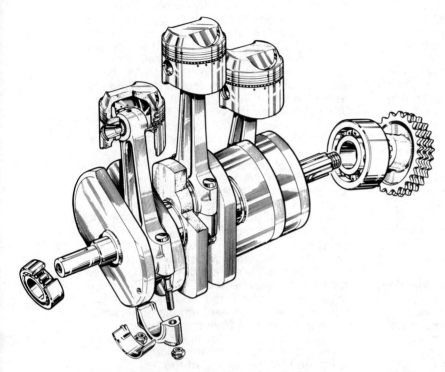

*Heart of the triple engine, its crankshaft with 120° throw.*

quite a job. Some sophisticated techniques were involved — the T160 crankcase castings, for instance, were passed through a vacuum chamber in which epoxy resin was drawn into the pores of the metal, to seal them — yet by then Small Heath's computer-controlled assembly track had been sold off, so the track was a 'pusher' one, and castings were moved from one machine to the next by hand. The Trident was a machine with Space Age performance largely put together by Iron Age methods.

The absence of tape-controlled machinery and the like had sometimes made itself felt, and had contributed to the early questions about reliability. An initial problem concerned primary chainwheel alignment, which was sometimes bad enough to contribute to chain breakages. Steve Brown, later the mechanic for racing ace John 'Mooneyes' Cooper, was working at Small Heath at the time on test riding the Rocket III, and on its rectification, and it was he who found that 'the wheels were out of line because the guy who was machining the chain wheel was putting 3 and later 6 at a time on his broaching machine in an attempt to get his money up'.

Harry Woolridge points out that the problem was not engine sprocket to swinging-arm sprocket alignment, as that was checked during the engine build, but the gear-cutting of the swinging-arm sprocket, which was on a helix.

Another problem was bad high-speed vibration on some of the early production bikes. This surprised Stan Shenton of Boyers, the manager of a successful Trident racing *équipe*, as the pre-production models he had been given by the factory had been as smooth as he could wish. He told *Classic Racer* recently that when Doug Hele investigated the matter, he soon found that 'someone at the factory had come up with a bright idea to speed up the machining of the crankshaft, which upset the balance factor'. Harry Woolridge confirms that the BSA machine shop were plunge-grinding the crankshafts without any thought to keeping the bobweights of equal thickness, and hence in effect changing the balance factors on some cylinders.

The tingles, from around 5,500–6,000 rpm, or about 85–105 mph in top, after which they usually smoothed out, would persist in some machines until the end. It was true that the triple's faults were always peripheral rather than fundamental, but they were irritating flaws in a gem of a machine. The temperamental triple contact-breakers and hence wandering ignition, the diaphragm clutch which Hele's man Jack Shemans called 'notoriously short of lift' and hence prone to slip and drag, the short-life shock absorber rubbers which Norman Hyde identifies as 'the Achilles' heel of these motor cycles', and which when they failed brought rough running or, at the worst, a broken crank at the drive end overhang, and the rapid-wear valve guides, were all crosses the Trident owner had to bear to the end, despite factory efforts to remedy most of them. Clattering valves and a reputation for oil leaks from the traditional Triumph sites of rocker box, pushrod tubes and inside the early gearboxes were further deterrents. All this obscured the fact that a good triple represented the fastest and smoothest British bike available, was one of the select number of Brits that could handle prolonged motorway speeds, and was

potentially capable of high mileages with minimum attention.

Early Trident finish could also be poor, with peeling paint and rusting cadmium-plated nuts and bolts being mentioned in a 1972 Rider's Report, though once again at a more fundamental level the welding of the chassis was excellent. The quality of paint and chrome improved after the Meriden blockade in late 1973 meant production in its entirety was shifted to Small Heath (previously Trident chassis had been built and the engines fitted at the Triumph factory), but a 1974 T150 tester noted iron sand casting imprints on the fork yokes as well as the footrests, brake pedal and stands, despite all the former items being enamelled, and the wiring was never properly tidied. Another exception to the general progress were the silencers: the early 'ray-guns' both sounded and lasted better than any of their megaphone, 'cigar' or 'black cap' successors.

Apart from their descent into industrial

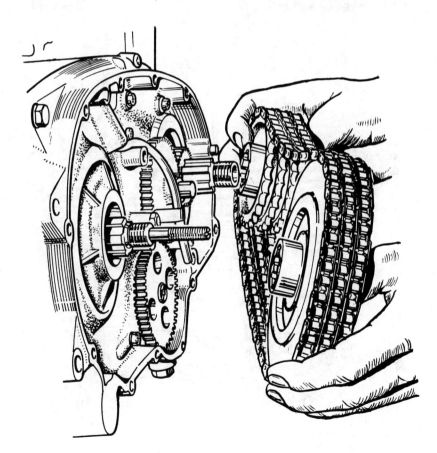

*Triplex primary drive was an early trouble source, due to manufacture, not design.*

turmoil at factory level, the other major negative factor during the Trident's lifetime, to be set against its dazzling background of race track success, was the way that the production triples became progressively slower and thirstier. It has been argued that this happens with most motor cycles, but in the Trident's case it was aggravated by a particular factor, as well as by the fact that it came just at the time when the first serious noise and emission restrictions in the USA and Europe were coming into force. The particular factor was that it was hatched in an era when, as Norman Hyde put it, 'Top speed was all', and hence produced with ports and carburation better suited to a 1,000 cc machine than a 750. Then, in the face of a certain lack of positive low-down pick-up, as well as other problems including American taste as well as their legal requirements, silencing and air cleaning became more restrictive, the gearing was lowered, and as a consequence petrol consumption plummeted to the mid-30s and below, with oil

consumption also often dropping far below 400 mpp. The reasons will be discussed later, but here it should be noted that the five-year period during which this took place also saw the price of petrol double due to the Arab oil crisis, so it represented another major disincentive to the biker on the street.

Finally, the Trident has to be seen in its historical context. There was a very marked contrast between the enthusiasm of the first, mind-blown road tests and the rather irritated tone of the final T160 ones, when despite its disc brake/five gears/electric start, as well as improved handling, these benefits were often accompanied by uneven quality niggles evidenced by smoking exhausts, restricted top speed, etc. One big difference was that in the intervening six years, the efficiency of the Honda and its brethren had changed expectations, and not just of performance; they had displaced the British industry's apparent philosophy, the one which expected the machine's owners to do its final development. Not for nothing did the famous

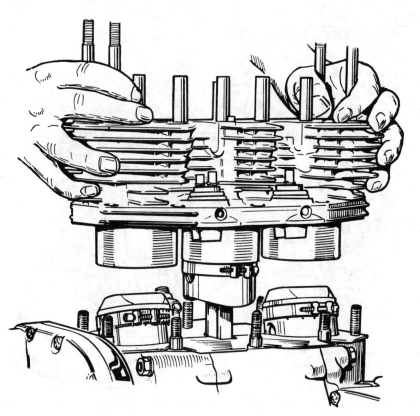

*Working on a Trident can be a complicated (and expensive) business.*

Bob Carlos-Clarke *Bike* cover photo of the first T160 and Mk III Commando pose them next to Stonehenge. During their production life a new age of motor cycling had indeed arrived. All this may help explain why the Trident falls short of a place in the ultimate motor cycling pantheon, despite being undoubtedly a very fine machine indeed.

In **1969** the new machine's engine, as well as its cycle parts, owed much to previous twin-cylinder practice. But the team at Meriden, wherever possible, had learnt lessons from the twins' problems and sought to remedy them. The traditional Triumph arrangement with two gear-driven camshafts fore and aft of the cylinders was employed. The layout was suitable for the three because of the symmetry it afforded, with two pushrod tubes on each side of the cylinders, the drive side pair containing a single pushrod each and the timing side a pair of rods each, all roadster rods being of equal length. The camshafts were positioned high up to keep the pushrods short, and unlike the cams on the unit C-range twins which ran directly on the crankcase alloy on the timing side, they were mounted in three plain bearings fed with oil supplied from small oil pipes running from the centre of the main bearing caps to the mouth of the crankcase under pressure, to the stems of the tappets, then passing through timed ports in the stems, to the tappet feet and thence to the cams. The camshafts were also of a new, tougher steel and were nitrided, which overcame the previous twin problem of rapid cam wear, and indeed was passed on to them.

A major step forward was the choice of alloy as the material for the cylinder block, which on the Trident was mounted upright, on the Rocket III tilted forward. Alloy kept weight down (Trident engines weighed around 180 lb) as well as width, owing to less cooling finning being necessary. But also, with the aluminium alloy's better dissipation, it did away with the twins' problem of heat distorting the cylinder head. The rocker box floor was also raised above the head joint to reduce head temperature. In prototypes, however, the use of alloy did create some trouble in avoiding fit problems and distortion of the bore for the press-fit alloy steel liners. Hence for production purposes the liners were pressed in and the complete block was then heat-treated, with the liners then being bored to their final size. As we shall see, this could

sometimes cause problems if the boring was less than perfect. The alloy block was very deeply spigotted into the crankcase.

The one-piece cylinder head, heavily finned, was of cast aluminium alloy, with hollow dowels both locating the head to the barrel and channelling oil from there to the bottom end. The head carried two Triumph-type separate well-finned rocker boxes, with their inner faces fitting inspection caps. Each valve was controlled by twin springs held by conventional collars and collets, and austenitic valve seats were cast into the head. The valve stem tips were of ultra-hard Delpha-B material and fused on, while the valve head diameters were the same as those on the current T100T twin. Pushrods were of aluminium alloy with hardened steel ends, and pressed-in aluminium alloy tappet guide books were housed in the cylinder casting. The tappet adjusters were of 0.25 in radius, with locknuts at the outer end of the rockers. The rocker arms were shorter than on the twins, which unfortunately would mean even greater side-scrub, and hence even more rapid wear of both valves and valve guides than with the twins' geometry. Lubrication for the rocker gear was by external oil-feed pipe.

The Hepolite pistons gave a compression ratio initially described as 9:1, though this was soon modified to 9.5:1. The three piston rings were cast iron to start with (later steel) and included an Apex scraper-ring assembly, which comprised two narrow rings in the same group separated by a corrugated spring-steel spacer. The pistons ran on Triumph-type H-section alloy con-rods, with bolted-on steel end caps, with the gudgeon pins running direct in the little end and white-metal-lined, steel-backed, big-end shells. Like the main bearings, the plain big-ends benefited from being modified during the development period by the use of special material from bearings specialists Vandervell.

The one-piece 120° crank provided the engine's built-in smoothness in contrast to the vibration inherent in a 360° parallel twin. A substantial item, the forged crankshaft was very rarely to be a source of trouble. It carried no flywheel, with bobweights taking care of balance, and it ran on four bearings. The centre two, like the big-ends, were plain bearings of the Vandervell shell-type, running in the centre crankcase section with their caps clamping the crank into position. The main bearings at each end of the shaft were a roller

*The 1969 T150's heavily finned alloy engine, with width kept commendably restricted. Note the oil cooler (a standard fitting) and the carburettor's operating shaft and levers.*

on the timing side and a caged ball on the drive.

The centre crankcase section had two substantial outer cases bolted to it. Despite the appearance of full unit construction, the four-speed gearbox and the primary transmission were housed in separate compartments within these cases. This brought the customary bonus that the gearbox could be dismantled without disturbing the timing gear housing. On the Triumph, this internal separation was emphasized, since in contrast to the BSA's more egg-shaped timing side cover, the shapes of the Trident's gearbox and timing cover were clearly delineated in the casting, in the tradition of the Meriden unit twins. This meant that the bottom end of the two triples differed in major ways. Keeping the cases narrow had been a prime design target, and was successfully achieved, with the Triumph triple engine being just $3\frac{1}{2}$ in wider than its 650 twin, though the extra width was somewhat emphasized visually by the fact that on the Triumph the engine overhung the frame substantially to the left.

Engine breathing was another area in which the triple improved on the existing twins,

which would adopt a version of the Trident's system from 1970 on. The Trident's crankcase dispensed with timed breathers and vented via the drive side main bearing directly into the primary chaincase. There a baffle made sure that the oil content of the vented mist settled in the case and kept up its oil level, before the mist was taken into the air filter unit to meet Californian legislation. However, when the twins adopted this system in 1970 they included three holes drilled between the crankcase and chaincase, which the triple could not do because of weakening the bearing housing. Breathing and its consequences could be a problem for triples.

The dry sump lubrication system began with a pump which finally abandoned the twins' vulnerable plungers in favour of a cast-iron gear-type item, driven by a gear-train from the crankshaft, and with the scavenge plunger having a greater capacity than the feed plunger. It was positioned on the drive side crankcase and protruded through into the inner primary chaincase. It provided an oil circulation rate $3\frac{1}{2}$ times that of the twins, to deal with the several plain bearings in the triple engine. Since the latter also caused oil temperature to rise, the system included an oil radiator mounted beneath the nose of the petrol tank, and in winter the triple was said to run at just 53°C against the twins' 78°C.

The oil tank held 6 pt, and since the oil cooler held about another pint, oil checks had to take place just after a run. There was one filter in the tank and another, Royal Enfield-style tubular one, lying across the engine in the centre crankcase casting below the gearbox, and accessible from the right. From it oil fed the two centre bearings. These connected to the other bearings as well as to the soon-to-be-deleted pipes to the tappets already mentioned. After being scavenged from the crankcase, which had a typically Triumph sump plate and filter bolted to its forward end, oil went through the cooler and back to the tank, which vented into the crankcase. From the return within the tank, oil was provided for an adjuster and supply pipe to lubricate the rear chain.

The gearbox had its own oil supply, and within it was a four-speed cluster, based on that of the 650 twins. Not every 650 gear will fit a Trident, but some interchanges are possible, with caution and reference to parts books. According to Harry Woolridge, provided that 1969 and later 650 gears are used, all are interchangeable with the triples, except the mainshaft which was shorter. The Trident 'box ran, however, at a primary drive reduction of 1.78:1, as opposed to the Bonneville's 2:1, which happily also resulted in a lower kick-start ratio. The mainshaft and layshaft bearings were exactly as the 650's, with the gearbox mainshaft running on heavy duty ball races, the layshaft on needle roller bearings pressed into the casing and the inner cover, and the gearbox input sprocket carried on independent bearings, to eliminate bending stresses on the gearbox mainshaft. The gearbox was rarely to be a source of trouble.

Positioned conventionally behind the triplex drive chain, the clutch was another piece of innovation, aimed at providing transmission strong enough to cope with the triple's power while still keeping the width down. A conventional multi-plate clutch would have meant a big overhang, so an all-metal, remote Borg & Beck diaphragm clutch was used, running on an outrigger bearing for greater rigidity.

The clutch ran dry in its own housing between the primary case and gearbox, with components being a diaphragm spring, a cast-iron pressure plate, and a driven plate.

All were enclosed within a pressed steel cover with a cast-iron drive ring bolted to it. Clutch release was via a pull rod, which acted on a ball-bearing in the centre of the plate. The clutch was operated by a sort of scissors mechanism, basically similar to the 650's with $3 \times \frac{1}{4}$ in diameter ball-bearings set between the clutch lever and the outer thrust plate and located in semi-spherical ramps. When the lever was operated, the balls rolled up the ramps, forced the plates apart, and operated the pull rod, which pulled the pressure plate outwards so that the diaphragm plate was compressed and the driven plate was freed. In practice, as on the Enfield, the mechanism provided only marginal lift and was prone to both slip and drag as well as burning out under hard use, unless adjustment was perfect. At the best of times, despite nylon-lined cables, Trident clutch action was often heavy.

The clutch also embodied another potential weak point, the shock absorber with its 12 rubbers set between the veins of a spider housing. The BSA and Triumph types differed, and these early Trident ones had a separate spacer which ran within its oil seal. The shock absorber rubbers, as mentioned, were short-life items, particularly since on the T150 they extruded between the outer edges of the paddles and inside of the hub. A knocking noise like a main bearing on the way out, which stopped when the throttle was opened, could be signalling that the rubbers had been crushed, so that the vanes were knocking together. Ignoring the problem meant harsh transmission, and on a few occasions the resulting snatch could snap the holding rivets on the clutch sprocket.

Primary drive to the clutch was by $\frac{3}{8}$-in triplex chain, which was tensioned by a rubber-faced slipper tension blade with a threaded adjuster, operating from behind a hexagon plug set in the front of the primary chaincase cover. From the start, in view of the triple's power, Hele had wanted a duplex set-up with more substantial chain, which he would get with the T160. However, the situation today has come full circle, for while the triplex chain is a car size and still available, supplies of the unique $\frac{7}{16}$-in duplex are drying up, and T160s perforce are being converted to the triplex system, even though with it primary chain life can be as short as 10,000 miles; though 30,000 is the average primary chain life according to Harry Woolridge.

The triplex chain wheel had plenty of room in the primary chaincase, as the triple Lucas RM20 110-watt alternator was mounted, unconventionally, on the right-hand end of the crankshaft, within the timing case, once again like a Royal Enfield of the 250 series. The 12-volt system, with its three coils rubber-mounted beneath the seat, was wired for alternative capacitor ignition. The standard system featured three contact-breakers, with their cam driven from the right-hand end of the exhaust camshaft. Unfortunately the camshaft, which also drove the rev counter, suffered from being an adaptation of the twins' camshaft, though supported by three bearings, and having to span a wider crankcase without the benefit of an increase in diameter. The contact-breaker back plate had three small adjustment plates carrying the three sets of 7CA contacts, which could thus be independently adjusted.

This was good, but unfortunately, torsional vibration of the exhaust camshaft at high speeds often caused bounce and chatter of the advance mechanism. There were also problems with the ignition timing wandering, due to the advance–retard springs being too weak; then, when the springs were changed to stronger ones, being over-retarded at high rpm; so that finally, in 1974, a mix of strong and weak springs would be tried. The later Lucas units were more robust, but the design could give problems anyway, as the contact-breaker heels sometimes caused drag and ignition retardation at full revs, which could lead to holed pistons. It was all unfortunate, as the triples were sensitive to their ignition setting. The racers adopted quill drive; and when systems became available, many triples would be adapted to electronic ignition, of which more later.

A final striking feature of the engine was the bank of three carburettors which fed it. A single carb would be adopted on the Quadrant, the four-cylinder prototype developed from the Trident, but this was not a possiblity for the triple, which would not idle with a single instrument. The carbs were special Amal Concentrics with 27-mm chokes. They were mounted to a manifold connected to the inlet port by short rubber clip-fitted pipes, and actuation was by a single cable. This connected to a shaft across the top of the Amals, bearing three operating levers connected directly to the throttle slide. There

These air boxes must also be used if 'ray-gun' silencers are fitted.

were also no throttle springs in the instruments, but a single scissor-type return spring for all three slides mounted on the cross-shaft. Balancing the three instruments, already a problem with the twin-carb twins, was still rather involved, requiring the removal of the carbs complete with manifold, but at least setting the idling speed was taken care of by a single adjusting screw on the shaft, which allowed tickover speed to be set without adjusting each one individually. The air slides at this stage were operated by a single handlebar lever.

The Trident's cycle parts, with the important exception of the square tank and ray-gun silencers, were recognizably Triumph. The frame was a single downtube, full cradle type, with a braced single top tube and a bolt-on rear end, all as on the twins, but the triple's downtube was of thicker gauge and an inch longer than the Bonneville's. The swinging-arm pivoted on steel-backed bronze bushes from a lug welded to the single seat tube, and braced properly as on the 1963-on 650s. The 61° fork angle embodied the experience from the twins, and the forks themselves, carried on cup and cone steering head bearings, were the same as those on the 650s but with stronger springs, with a steering damper topped by a Triumph badge, rubber gaiters, and brackets on the shrouds for the new flat 7-in chromed headlamp, which was similar to the one that would be found on the early oil-in-frame twins, but differed from it in lacking the twins' warning lights, or lightswitch, until 1971.

The Triumph frame was claimed to be an inch lower than the Rocket III duplex downtube version, which Meriden men also said was heavier, though the factory figures gave the two machines identical 32-in seat heights, 58-in wheelbase, and 468-lb dry weight. Opinions would differ about the relative handling of the two versions: *Motor Cycle's* David Dixon found the T150 steadier than the Rocket III in 1969, while a 1972 Rider's Report found that the BSA seemed to have a slight edge on the Triumph for steering. In practice there seems to have been little in it. The Trident did give the impression of being a more compact machine than the Rocket III.

One thing they both shared from the start was Unified Threads for the vast majority of bolts, etc. Otherwise, as well as the upright engine — the BSA's cylinders were tilted 12°

forward — and the frame, further differences from the BSA included the Triumph's chrome-trimmed seat being ribbed, its three-position Girling rear units being traditionally shrouded where the early Rocket III's lower springs were exposed, a Triumph blade-pattern front mudguard with three sets of tubular stays, and different side panels, plainer shaped and unribbed, which carried for this year a stick-on 'Trident' motif and ran forward to enclose the one-piece rectangular air filter. The Triumph's oil cooler was unshrouded (the early Rocket IIIs fitted alloy end casings), carrying the US-regulation rectangular side reflectors directly on its ends. On the 4¼-gal petrol tank, the shape of the badge background plate and kneegrips were different, and the Trident's tank lacked the step halfway along the bottom which was found on the BSA. Another detail was the Trident's rather inelegant grab-rail with its squared-off hoop bolted to the mudguard, in contrast to the Rocket III's BMW-style hoop fastened to the frame.

From both these chromed rails were suspended the support brackets for the oval-shaped ray-gun silencers, with their reverse flow internals, central seam, raked end plate and three distinctive stubby tail pipes. The sound they produced was a civilized enough but very distinct snarl as revs rose, though the famous true triple wail was reserved for the racers, which according to Les Williams was because of their valve timing. Today the presence of ray-guns just means that the owner knows that they make the triple go faster, but at the time the unusual silencers with their bracing struts looked off-puttingly weird. At the other end of the exhaust system, the frame's downtube meant that the middle exhaust pipe had to split into two as soon as it emerged from the screwed-in exhaust stubs, so this first system was three into four into two, with all the junctions completed by the base of the cylinder block.

The wheels (3.25 × 19 front and 4.10 × 19 rear), their bearings, the tyres and the brakes were all in common between the two machines, though the chromed cover plate on the Triumph-originated 8-in TLS front brake, like the ones on the 650s and the Daytona, had circular flutes on the Trident and radial ones on the BSA. The original front tyres were 3.25 × 19 in Dunlop K70s, soon to be changed to 4.10 × 19 in TT100s, renamed thus to commemorate Malcolm Uphill's 1969

ammeter and warning lights were carried in a neat fork-top binnacle, with the ignition switch conveniently placed on the right-hand headlamp bracket (scoring over the BSA's less handy underseat switch), and the toggle lightswitch on the left one. A steering head lock was also found between the forks. The handlebar, originally the high US Western pattern, but later somewhere between a Triumph pullback and a 'flat', was rubber-mounted like the later twins, and with the same slightly unnerving effect under heavy braking. Its controls were decidedly dated, with the traditional pressed steel horn button/dip switch bolted on one side, and a matching cut-out button on the other. The bars fitted the current awkwardly fat grips, and ball-ended control levers. The petrol tank had a padded tank top strip down its centre between two chromed beads, with the filler cap offset to the right. The tank fitted twin taps, and though the left one provided a nominal reserve, it was advisable to run a triple with both taps open, as otherwise fuel starvation at high revs could lead to a holed piston. The twin Windtone horns were mounted down by the base of the suspension units on the downtubes of the rear sub-frame, where predictably their performance was not very impressive. Neither was the first T150's Aquamarine paint colour for tank and mudguards. It somehow reflected the Trident's identity problem, for in contrast to the integrity of the Rocket III's deep red, it was neither green nor (Triumph) blue. The Triumph racers were to get it right with their blue and white finish.

But every sort of detail and reservation could be forgotten once astride this Triumph. The Trident produced 58 bhp at 7,250 rpm, and the performance package this created was the overwhelming first impression. There was very, very vivid acceleration, so that despite the seat's ribbing *MCM*'s tester, his helmet blowing loose, had to struggle to retain his grip, while *MCN*'s was thrust backwards so much under a rising throttle that he found it hard to reach forward and pull in the clutch lever. *Motor Cyclist Illustrated* ran 50 mph in first, 80 in second, 110 in third, with a standing quarter of just under 14 sec already come and gone, and just over 125 mph in top. This was production performance virtually in a class by itself in late 1968. It was also achieved with an incredible smoothness hitherto unknown on post-war

100-mph Production TT lap and developed with the triples in mind, because as 'Polly' Palmer recalled, such was the motor's torque that 'put an Avon SM on the rear and large chunks would rip out of it'. As it was, rear covers had to be renewed every 4,000–5,000 miles, which was also about the life of the ⅝ in rear chain. The rear wheel carried a Triumph 7-in SLS brake, and was not quickly detachable.

At the sharp end, the twinned 150 mph speedometer and rev counter plus the

British machines at high speed.

US gearing in a *Cycle World* test provided a 13.028 standing quarter but a top speed down to 117 mph. On the European version the only reservation, which the smoothness accentuated, concerned a certain lack of bottom end punch, in contrast to the accustomed big parallel twins, with the triple's power beginning to come in, deceptively smoothly, from 3,000 rpm, and serious power stepping in around 5,000 rpm. But medium- and high-speed acceleration was the name of the 750 triple's game, and though it might have been true that Norton's Commando twin would run quarters a shade faster due to its outstanding low-speed torque and hence speed off the line, at 90 mph, when any parallel twin engine was getting very busy, and every British one bar the Commando was subjecting it rider to bad vibration, the European-geared triple, despite some increasing high-speed tingles, was accelerating, infinitely more smoothly, at the same rapid rate it had done from 50, and would keep on doing so for another 20 mph or so. The engine revved freely to its 8,000 rpm bloodline and beyond.

Very precise steering and excellent roadholding by and large matched the speed. 468 lb dry was a heavy motor cycle for that time, and the feel was of a large bike with a firm footprint, rather than Triumph traditional nimbleness; it could be swung fast through bends, but it they were bumpy ones some muscular effort was required. Despite this, as *UMG*'s Molloy observed, 'On the right road, the bike really shifts for a heavyweight multi'. One limit was ground clearance: both silencers and the centre stand could be touched down quite easily. In a straight line a slow weave set in after 100 mph, and while the handling was good, the T150 was enough of a Triumph for back end wriggles to set in if the power was backed off on bumpy curves. Some T150 owners I talked to also noted a tendency for their machines to pull to one side, which they thought might be due to the engine's overhang to the left. Used Tridents are as sensitive as the twins to the condition of their swinging-arms, and imprecise handling over bumpy surfaces usually indicates a worn pivot and bush assembly, while a slow roll at low speeds means that the cup and cone steering head bearings have been overtightened.

The footrests were set wide, as well as fairly far forward, in a compromise between touring and sports riding position, and like the rather awkward-to-use centre stand, this added to a feeling of bulk when the bike was at a standstill. But once under way, the feeling of weight instantly dissipated. Though

**Left** *The good 8-in 2LS front brake, but not really good enough for 120 mph and 490 lb kerbside.*

**Right** *Some dubious styling, but for 1969 the Trident could really go.*

the riding position was comfortable, especially on the earlier better-quality seats, and the Trident's seat height and reasonable width allowed *MCM*'s tester 'with a 29" inside leg' to get both his feet on the ground, the Rider's Report did note that comfort, otherwise excellent, was not too good for the smaller rider.

Other ways in which the triple proved itself an easy machine to ride were fairly easy starting (as long as the ignition timing was correct), the outer two carbs tickled and the air lever set precisely. Gear changing and clutch action were smooth, though if the latter was out of adjustment, it could be a heavy pull. The engine was flexible, ticking over easily and capable of burbling along at 30 mph in top gear, though it would need a down-change to take off, and third gear was its favourite for town work. It did not much relish the latter, however, becoming fussy and lumpy in traffic. In fact, prolonged slow running caused an overall drop in oil pressure. Fast open roads were the Trident's patch, and the Rider's Report confirmed it as a superb machine for long, fast touring, with two up and luggage representing no problem, though the standard rear springs were found a little soft for pillion work. The lights were relatively good, but the early brakes less so: both the 8-in front and 7-in rear drums were good of their kind, the front very good, on 400-lb twins, but hauling down triples with a kerbside weight of around 490 lb from speeds of 110 mph and more was asking too much of them.

Other niggles included a relatively noisy engine mechanically, as well as the early reliability problems, already mentioned, principally from chain-wheel alignment, crankshaft lubrication, clutch and ignition troubles. Very hard usage could occasionally result in a con-rod letting go, usually caused by a seized big-end.

Internally, the principal problem centred on high oil consumption, evidenced by smoking engines — smoking on the over-run indicated worn valve guides, while smoking in general indicated piston ring wear, particularly on the centre pot. The origins lay with rapid wear of the bores and/or the valves, valve guides and valve seats. Some believe that the engine's breathing holds one of the solutions. There has never been a definitive answer either on the cause or the cure of these interrelated problems, though it is possible to identify

some ways of minimizing the effects. The tolerance of piston to barrel was critical, and could be thrown out either by cylinders originally bored inaccurately so that they went oval, or run in too gently so that the necessary roughness had not been achieved, or by the original fairly fragile cast-iron piston rings; Harry Woolridge also points out that the Apex oil control rings fitted were never really suitable for Triumph engines. There could even (a Norman Hyde tip) be piston problems from faulty taps letting petrol through to the cylinders and washing the oil off; one way to avoid the latter is to disconnect the taps if the bike has to stand for a while. Visual evidence of excessive bore wear was usually provided by a deep ridge at the top of the bore. Today, rebores to a high standard can be had from the triple specialists.

Heavy wear of the valves and guides may well have been endemic to the design, though it did not occur with every triple. Arthur Jakeman wrote that he had seen it occur between 5,000 and 50,000 miles, though I have privately overheard him jokingly expressing surprise when a Trident engine brought in for work had managed 10,000 miles without it! Checking the diameter of used valves against new ones will reveal a badly worn stem, which in turn indicates a probably worn guide. Modern high-quality stellite-tipped valves, with Norman Hyde stainless for the exhaust and with chrome-plated stems, as well as better fitting guides with sealing rubbers on the inlets, can all help with, if not infallibly cure, the problem. Valve guide life can also be lengthened by the use of Hyde's mushroom-headed tappet adjusters, which will be discussed later, as these tend to roll rather than scrape over the valve ends. The early tappet adjusters could eventually wear holes in the top of the valve stems. Les Williams provides reground cam followers on an exchange basis, and these are ground to 1 in radius rather than the standard $1\frac{1}{8}$ in, as there is then less likelihood of the cam knocking the edge of the follower and breaking it. The early inserted valve seats were also very prone to pocketing, and the situation was not remedied by the factory until 1972.

To return to the rapid valve/valve guide wear and consequent smoking, one theory among users was that insufficient engine breathing possibly contributed; that in practice the crankcase might not have been able to breathe well into the chaincase through the drive side ball-bearing, as once the engine was running, a screen of oil would obscure the bearing; and that this pressure might have helped cause the rapid valve/guide wear. It could also have contributed to the oil leaks from the cylinder base (the race-developed practice of fitting the base gasket dry can help here), the cylinder head joint and the rocker box, as well as sometimes the traditional ones from the pushrod tubes, plus from the gearbox spindle housing and from inside the gearbox until a 1970 modification. On the head, the retention of the original solid copper head gaskets in place of the interim Klingerite composite ones has been found to be the best way to go, as well as replacing the hollow dowels with new ones when rebuilding, while some have supplemented this with separate breathers on the rocker boxes, or tried altering the basic crankcase breathing dimensions. Another culprit could sometimes be the oil pressure release valve which was only held into the rear of the crankcase by a very few threads; if it leaked, the crankcase filled up with oil and oil gushed from every joint. Jointing compound on the thread and a new washer every time were recommended. Recognition that the head sealing problem was a design one came with the new fixings for the final T160, and substituting the later studs and bolts on a T150 can be a good move.

The problem of smoking and high oil consumption (it could drop to 200 mpp) on some, but not all, Tridents never really went away, but then, as we shall see, right to the final T160s, neither did the problem of quality control on matters like oval bores. What should also be noted is that Tridents were very much Triumphs in that a 'properly put together' example could transform almost every aspect of them, i.e. a skilfully prepared engine eliminated many of the typical problems like engine noise, carburation flat-spots and oil leaks, while carefully set-up cycle parts could have unexpected benefits in addition to good handling — one tester found that the simple act of tightening his rear chain virtually eliminated the previously experienced high-speed vibration.

These early four-speed T150s may have had their teething troubles, but in practice their relatively high gearing (for home and European models) and de-restricted silencing and air cleaners mean that they can often still

be among the toughest and quickest of all the triples. They also returned around 40 miles to the gallon of four star, something that would change on subsequent models. The five-speed 'box would have to come, however, both to keep up with the Japanese Joneses, on and off the race track, and because on the four-speed 'box the big gap between second and third was quite noticeable.

There were a few mid-year modifications to 1969's T150. In the gearbox, the selector fork rod was shortened, and the pin location of the layshaft's shift selector fork changed. Also, on the transverse crankcase oil filter housing, loose steel sleeves were added at either end of the centre crankcase section to retain the O-ring seals there more effectively.

**1970** saw little change to the cycle parts. The rear drum brake threads altered to UNF, while stronger Windtone horns, and a Dark Orange colour scheme for tank and guards, with white side panels on the tank and a white centre stripe on the guards, were all introduced. The springs on the rear dampers were now exposed, and the lower stay of the front mudguard attached to the guard by two bolts instead of one.

In the engine, attention was directed principally at oil-tightness, and there was one significant change to the lubrication system in the light of some early mains bearing failures. This consisted in the blanking off of the original feed pipes from the two middle main bearing caps to the tappets and cams, as the latter were found to be adequately oiled by splash, as well as by the provision of a larger bore external feed pipe to the rocker gear. The new arrangement left the crankshaft significantly better lubricated. and any remaining examples of the old should be blanked off accordingly. (Another measure already undertaken on the Rocket III and often done retroactively on Tridents was a small ledge built up in the crankcase to trap oil and provide an additional feed to the bearings.) The idler gear spindle to the oil pump was also lengthened, with the pump spindle relocated from its previous position on the primary chaincase inner cover to the left-hand crankcase, and the crankcase strengthened locally at the pump mounting.

On the oil-tightness side, the engine joint faces were broadened. The cylinder base nut design was altered to permit greater clamping force. Gaskets were fitted between the gearbox outer and inner covers, and the inner

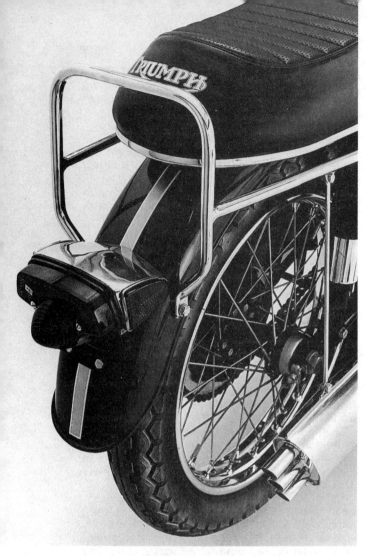

$\frac{3}{8}$ in, and this second type was also longer, at $\frac{15}{16}$ in, and identifiable by a cross milled on its square end. In mid-year the hub diameter of the shock absorber was changed and the rubbers revised. There was also an attempt to counter clutch slip by ventilating the clutch housing with holes drilled in the casing. To close up the gap in the gearing, third gear ratio was lowered slightly (from 1.19 to 1.24:1), which involved fitting new layshaft and mainshaft gears. And in a first move to provide more positive pick-up, the overall gearing was lowered a little, with the number of teeth on the rear wheel sprocket being raised from 52 to 53; like all such subsequent moves, this slightly increased petrol consumption.

The gearing between the kick-start and crankshaft was also slightly raised, using 650 parts, for even easier starting. The camshaft pinions became identical for both inlet and exhaust, and an earth lead was fitted from the centre bolt of the rectifier to the coil platform. But major changes to the Trident would always be limited: Meriden triple fans said this was because it was very nearly right from the start, though the ongoing chaos of the Group's situation and finances also contributed. An electric starter, for instance, according to Al Cave, had been in the pipeline from early on – but because it would not fit in the limited space behind the Triumph's upright cylinders, only on the inclined-engined BSA, it was not judged 'politically acceptable' as BSA's fortunes declined, and was thus delayed for another four years.

1971 saw the infamous last-ditch oil-in-frame BSA/Triumph range, which halted Triumph twin production for three months and left no model unaffected. For the Trident the changes were mainly cosmetic, though they did include the new ungaitered alloy front forks, which reduced the wheelbase by 1 in, to 57 in, as well as the conical 8-in front and 7-in rear brakes. Otherwise there were minimal mudguards, smaller side panels with transfers, not nameplates, which no longer covered the air cleaners, the flat headlamp carrying a twist-on light main beam switch as well as warning lights, which now included an amber one for the new chromed plastic direction indicators, and a new four-position ignition/light switch. All this was aimed at America and, except for the side panels, all was as for the twins, including the skimpy

cover and the main casing. They were of a new asbestos and synthetic rubber material. A seal was added to the primary chain adjuster plug, and the adjuster became a hinged design. Early in the year a Klingerite head gasket replaced the solid copper one; it did give a better seal around the dowels, though worse gas sealing, and a point to watch with the composite one was trimming any loose strands of wire from where they might protrude into the bore, and there cause pre-ignition and a holed piston. In mid-year, the gearbox sprocket lock nut assembly was modified and fitted an oil seal, with the clutch hub now featuring a recess to accommodate the nut.

There were also attempts to deal with other problems. Early in the year the radius of the tappet adjusters was enlarged from $\frac{1}{4}$ in to single rubber mounting for the front guard, the chrome bracket mounting of the instruments in their rubber cups (no more consoles for a while), the unpopular bent chromed wire mounting for the headlamp, the new-style combined grab-rail and lifting rail which also carried the circular rear side reflectors, and the new elongated mounting for the 'teat'-type tail lamp.

Details of all these items will be found in the oil-in-frame twin section, and fitting them to the triple resulted in a catalogued 8-lb weight loss, with claimed dry weight now 460 lb. Further major items in this transformation of the triple's style were the twin-type megaphone silencers. Despite a brasher appearance, the silencers were matched to revised air cleaners, with carburettor slides changing from 3 to $3\frac{1}{2}$, and with the catalogued compression dropping to 9:1. A cumulative result was a marked falling-off in top speed, accompanied by an increase in fuel consumption, which fell to 35 mpg and below from then on. This was coupled with the 1971 $2\frac{3}{4}$-gal 'conventional' rounded petrol tank, offered in greenish-tinged Spring

Gold with gold-lined black swept-wing scalloped panels. The tank not only provided a range of under 100 miles, but being waisted at the rear, exposed the tops of the two outside carburettors, so that when the rods that lifted the carburettor slides became a sloppy fit through their rubber top covers, rainwater could enter the carbs.

With the increasing disorder at Small Heath it seems that few of these triples reached the UK market, but those that did were roundly loathed, for the tank with its impractical range, the skimpy mudguards, the fracture-prone front mudguard stays, the rear wheel which was still not q.d., the fade-prone front brake which was no improvement on the old one, and the not-too-effective rear brake (Meriden offered a kit to improve it which included a new upward-pointing cam lever). The only features which were appreciated by the '72 Rider's Report were the new forks, though their exposed stanchions made their oil seals vulnerable. The Riders also liked the new switch gear in its alloy housings, despite the stubby thumb switches and poor waterproofing. Tridents may have avoided the

**Left** *The view most other bikes got of the T150 Trident in 1970.*

**Right** *The 1971 T150 Trident, considerably restyled. Alloy forks, megaphone silencers and the new 2LS conical front brake, with a conventional petrol tank.*

'71 Rocket III's dove-grey frame (but also its pretty chrome, cream and red tank), but all the Umberslade Hall-dictated restyling had succeeded in doing was making the triple resemble the twins in the year when the twins' name was in decline, while the triples were establishing a resounding reputation for themselves on the racetracks of the world. It was a prime example of the BSA Group 'snatching defeat from the jaws of victory', and the absence of a faired race replica was not just a failure to capitalize on track charisma, since several testers would note how the unfaired triple's top end performance could not be explored much above 95 mph

for long, with its existing riding position and in the teeth of its self-created howling gale.

One further development may have come in mid-year. The five-speed gearbox was certainly announced during 1971, but does not seem to have become available in the UK until June of the following year.

**1972** saw the last Rocket III built, and all Group motor cycle production bar the triple engine transferred to Meriden, where Hele and Hopwood tried among other work to turn the range back into relatively practical motor cycles. The slab-sided tank was back for the UK, in a version catalogued as slightly larger at $4\frac{1}{2}$ gal, but fitting the previous kneegrip and

**Left** *1973 brought the very welcome 10-in Lockheed front disc brake, as well as five gears for the T150V.*

**Right** *Basically a five-speed BSA Rocket 3 but none the worse for that, the slanting pipes and flowing fibreglass of the X75 Hurricane, for 1973 only.*

badges with the Triumph name on a white background. Like the side panels, the tank was finished in fizzingly trendy Regal Purple, while the small mudguards became chrome.

In the pursuit of better low-down acceleration, the gearing was lowered again, this time by fitting one tooth less on the gearbox sprocket, which dropped from 19 to 18 teeth. The measure was effective in improving acceleration between 40 and 70 mph, though petrol consumption stayed high, and for fast touring, to lower the revs at sustained high speed, reverting to the 19-tooth sprocket can be a good idea. Within the engine, the cylinder head now had inserted valve seats to overcome the bad pocketing experienced on the previous model with its cast-in seats.

With the ongoing Group confusion it is hard to pinpoint changes accurately, and the position was further complicated by the fact that Meriden's efforts on the triple were concentrating on a long-stroke 830 cc version, the Thunderbird III. Based on experience with oversize race engines such as Norman Hyde's world champion side-car record-beater, and scheduled for release early in 1973, the calendar of BSA troubles would mean that all that reached the market were a few Thunderbird III-type badges which turned up on some T150s exported to Australia. But July 1972 did see the introduction of the five-speed cluster adapted directly from the Quaife gearbox developed for the racers. Though it did not make the engine any more tractable, the five-speed 'box brought greater flexibility and better responsiveness, as the gears were brought closer together and the engine closer to its optimum power band in the next ratio. And by November came the full house T150V with disc brake and revised silencer, as well as the wonderfully flamboyant X75 Hurricane, both for **1973**.

A prototype Hurricane had been exposed in America as long ago as September 1970, the year after the film *Easy Rider* had seriously launched the chopper cult. Though shown as a Triumph at that time, it is now known that the production Hurricane was originally intended to be a BSA. This seemed only fair, as Illinois automotive stylist Craig Vetter, who went on to design the Windjammer fairings, had selected the inclined Rocket III engine for this factory custom. The BSA's tensely tilted cylinder angle matched that of the BSA frame's twin downtubes and of the exposed-

spring rear damper units. BSA's troubles delayed the Hurricane's launch until 1973, by which time the BSA name was defunct, and the X75s were built at Meriden. These BSA origins probably contributed to the fact that the Hurricane was resented by many at Meriden (see Volume 5) as a typical Group attempt to muck about with a fine Triumph roadster and associate Triumph's name with something expensive (nearly £200 more than a Trident) and impractical.

This was unfair. Always intended as a top-of-the-market, limited edition machine, just 1,152 Hurricanes were built, and they represented in my opinion the finest factory custom ever. Vetter fulfilled his own parameters, an eye-catching boulevard cruiser with both a comfortable ride and terrific acceleration. He created a lean racy sportster

# The 1973 Hurricane X-75 (TRX75).

1. Custom-styled and chromed front fender.
2. Teardrop front headlamp.
3. High-rise handlebars, and steel clutch and brake levers.
4. 2.6 gallon steel gas tank enclosed in fiberglass tank/seat combination.
5. Custom-styled tuck-and-roll seat.
6. Custom handrail/lifting handle.
7. Chromed rear tail lamp mount.
8. Three custom-styled megaphones—low level exhaust tones.
9. Dunlop K81 4.25x18 tire. Highly-polished alloy conical-shaped rear hub.
10. Three individual exhaust pipes.
11. 750cc three cylinder engine, fitted with heavy-duty five speed gearbox.
12. Oil radiator.
13. 8" double leading shoe front brake.
14. 3.25x19 Dunlop Rib Tire.

with minimal touches: as well as the frame and engine, the wheels, brakes, chrome mudguards and polished alloy tail light were standard 1971/72 Rocket III, though the wheel rims were alloy and the front one wore a ribbed 3.25 × 19 tyre where the rear was a fat 4.25 × 18. The engine did have one variation from standard, strictly for styling purposes, as the finning on the head was extended sideways by $\frac{3}{4}$ in at some points. The Hurricane ran at 9.0:1 compression, and the five-gear cluster was fitted. Both gearing and weight, at 420 lb dry, were right down, a combination which reputedly provided 12-sec standing quarters but meant power began to run out early after 90 mph.

The main styling exercise was embodied in the sleek curves of the narrow, angular, radically waisted bright red and yellow high quality fibreglass seat/tank unit, with its short tuck-and-roll seat and concealed 2.2-gal steel gas tank. Beneath the unit the HT coils and

oil tank were moved inboard. The other eye-grabber was the exhaust sytem. Not the stock three into four into two system but, with a curt nod to Honda's new 400-4, three streams of chromed steel snaking across and under the power plant to fan out into a stack of short chromed custom megaphones on the bike's right-hand side, with the top one bearing a perforated chromed heat shield, and the right pillion footrest angled neatly below it.

The front end was kicked out $3\frac{1}{4}$ in over stock, using naked, polished forks (the prototypes had been Cerianis), topped by a teardrop headlamp on a U-shaped mounting of chromed wire, and instruments in their own plain rubber binnacles on chrome bases, with uncluttered high and wide handlebars. Otherwise, there were just deft small touches like polished hubs and chromed spokes and sprockets, plus a chromed sidestand, skimpy rear chainguard and own-brand grab-rail, with round red Triumph badges, as on the steering damper, also topping the rear units, where they covered the knobs releasing the seat/tank unit at the back.

The Hurricane was a stirring experience, and not just visually. The three open megas produced a thrilling howl, especially at eight grand, which the Hurricane revved to as willingly as any other triple. Dynamite off the line, the X75's handling limitation was a slight front end instability at 70–80 mph under some circumstances, due to a combination of the extended forks and the impractically high bars. Otherwise the Hurricane was an experience not to be missed, and having been lucky enough to ride a well-used but well-sorted example, with a clutch and gear-change that showed just how good they could be, I can confirm that the Hurricane's low weight, basic smoothness and agility (except for a wide turning circle) made it a delightful ride in stop–go town traffic and on fast A-roads. At speeds up to 80 at least, the conical brakes were good performers, once again in view of the bike's reduced weight—it's no wonder that so much subsequent customizing effort on Tridents has gone into trimming their avoirdupois, which is what the factory should have done with a race replica. Today homage to the Hurricane can be found in the form of X75-style seat/tank units being marketed for T140 twins. The 1973-only original machine was the quintessence of one kind of biking—pure distilled street summer fun.

Meanwhile the 1973 T150V attempted to claw back the basic Trident into the realms of the practical, with many of its changes also appearing on the twins. The chrome front mudguard became full length and reverted to three-stays tubular brackets, now themselves chrome. The chromed rear mudguard became more substantial, and carried a neater and chunkier squared-off polished alloy mounting for a large new rectangular tail lamp. The front forks, which took the wheelbase back to 58 in, now wore clipless rubber gaiters plus black-painted dust shrouds on the stanchions, with conventional mounting lugs for the headlamp. The light became a teardrop shape, as on the pre-'71 twins, but bearing the warning lights as well as a popular three-position toggle switch, though unlike the twins, the four-position ignition switch, which actually turned on the lights, moved down to the right-hand side panel.

The alloy fork legs were polished, and the left one carried an integrally cast lug for the 10-in Lockheed disc brake, with chromed disc and caliper covers, itself mounted on the left side, as Commando experience would prove to be preferable. The handlebars were altered to accommodate the master cylinder for this most welcome addition, with the choke air lever also being moved down by the carburettors on the left. The disc may have had a rather wooden feel, but it was powerful, and in conjunction with the triple's good engine braking, finally provided stopping appropriate to the T150's performance.

Another major change was to the silencers, which for UK and European models became

**Above left** *Points to ponder on the X-75 Hurricane, a fine-looking factory custom.*

**Right** *A rare nearside view of the Hurricane—most photographs go for the pzazz of those silencers.*

cigar-shaped to cope with increasing noise legislation, and were fitted in conjunction with new air cleaners and housing. Though the silencers were still quite loud on full bore, the total effect again was restricted, with top speeds now down to around 115 mph. The finish of the square-sided petrol tank was restyled, with the padded tank top strip deleted and a square, gold-lined painted side section leading back into winged scallops above and below the large rectangular kneegrips. This gold-lined side section was either in a deep golden yellow or in red, and in the latter case, for this year, the background of the new alloy name badges now fitted to the machine's side panels would be red too. The conical rear hub was now polished and lacquered rather than painted silver as previously. The new T150V was a compact, practical-looking, if rather uncharismatic motor cycle.

By now, from engine no. 04571, the tappet adjusters had changed to their final, Ducati-type ball-ended form, with the valves shortened to suit. Well-engineered, mechanically quieter in operation, and providing potentially increased valve life by

sparing the tip, the ball-ended adjusters had one important flaw—they were very difficult to work with. In this system, a ball-bearing with one side flattened off sat in a cup at the bottom end of the square-ended adjuster. The intention was that the flat section should bear down on the top of the tappet stem, while the ball rotated constantly as it did so, making for even wear. The problem was that as soon as the feeler gauge was inserted, it tended to be pinched up, so an accurate adjustment was virtually impossible without backing off and starting all over again. In addition, the flat often rotated away, so that adjustment was being attempted on the spherical bit, which gave an inaccurate gap. Service bulletins recommended lightly tapping the adjuster screw to seat the ball, but the thing was just not user-friendly, and incorrect clearances were all too easy to achieve. As the triple's valves were such a critical area, and adjustment was advisable every 3,000, if not every 2,000, miles, today Hyde's mushroom-headed adjusters, which also have an easier-to-use slot for a screwdriver at their top end, have been fitted by many.

With Meriden in turmoil over the NVT

takeover, the Thunderbird III was cancelled and Trident production ceased with everything else by October 1973. There was then a gap until April **1974**, after which Small Heath was tooled up to make the Trident cycle parts as well as its engine, and production, by a workforce which swelled to 1,000, began again in full swing. The triple's continuing exploits on the racetracks meant that demand for them was healthy, and output shortly rose to 200 a week, so that in the following 12 months probably as many T150s were made as in the preceding four years.

Specification changes were few. The most important was the fitting of a crankshaft with

the rotor key relocated to give the optimum flux between rotor and stator for kickstarting when the battery was low. Where the earlier version had a common flat key for both the alternator rotor and the pinion, the later had two separate Woodruff keys. Most rotors have two marks, 'A' and 'B', with 'A' to be used for timing on the first type of crank as it represented 38° BTDC, and 'B' fulfilling the same function on the second type.

Otherwise, catalogued compression ratio was dropped to 8.25:1, though it is unclear whether this was for US export or for all models. In mid-year, the contact-breakers' advance-retard return springs returned to the mix of one strong, one weak. But with Hele

**Left** *By now quite a handsome if conventional motor cycle, a T150V for 1973 on show in France late in 1972.*

**Right** *A trio of British bobbies campaign a T150V in the 1973 Circuit des Pyrénées.*

and his team at Kitt's Green working on ohc, rubber-mounted and four-cylinder versions of the Trident, as well as on the upcoming T160, the T150V stayed much as before. A few T150s with poor top end performance were found to be suffering from a casting restriction in the exhaust port shape around the valve guide support boss, particularly on the centre cylinder. Machines tested around this time were all noticeably free of oil leaks.

An interesting insight into the strengths and weaknesses of the production T150V was afforded by a *Motor Cycle* account in the autumn of '74 of a Land's End to John O'Groats run by a Commando and a Trident. On the triple, rider comfort was not good, due both to the forward footrests, and in particular to a feature much noted from 1971 onwards, namely seats which subsided quickly to leave the rider sitting on the hard pan. The Trident proved a difficult starter, and consumption and wear on what was evidently a hard 1,200-mile ride were awesome, with the $4\frac{1}{4}$-gal tank returning just 90 miles, with a further $2\frac{1}{2}$ on reserve, plus three-quarters of the tread gone off the rear tyre, and a brand new rear chain ending up worn out. Oil consumption was acceptable at 2 pt. 1974 tests in *MCW* and *MCS* would also confirm that petrol consumption dropped into the 20s with high-speed running. On the straights there was sustained high-speed vibration, with the tool box coming loose on the first day and the rider's feet being pushed off the footrests; using the pillion rests was found to be best, and they were ready, having already vibrated down. But the triple's excellent

handling and cornering meant that it led the Norton on the twisty bits over the Highlands, with clutch and gearchange fine and the brakes normally excellent, though the front disc performed badly in the wet.

**1975** saw a few changes for the T150V in the remaining months of its life, the principal one being an attempt to remedy the triple's thirst by raising the UK gearing, substituting the previous pre-'71 50-tooth rear wheel sprocket for the 53-tooth one. The result was a track top speed of 118 mph but very slow and gradual acceleration from 100 mph onwards. Also, despite the headlamp's performance not having been spectacular, the size of its bulb was reduced from the previous 50/40 to 45/40 watts.

Dave Minton, writing for *Motorcyclist Illustrated*, had a T150V for a month's appraisal over 2,000 miles, during which time his only problems were a side panel screw falling off, and one set of contact points closing up. He found the Trident performance faultless but unostentatious, because tyres, brakes and suspension complemented each other too well to isolate any one of them, yet together provided a flow of input that permitted fast riding as well as 'a ragged style' — line-changing and braking in bends, brake-snatching and then accelerating, etc. — ignoring the rule book and still getting a faster and safer ride than on a bike that could only give its best under a disciplined fist. This was combined with a 'peaceful' bottom end performance, with the engine ticking happily at 1.500 rpm/21 mph in top (the test machine had US gearing). But like everyone else,

*The 1973 T150V with interim 'cigar' silencers.*

Minton disliked the riding position and the uncomfortable seat, and criticized the poorly waterproofed switch gear, which in addition was irritatingly different from the similar-looking Commando's, with the triple's dip switch being on the right and its indicator switch, awkwardly, on the left.

Then early in 1975 came the end of the T150, as on 20 March the final T160 was launched in the UK. The new Trident was still a 750 but, like its companion 850 Commando Mk III, sported an electric starter, a rear disc brake, and left-side gearchange to satisfy US legislation, as well as over 200 other alterations and improvements.

Probably the best as far as the rider was concerned was the race-bred frame. This was not the Rob North type on the F750 racers, but the 'short' frame as fitted to, and homologated for, the works production racers. The lower frame tubes were raised for improved front ground clearance, the front forks, now mounted at a 62° angle, were shorter and had a shorter action, and the swinging-arm was lengthened. The front forks now pivoted on taper-roller steering head bearings, which represented a big improvement. The result was a wheelbase which measured the same 58 in but changed significantly in weight distribution, lifting the Trident's handling from the good to the outstanding.

Part of the weight shift was achieved by the use of an engine with the familiar Triumph-style bottom end, but with its cylinders now tilted forward in Rocket III style, though at 15° against the late BSA's

12° angle. The more-or-less hybrid Rocket III/ Trident had been known to the team developing it at Kitt's Green as 'the Rodent'! This engine was moved forward $\frac{1}{2}$ in on handling grounds, and raised 1 in to help ground clearance. The extra room behind the tilted cylinders was used to accommodate longer inlet tracts and a bigger air box, with a larger paper air filter inside it, which was claimed to cut induction noise by 30 per cent.

The extra space behind the cylinders also housed the solenoid-operated Lucas starter, an approximately $\frac{1}{2}$ hp device. This sat in a circular housing on top of the gearbox and was of the pre-engaged gear type, meshing with a gear on the back of the clutch. This meant that it could be started with the bike in gear, but there was no starter lock-out device in case one did so inadvertently. It was operated by a button on the right-side handlebar, and a more powerful 12-volt battery and 6-volt ballast resistor coils were part of its system. When the starter was switched on, the resistors were cut out and the full battery voltage went across the coil, to compensate for the voltage drop caused and ensure enough was left for the motor. A more powerful RM21 127-watt alternator assisted this. The kick-start was still fitted, but in practice the Trident's starter worked quite well, and certainly better than the Mk III Commando's.

The crankcases had been modified to accept the starter, as well as the left-hand gear shift. There was now a circular bulge in the front of the gearbox's right-hand face to accommodate part of the cross-over linkage,

*The NVT-built 1974 T150V. Note the variation from previous silencers.*

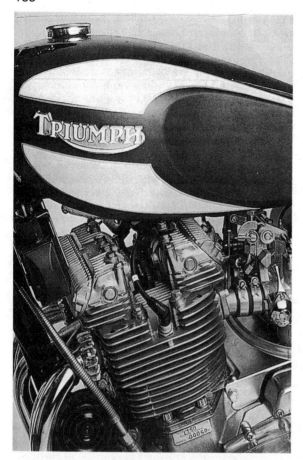

and this was decorated with a '5-speed' sticker. The long cross-shaft was supported on a steady bracket, splined at the gearbox end, and with two flats at the other end. If the cross-shaft was disconnected at the gearbox end, it had to be 'retimed' correctly when rebuilding, or only exclusively upward, or downward, changing would be available. Unfortunately, the new gear pedal's position dictated that the footrests, which would shortly be capable of conversion to rubber-mounting by means of an NVT kit, were still too far forward.

A useful change in the transmission involved the troublesome clutch shock absorber. Where it will be recalled that previously the shock absorber rubbers had extruded between the outer edges of the paddles and the inside of the hub, the T160's reduced the clearance by half with a modified hub. This replaced the previous separate spacer which ran in the oil seal by an

extended nose which did the same job. The unit was now fitted with its six cover screws facing inwards, but was interchangeable with the previous one though only with machining and difficulty. The other major transmission change was on the primary drive, which changed from $\frac{3}{8}$ in triplex to $\frac{7}{16}$ in duplex chain, which as Hele intended could cope better with marginal misalignment (as Harry Woolridge points out, alignment was held to .010 in which is good enough for any chain), and wore better, though still fast. Today, particularly in view of the $\frac{7}{16}$ in chain shortage, belt drive is a possibility. Finally, the lift action of the clutch was increased with a view to making adjustment of it less crucial, though the T160 could still have a heavy action like its predecessors, and T160s were known for getting through their (nylon-lined) clutch cables at a fair rate.

Elsewhere in the engine, oil circulation was improved by opening out the internal oilways to the oil pump from their previous $\frac{1}{4}$-in bore to $\frac{5}{16}$ in, with a small diameter pipe to the oil pump also replaced by a suitable $\frac{5}{16}$ in one, and the holes in the pump enlarged to suit. All this can be done retrospectively to a T150, but only by a skilled operator. A principal benefit of this race-bred measure was that it helped oil get round easier when the engine was cold. Another after-market aid to that process is fitting a Norman Hyde thermostat, which only brings the oil cooler into action when the oil has reached a reasonable operating temperature (74°C). This helps eliminate the internal condensation these engines are otherwise prone to, especially on frequent short runs.

Compression was raised 'in the American specification machines' back to 9.5:1, and that seems to have applied to the earlier UK T160s also, though from engine no. 04075 it was announced that 'lower [8.25:1] compression ratio pistons would be fitted to all engines', – excepting those for the American market, with engines with the new 8.25:1 pistons identified by an 'L' stamped on top of the front engine mounting lug, though in practice it seems this may not always have been done. The T160 Cardinal Police export versions were certainly to this specification, but many reimported examples have been changed to 9.5:1 either for preference, or because of the fact that 8.25:1 pistons for the 750 had not been available in oversizes.

Another change was that both camwheels

were marked IN and EX, and should be fitted to the camshafts using the keyway which is in line with the appropriate IN or EX. What this indicated was that while the T150's cam timing had been done on the production line, by putting dial gauges on the cam followers and then setting the cam timing for each individual machine, on the T160 the camwheels were marked up earlier in the production process, so that cam timing was always more approximate with them. The T160's rev counter drive was now taken off the left-hand end of the exhaust camshaft, as on the twins, via a right-angled drive box, and it should be noted that the bushed screws securing the drive box now had a left-hand thread. On early T160s the rev counter drive gearbox had proved an oil-leak point, and from T160 engine no. 02085 the crankcase was modified to relieve the pressure which caused this; prior engines were offered a modified securing screw assembly with an O-ring and washer.

Gearing on the T160 was altered again in a variety of ways, as well as the gearbox itself being revised, with a different-sized inner cover bush for the gear shift fork. The engine sprocket's teeth changed from the previous 28 to 23, the shock absorber from 43 to 50, and the gearbox sprocket from the recent 18 back to 19, while the rear wheel sprocket remained at the recent T150's 50. The effect was to lower the overall gearing a little, which in turn contributed, together with restricted breathing and silencing, to true top speeds of around 117 mph. (A *Bike* magazine test T160 did clock 126 mph in May 1975, but Brian Tarbox, writing in *MCN* in 1978, blew the

whistle on the fact that this machine had first had its engine stripped and rebuilt by one of Jack Sheman's colleagues in the development team!)

Another modified item was the carburettor operation, which was no longer by scissor-spring on the external throttle linkage. Though still using a cable-operated alloy cast beam with three arms operating the slides directly, the T160 had more conventional slide return springs.

The T160 was around 40 lb heavier than its predecessor at 503 lb dry, and it looked it, largely due to the major new styling feature, a big, handsome waisted tank of 4.8 gal for European models, though a 3.7-gal American version was also available. The tank uncannily resembled a slightly more angular version of the one Bert Hopwood had designed for his first Norton Dominator twin over 25 years previously. Its cap was usefully offset to the right, so that as well as being able to check the level visually, it could be filled right up (a very necessary procedure) while on its side stand. The tank was handsomely finished in either standard Cherokee Red, with gold-lined white flashes and tank badges with 'Triumph' picked out in white, a scheme later to be associated with the T140 Bonneville, or in the very nice export version of white with gold-lined bright Sunflower Yellow flashes. For me these tanks, with the raked engine, naked forks with chrome dust covers and headlamp brackets, and everything else black or chrome, really defined the Trident.

The forks carried a new front mudguard, attached by just a single chromed bent tubular bracket at the rear, and a substantial

**Above left** *Tilted engine and restyled tank were the signatures of the electric-start T160, from April 1975.*

**Right** *The 1975 T160, a big, beautiful motor cycle that handled as well as it looked.*

central bridge piece to the fork legs themselves. The T160's engine was also polished, and the caliper covers and brake discs themselves still chromed, with the same drawbacks concerning the discs which this entailed for the T140. The right-mounted rear brake had become the same 10-in Lockheed disc as at the front, with an underslung caliper which could be swung away when wheel changing, which was still not an easy job. The decision to go to a disc had evidently been taken on cost rather than fashion grounds, as of the Japanese machines, only the Gold Wing had one at that stage. The new brake with right-side pedal, though still vulnerable to the wet, worked well. *MCN's* tester John Robinson found it

controllable, with the right amount of leverage and feel. Pad life would be around 7,500 miles.

The other restyled area was the exhaust system, with the three exhaust outlets from the cylinder head immediately going to four pipes, which were lengthened to run in pairs down the front of the engine and out of sight. The four longer primary exhaust pipes were claimed to improve gas flow for low-down power, as well as visually mimicking the massed exhaust pipes of Japanese Fours. Each pair then joined via a collector box into a single pipe, just before the junction with the uptilted Norton-style 'black-cap' silencers. While handsome enough visually, and meeting noise emission requirements, these big silencers both muted the engine's song and did not suit the Trident's requirements, stifling it. The silencers had been foisted on the Triumph by NVT management; possibly reflecting their recent Production TT defeats, as well as other projects dearer to their hearts, there were voices in that quarter not well disposed towards the triple, with Norton man Bob Trigg referring publicly to 'that rather oily engine', and NV's managing director Geoffrey Fawn being the one to bring the hammer down, due to somewhat spurious costing exercises, on Hele's four-cylinder Quadrant version. Though the 'black-caps resembled those on 850 Commandos, they were not identical, and confusing the two can mean incorrect carburation and piston problems. The Norton versions had a small point in the centre of the end cap, while the Trident's had a circular depression.

At the fork top area the instruments, their faces bearing the NVT 'wiggly worm' and now mounted in fatter rubber binnacles, were linked by a new console fitted between them, carrying the ignition switch as well as the standardized instrument lights required by US legislation. These were for the direction indicators, plus an (intermittently effective) neutral indicator, as well as high beam and oil pressure warning lights. There were revised handlebar controls with longer thumb switches, which were still vulnerable to the wet. Finally, the hinged seat was also modified, fitting a cover which extended its ribbing down the sides of the rider's portion, with the seat still having to be lifted to reveal the left side panel's top fastener. Unfortunately, the seat was still not lockable, and was little more comfortable than before, with the foam squashing down to the seat base in a way that became painful after a couple of hours. It was also a poor proposition for the pillion rider, being too low at the back, and coupled with a badly positioned grab-rail plus a footrest evidently designed for dwarfs, which shortly gave a normal-sized passenger cramp.

Road impressions of the T160 were fundamentally good, but marred by a lot of detail niggles. Several test bikes burned oil at 200 miles to the pint or less, which seems to have been due to a combination of some oval bores plus an early piston ring problem. The clutch on John Robinson's T160 burned out on the test strip and slipped after that. There were some oil leaks due to early gasket sealing problems, though as mentioned the revised cylinder head fixings were an improvement. Some test bikes also displayed a carburettor flat spot which meant the engine fluffed when the throttle was opened: NVT would say this was curable with richer slides, but the latter would do nothing for the petrol consumption which was already around the 35 mpg mark. And in an age of rapid inflation, the battle of price had been lost: at

£1,215 against the last T150s at £971, the then psychologically significant £1,000 barrier had been breached and the Honda-4 at £979 left far behind, and, combined with the Trident's weight and performance (and the left-foot shift), this put the triple outside the calculations of most of us at the time. At around the same price as a Ducati 860GT, the new T160 was the preserve of relatively well-heeled enthusiasts who didn't mind a performance package with some rough edges.

The rest of us were the losers, because this proved to be a final chance to buy new what was, with its flawed but likeable Commando stablemate, the last of the classic British thoroughbreds, the current crop of new Hinckley Triumphs representing a very different ballgame. The triple engine's potential could always be liberated, and the race-bred T160's handling was truly sorted—not for nothing is Les Williams, the Meriden man who maintained and backed the legendary Slippery Sam in its 1973-'75 Production TT victories, content to base his beautiful Triumph Legends firmly on the T160.

As *MCM*'s Robinson wrote, 'At the [test] track we discovered that it could be run

**Left** *The T160 rear wheel disc brake with underslung caliper.*

**Right** *Last of the production triples, the 1975 T160.*

*A postscript. Bob Currie rides the Cardinal, a Police triple targeted at the Middle East, but as NVT collapsed, some were sold in the UK.*

increasingly harder through the turns and its behaviour actually got better'. Previously the T150's handling at around 100 mph could threaten to turn nasty if the power was backed off, and bumpy curves plus the sudden need to change direction could occasionally reveal a certain top-heaviness, with the back end wriggling and the bars having to be wrestled into submission. Though it had never been a serious problem, with the lower, more forward-mounted engine John Robinson found that despite its neutral feel and its bulk, the T160 coped with bumps even better heeled over than when upright; that the lack of feedback meant the left footrest in particular got worn away without him realizing; and that over a test hill where most bikes went airborne, the Trident's front wheel tracked all the way, and though the rear one went light, the Triumph went through the following hairpin bend without a twitch. Such were its reserves of handling. Nimble and usable was the final verdict.

For *Bike* Mike Nicks again found that

despite its weight, well-matched suspension meant that it could be peeled into corners and hustled fast around the lanes. The ratios of the T160's five-speed 'box were well spaced and, unlike most Japanese machines at the time, fifth was not just an overdrive gear, and pulled well. And once they settled in, T160s could also prove very reliable.

NVT's collapse late in 1975 meant that production finished after something less than a year, though there was a coda in the form of the Cardinal. This was a white-finished Police machine with a main production run of 450 destined for Saudi Arabia in a deal engineered by Neale Shilton. In the end, many were reimported, as well as 130 more stored in the Midlands and sold off in 1977, together with 288 British-spec. Tridents with KPH speedos (they had been intended for Australia) plus 244 US-spec. machines.

The Cardinals had featured low compression (8.25:1) engines, a lowered exhaust system, a Tri-point windscreen, crash bars, Craven panniers with one having air

*Within certain limitations, the T160 Cardinal could make a good tourer.*

horns mounted on the outside, high Western bars, spotlamps, and a comfortable single seat. A dualseat and pillion rests could only be fitted with difficulty, due to the panniers, as mounting them had meant cutting off the seat's rear hinge. *Bike* judged the Cardinal a superb tourer, which was now a neglected area for the triples as NVT were marketing the Mk III Commando for that function, with the T160 as their fast roadster. The Cardinal was comfortable, good for rapid stop-go town work, and kept its handling intact until over 80 mph when the fairing and panniers caused the usual slow weave, which *Bike* judged more controllable than on the contemporary state-of-the-art BMW twin. The T160 Cardinal was the last of the line.

The Trident's story is a sad one in that it involves much potential lost to events beyond the control of the men who engineered this fundamentally superb machine. The happy ending today is that a lively Trident sub-culture still exists, and has succeeded in unlocking much of that potential. Norman

Hyde and Les Williams have already been mentioned. Twenty-eight-year Meriden man and Hele cohort Jack Shemans, once Hyde's assistant, now works for himself, while Phil Pick at Triple Cycles will prepare road as well as racer engines, and Miles Engineering Rob North race frames can also be adapted for road use. Hyde, too, has provided alternative chassis in the form of his previous Missile and current Harrier kits, but for road riding probably his greatest contribution has been the various big bore conversions he offers. These deal with what was and remains, when all the detail faults are discounted, the fundamental stumbling block for many about the smooth triples, namely lack of bottom end grunt compared to a traditional British twin. Various combinations of barrels and cranks give up to six capacities from 831 cc up to the ultimate 1,002 cc, and it is the latter, with Hyde half-race cams and 3-into-1 exhaust, despite the latter grounding rather too easily for scratchers, which is usually judged the ultimate for the road, providing built-in

144

**Left** *Trident development keeps right on. Here for 1982 was triple specialist Norman Hyde's Missile, something of a symphony in sheet metal.*

**Right** *Another way to go. Les Williams' Slippery Sam replicas became the basis of his wonderful T160-based 'Legends'.*

pulling power all the way.

A Trident is not the most convenient of machines to work on. The centre spark plug, at a different angle from the outer two, is difficult to get at with the tank on, and the tank has to come off for accesss to the oil cooler. Very thin spanners are needed for the cylinder barrel nuts, and most head bolts and base nuts are inaccessible to a torque wrench. The centre exhaust pipes have to come off in order to remove the sump filter. Having said that, for the enthusiast servicing is lengthy rather than complicated, with the only special tools needed being a camshaft timing pinion extractor and a clutch centre extractor.

As with the twins, regular attention to the swinging-arm is vital to maintain handling. In addition to items already touched on, useful after-market buys include Hyde's improved clutch hub and sintered iron clutch friction plate with a steel centre, as the bronze internal splines on the standard driven plate could wear quickly. Electronic ignition is pretty well a must, and Mistral now offer a special system used by Les Williams on his Legends and particularly good for the T160 with its electric starter, since the system is not subject to voltage sensitivity and so will not baulk when the starter is operated. Modern rear suspension units allow full exploitation of the handling, and finally Hyde sells a stepped seat that offers improved rider location and comfort.

None of this kit is cheap, and neither are T160s, though T150s remain reasonable for the moment. As noted, on a Trident consumables get used up fast, and trouble with the clutch, valves, especially the exhaust valve, or with the ignition, can all mean hefty repair bills. Though with its race record the engine's basic ruggedness has never been in question, this colours the Trident reliability picture. The frames and cycle parts, bar '71/ '72 ancillaries, are tough enough, with the only point to watch for, on the T160 only, being the very occasional crack in the front downtube, just above the mounting lug. *UMG*'s Molloy says 35,000 miles is the most he's heard of for a triple before a rebuild has been necessary, but one Cardinal, with the Devon and Cornwall police, covered 52,000 miles with few problems outside clutch cables, the American magazine *Motorcyclist* in 1975 knew of several T150s that had covered 80,000–100,000 miles without the head coming off, and Harry Woolridge knows of one with 150,000 miles up and only head and transmission having been attended to. Perhaps the wide open spaces suit them. The picture seems to emerge of a machine not without flaws, but untemperamental once these have been sorted out, and basically rugged; expensive but rewarding, with smoothness, medium- and high-speed acceleration and handling, the Trident transcended the very difficult circumstances

under which it was designed and produced, to create, against great odds, the basis for a genuine British superbike.

## Triumph: The Trident T150, T150V, X75 Hurricane and T160 — production dates and specifications

### Production dates
T150 Trident — 1969–71
T150V Trident — 1972–75
X75 Hurricane — 1973
T160 Trident/Cardinal — 1975–6

### Specifications
Capacity, bore and stroke — 740 cc
(67 × 70 mm)
Type — ohv triple
Ignition — coil
Weight — T150 (1969) 468 lb; (1971) 460 lb;
X75 (1973) 444 lb; T160 (1975) 503 lb

## Triumph 650 and 750 oil-in-frame twins, 1971–88: T120 Bonneville, TR6C Tiger, T120R, TR6R, T120RV, TR6RV, T140V, TR7RV, T140 Jubilee Bonneville, T140E, T140D Special, TR7VE, T140E Executive, T140 ES Electro, TR7VS Tiger Electro, TR65 Thunderbird, TR7T Tiger Trail, TR6T Tiger Trail, TSS Eight Valve, and TSX Custom

The oil-in-frame Bonnevilles were the last of the line, and after a near-disastrous start, settled down for a long if fluctuating production run. During a life which saw them go from 650 to 750 capacity, as time moved on, despite the addition of modern ancillaries like disc brakes and an electric starter, they changed from competitive motor cycles to the high-priced embodiment of a fading but still admired tradition. Their troubled history and many detail faults make it easy to overlook some solid virtues. At base these are rideable motor cycles and potentially quite good all-round machines.

The birth of the oil-in-frame twins was tumultuous. They came in twin-carb T120 Bonneville form and in a single-carb version now known as the TR6C and TR6R Tiger rather than the previous Trophy, which name was now reserved for the single-carb 500. Early problems at Umberslade Hall, the Group's design centre, can be found detailed in Volume 5. Then in late 1970, because of Umberslade's disorganization, there was a delay in Meriden's production schedule of three months, when only the 500 twins and the triples were built, until the start of **1971**.

At Meriden it was already known that Umberslade had needed to make 12,000 modifications before the final drawings of the P39 frame were released, but when at last the drawings arrived and the first frames were completed, incredibly enough it was found that the 650 engine would not fit into them. After some experiment it came out that the engine could be shoe-horned in if the rocker boxes were removed – but once the engine was in the frame it was then not possible to refit the rocker boxes. Meriden took matters into their own hands by redesigning the 650's cylinder head with 18 modifications, including the rocker boxes themselves, as well as covers, studs, bolts and gaskets. Even so, the engine still proved awkward to install and work on.

In the engine, the redesigned rocker boxes adopted an extra fixing hole, as well as new access plugs on each side, in addition to the caps on the top, which finally made setting the valve clearances easier; the days of the bent feeler gauge were over. The new cylinder head needed four extra locating dowel pegs. The pushrod tubes lost their castellations at the top but gained drain holes to compensate, and continued with the '69-on silicone washer and its sleeve at the bottom. On the crankshaft there was another change of flywheel, which again involved new bolts and flat washers. The engine sprocket's oil seal face was removed and a modified distance piece fitted, to allow the use of shims to help with the long-standing problem of primary chain alignment. The oil pressure relief valve became a single assembly and adopted UNF threads. In the gearbox, the inefficient leaf camplate index spring continued.

Finally, in mid-year, due to a worldwide shortage of bearings, from engine no.

GE27029 the timing side crankcase and the crankshaft itself were modified to take a metric timing side ball main bearing, with the crankshaft timing gear nut also revised. Both crankshaft and cases were initially supposed to be distinguished by an 'M' denoting the metric fixings, but this was never implemented. Unfortunately, this would usher in an era of epidemic main bearing failures. In the 1971/72 period Nelson confirms that no less than one in three main bearings were failing while still under warranty, though Harry Woolridge does not believe that failures were so common. As with pistons, Service at Meriden carried a range of options, since bearings are defined '2 dot', with normal clearance down in the $\frac{10}{1000}$ th in range, or '3 dot', with larger clearances than normal. Nelson knew of a previous bout of mains trouble with the pre-unit machines in 1948, but that had been due to inconsistency in manufacturing. In this case he felt the cause to have been selection of an inappropriate 'dot' bearing. By the end of the period the '3 dot' type was being favoured, though then again, being a loose fit, this could cause rumble, in which case a '2 dot' replacement was substituted by Service. (There was also disagreement over the optimum number of ball-bearings in the timing side ball race, with eight allowing a bigger space for oil, while nine provided a greater bearing area to take the load.) The situation would briefly worsen with the increased torque of the 750, which had to be detuned accordingly.

Also in mid-year, the clutch shock absorber front and rear plates changed to a through-bolt design.

This 650 engine was fitted into a duplex

**Left** *Time for a change – the 1971 oil-in-frame T120 Bonneville.*

**Right** *The new alloy front forks proved comfortable, and fine performers.*

downtube chassis, with a large central 3 in × 16G central spine tube running down from the steering head and bending downwards to form the seat-tube. This thin-walled spine contained 4 pt of engine oil, and at its base was an inspection plate embodying a 'top hat' gauze filter, plate and filter being integral at this stage, though in mid-year it altered to a two-piece design. Also at the tube's base was a pressing linking the 1¼ in × 14G duplex cradle tubes. Raising the hinged seat gave access to a threaded oil filler cap and an awkwardly separate dip stick.

Also below the seat, which hinged on the right at this stage, was a pair of side panels ornamented with louvres, which were dummies, since the filters they concealed drew their air from beneath the seat. The two-piece panels, of which the main rear tin pressing was awkward to detach, behind filter covers held by a nut each side housed the rectangular dual wire mesh/cloth element air filters and their rubber tubes to the carburettor(s). They also concealed the Zener diode, which used the right-hand panel as a heat sink. With another step back in terms of convenience, this right side panel also housed the four-position light and ignition switch. The front panels were light alloy die-castings and the rear portion tin pressings, decorated by transfers. The panels' design varied on the single- and twin-carb models.

The frame was similar to the one provided for BSA's A65 twin, but the engine mounting points were different: the Triumph motor sat lower and further back, with the engine itself bracing the frame at the back. The Triumph was also distinguished, thankfully, by its black finish frame, which probably helped it sell while BSA's Dove Grey version proved unpopular. The new chassis fitted new side and centre stands (the latter in particular, as we shall see, was to be a source of trouble), footrests, engine plates, rear chainguard, rear brake pedal and swinging-arm. After development trouble with the latter tearing out of the oil-bearing tube, the arm was firmly located between two plates welded to the frame, and it pivoted on steel-backed bushes, with two in each half of the pivot.

At the front end, pivoting luxuriously on Timken needle roller bearings were new all-alloy front forks. Their design derived from BSA moto-cross experience, and internal damping was by clack valve rather than the previous shuttle valve. They provided 6 in of

movement, and rear springing was softer than previously too, with 110-lb rate springs fitted on the exposed-spring Girling units. The chrome-plated upper parts of the slim precision-ground fork stanchions were exposed, while the light alloy sliders featured four-stud cap fixings for the wheel spindle. At their top end, the fork cap nuts secured separate chrome carrier plates for the rubber-mounted speedometer and rev counter binnacles. The handlebars were still rubber-mounted. Though good performers, the forks' problem was that unlike Triumph's previous ones, the new aluminium sliders bore directly upon the stanchions, and hence could not be rebushed, though [in practice] wear was minimal. Furthermore, in the short term the exposed stanchions quickly let grit rupture the sliders' oil seals, invariably causing noticeable oil leaks and ultimately affecting the handling.

The actual action of the forks combined soft springing with stiff damping, so that the

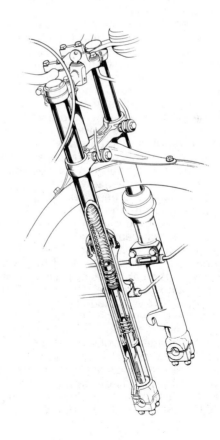

front end dived under heavy braking, and also, being unbraced, the braking forces acted on the right leg so that it could fail to rebound until the brake was released, which could lead to some alarming pogo action on bends. Personally, I found the fork legs a little too close together to feel completely secure, but appreciated the comfort of the soft springing.

The forks supported a minimal painted front mudguard in rubber mountings attached to the stanchions by a single, somewhat fracture-prone stay on each side, though it was the BSA version which suffered the worst of the breakages. They housed a 3.25 × 19-in wheel and a new 8-in TLS front brake mounted in an alloy conical hub. There was a prominent front-facing air scoop on the brake plate, which unfortunately could allow the drum to fill with rainwater. The brake featured Lockheed-designed Micam click-action adjustment of the shoe pivots, with the adjusters reached by a screwdriver via a hole beneath a rubber plug in the conical face of the hub. This relatively simple procedure was welcome, because the brake would prove to need frequent adjustment if it was to give of its best.

The brake incorporated two dubious design features. As Ariel and BSA man Clive Bennett pointed out to Umberslade at the time, the new brake used steel brake shoes within an alloy hub, instead of the other way around, as on the previous Hele brake. The different expansion rates of aluminium alloy and steel meant that the alloy hub expanded away from the steel shoes as soon as it got hot in operation. Although an Umberslade man has subsequently pointed out the presence of a steel drum liner in the design to obviate this effect, the brake did undeniably fade fast under hard application. The other design problem was that while the brake's front cam lever was operated by the inner cable's nipple pulling it on, the rear cam lever had the cable's outer casing abutted to it (rather than, conventionally, to a fixed stop), and this rear lever worked by the cable casing 'pushing' it. This was intended to provide a 'caliper' action on the two cam levers, but equal pressure should have been exerted on each lever, and in practice the cable casing, which beneath its PVC sheet was made of wound circular section wire, like a spring, compressed like a spring when the brake was applied, ultimately becoming squeezed up and losing potency. The squarish cam levers themselves were too short, which meant a lot of pressure was

necessary, particularly as the set-up meant that the brake lacked initial bite. Meriden soon added a spring on the exposed portion of the inner cable between the two cam levers, to help keep the cable properly seated on the levers.

On the fat 4.00 × 18-in rear wheel, which no longer offered a q.d. option and was difficult to change, there was also an alloy conical hub, with a bolt-on 47-tooth rear sprocket. This contained an SLS 7-in brake. Although giving the appearance of a fully-floating brake, it was not — its long strip-metal torque arm bolted to the front of the swinging-arm. It too gave problems when first introduced, so that in April 1971 thicker linings and fulcrum pads were fitted, as well as a longer cam lever now fitted pointing upwards, plus a new return spring to increase the leverage. In this form it worked well, as indeed did the front brake when it was in good condition and well adjusted.

At the top of the forks, rubber-mounted on brackets of bent chromed steel rod, was a flat chromed headlamp, lacking an ammeter (which was gone for good) but incorporating warning lights for ignition, main beam, and for the Lucas winkers which were now fitted as standard. No friends to parallel twin vibration, these winkers usually malfunctioned quickly, or loosened off to point skyward before detaching themselves. Also on the headlamp was an unpopular twist-on rotary light switch. US legal requirements meant that the 50/40 main bulb was replaced by a 45/35 watt item. On the high and wide US-spec. bars fitted to all models at first, there were cast-alloy brake and clutch levers, and new Lucas alloy switch housings with impractically short thumb switches, the right-hand one for the indicators being mounted just above the engine kill button. The 'teat'-type tail lamp was now mounted at the end of an unsightly elongated pressed steel housing which also supported the rear winkers. A single Lucas 6H horn was fitted in place of the previous twinned Windtones.

The petrol tank was a US-styled 3-gal one with a BSA-type single central mounting bolt and its own central chrome trim strips. Petrol caps were the plain twist-on type, and from then on would be prone to leaking. Finished in Tiger Gold for the Bonnie, the tank was decorated with white-lined swept-wing scallop panels in black, above and below the 'picture frame' tank badge. The louvred side panels were black, with a plain name transfer on the black tin pressings to the rear of them. The ribbed seat featured an external 'ammunition-box' wire clip catch which could be secured with a padlock. The seat was thickly padded at first, though by mid-year this would change. The chopper-style image was reinforced by new exhaust pipes, though still with the linking cross-pipe, running into quite short megaphone silencers. The overall effect of the new twins with their kicked-up front ends, skinny fittings and chrome was a bit like a child's (or a young American's) idea of a motor bike.

Aside from the impractical details already mentioned, the oil-bearing chassis was already known to be too tall, in Triumph's case having a seat height of 34 in (see Volume 5 for details). The height was not the only problem. Engine vibration had increased dramatically. Accessibility for working on the engine remained poor. Though it was no longer a large matter, the factory announced that side-cars could not be fitted to the new frame. While since then individuals have done so without apparent ill-effects to the oil-bearing tubes, and the co-op would give their blessing to the practice in 1981, it remains true that crash-bars should not be fitted for fear of their rupturing the oil-bearing frame on impact. The overall styling of the bikes echoed the chopper cult which had taken hold with the 1969 movie *Easy Rider*. They featured the impractically high handlebars, minimal underseat storage space for tools, the naked ungaitered stanchions meaning vulnerable oil seals and leaking forks, and the very small mudguards which splashed English weather all over the rider's legs and up his back.

More fundamentally, the oil-bearing chassis sometimes fractured and leaked. Examples arrived in America with split seams on the main tubes from faulty assembly, despite being pressure-tested during manufacture, but a more common cause was the centre stand, a poorly designed item with its pivot cross-tube attached directly to the bottom of the oil-bearing tubular spine (though not to the actual oil compartment), which when it twisted in use could soon also crack and fracture the frame, with any failure leading to persistent oil leaks around the sump filter. The remedy was $CO_2$ welding for the crack, and then fitting two flat stays from the pivot tube forward to the main frame tube. The factory

were soon doing this.

The stand remained very awkward in use, both to pull the bike on to it and, once there, to push the bike forward off it when the rider was in the saddle. This was caused by the cross-tube which located the stand pivot ears being prone to twist or partly rotate in use. The answer was to reposition the pivot ears, and then weld a small pair of fabricated bent brackets between the frame cradle tubes and the pivot ears. Meriden would do this after 1973. The swinging-arm pivot was also strengthened by extending the rear guard mounting plates to the oil-bearing main frame tube.

Meanwhile, by the end of 1971 a squared-off 4-gal tank with a plain Triumph name badge was introduced to supplement the 3-gal export job, but another problem remained. The Triumph version of the oil-in-frame chassis only held four pints of oil, a borderline capacity that would condemn the Bonnie to hot running from then on. The origin of the restricted capacity had been frothing problems which had forced the frame's designers to move the oil-filling aperture from its intended position behind the steering head to a much lower point just ahead of the seat. Harry Woolridge believes that petrol tank design also played a part in this decision.

The weight saving involved from the use of an oil-bearing frame, incidentally, appeared non-existent, as a 1970 T120 was listed at 363 lb dry, while a 1971 T120R was catalogued at 387 lb. In fact, this seems to have been selling the new bike short, as *kerbside* weight for a 1971 Bonnie on test was only 382 lb, meaning a dry weight some 20 lb lighter. The frame's excess height was slated not only in England and Europe, but in the USA, and the seat height did get lowered, but Nelson records that it took three variations to do it before the Series 3 version which was, according to Hopwood, finalized only by April 1972.

The changes, with interim 'Series 2' variations during 1971 as well, involved for the Series 3 version new side panels, air filter assemblies and battery fitting, slightly different rear mudguards, and a seat which was eventually narrower, with thinner padding, and hinged from further back and on the left. Jim Lee has confirmed that the main change involved lowering the rear sub-frame where its tubes were welded on to the main oil-bearing spine. From then on this was to remain a potential stress and fracture point on oil-bearing frames, as confirmed to me by, among others, Police riders of the time. In addition, the Series C rear suspension units would shorten by $\frac{1}{2}$ in, with their previous 12.9-in centres reduced to 12.3-in ones.

The front forks too were lowered, and fans of a '60s look feel that this meant some loss of the original flamboyant line at the front. It certainly had one irritating effect in conjunction with the 4-gal tank. This now tilted forward slightly which meant that when petrol got low, you could hear and see a pint or two still sloshing about in the bottom, which was too far forward to reach the taps . . . The new seat height was claimed to be $31\frac{1}{2}$ in. The riding position remained not very comfortable. Few dispute that in the most important area, steering and roadholding, the new frame was and continued to be excellent, and in the opinion of many, marginally superior to its predecessor. But having owned an oil-in-frame bike I do not now feel that the handling advantage over a conventional frame was worth the problems. I have gone out of sequence on this to emphasize the importance for a '71 owner of checking replacement components carefully against the original. It should be noted that much would change again for 1973's 750.

Meanwhile, though the above may help to explain Meriden's exasperation with the new twin, few of these problems except the seat height were immediately apparent to the public. *Bike* tested a late 1971 Bonneville and judged that the frame and forks were 'about the best available on a big bike anywhere'. Despite noting little vibration, they criticized the electrical equipment, losing the use of the winkers after 150 miles, then the rear light and then the parking light. The gearing was lowered by the rear wheel sprocket with its 47 teeth, one more than previous, but top speed was much as before at 111 mph, and with the 9:1 c.r. engine returning a claimed 50 bhp at 7,000 rpm, the plot could be cruised at a steady 85 and could carry a passenger with no sweat, though in practice the dualseat was rather short to do this. The conical front brake needed constant adjustment to stay fade-free. Petrol economy was down a little at 46 mpg overall, but the roadholding was perfect and it 'could be dug into corners at almost any speed you cared [dared?] to try', though they noted that 'a somewhat thinner swinging-arm member than

we've seen on earlier Bonnies seemed prone to just a little flexing now and again'. But the conclusion was that this was a great all-purpose bike and 'a better machine than the good old Bonneville you always wanted'. In truth, the new generation of riders which *Bike* catered for, whose tastes and attitudes had been formed in the '60s, would not be too bothered about practicality as long as a machine looked and sounded right and could be driven hard and hurled around when they felt like it. For them, from now on, the US-spec. Bonneville in particular would be quite a dream machine.

**1972** saw the lowering of the frame already mentioned completed by early in the year. The lowering of the forks involved new fork top nuts, fork legs and lower crowns, plus shorter springs, and for 1972 the fork crown stem threads were made finer for ease of head race adjustment. The raised ribs of the fork sliders were no longer polished. In addition the 4-gal tank, now standard for the UK, sported kneegrips and a gold finish with white lower stripe, while the side panels carried new transfers in Edwardian 'Tombstone' lettering. The big tank was also accompanied by flat pull-back handlebars. The front mudguard was now fitted with a reinforcing central stay assembly to combat the frequent previous fractures. This practicality was necessary for Meriden's fleet customers, because the single-carb Saint was still being supplied to the police, and indeed the AA returned to motor cycles that year on versions of the Police 650. The problems set limits to the practicality, however, as *MCS* found when they talked to some despatch riders with new TR6s early in 1972. Several had already ripped their prop stand lugs out of the frames, and every one had gone through its fork seals and scarred the fork tubes.

In the engine, a new cylinder head was fitted. It replaced the traditional four rocker inspection caps with a pair of flat finned covers, bolted on fore and aft, which was a cause for some mourning among the spares shops. It also featured bolt-on inlet manifolds in place of the previous screwed-in stubs, and likewise the exhaust pipes were now a push-fit directly into the head, instead of over the previous steel screwed-in stubs. The latter was a retrograde move as the pipes proved all too ready to detach themselves. The head redesign required four new internal cylinder head holding-down bolts, and associated

*A 1972 T120 with lowered frame and 'sensible' slab-sided 4-gal tank.*

rocker box bolts. Elsewhere, the con-rod cap nuts were revised again, and there was a reversion to the 1966 gudgeon pin circlip. From CG50464 the oil pressure relief valve changed back to a two-part assembly. At the same time, full-width timing gears with two holes for an extractor puller were fitted.

On the electrical side, the switchgear was revised, with the dip switch, headlamp flasher and horn now on the right, and the winker switch, still paired with the kill button, on the left. The alloy brake and clutch levers were given an increased fulcrum radius. The winker stems were commonized with those on the Trident, and a louder 6H horn was fitted. From CG50414, under the seat there was a new electrical coil mounting plate incorporating a tool shelf.

The major development during a troubled and somewhat chaotic 1972 model year was the introduction of the five-speed gearbox as an option on the T120RV and TR6RV models, available in fact since June 1971. The only external clue would be a small 'V' on the side panel transfers. Developed by Rod Quaife for the racers, the design was interchangeable

with the old, with a little work, and featured a roller race for the sleeve gear. In addition, in the clutch mechanism a new three-ball clutch lever was fitted in an attempt to eliminate lost movement. Some felt this fifth gear was superfluous, but it was in line with current fashion and, particularly with the current lowered gearing, did away with the need to run up the revs in each gear. Indeed, many rate these late five-gear 650s very highly.

*Motor Cycle* tested a five-speed T120RV Bonneville in August 1972. Interestingly, they remarked on how the E3134 cams, once a racing grind, narrowed the power band, with real power only coming in at 5,000 rpm. The official rev limit was 6,700 rpm, but with the free-revving Bonnie it was easy to surpass this, and the test machine reached 7,700 rpm during a (wind-assisted) best one-way speed run of 117 mph. The bike was clearly undergeared. Over 2,000 miles, good points included an absence of oil leaks, satisfactory lights, controls, clutch and brakes, and the five-gear ratios, which they found well-chosen to make best use of the power band. Minus factors were vibration, which fractured an exhaust pipe bracket within 1,000 miles, high oil consumption (a pint every 160 miles), inaccessible spark plugs, and footrests too wide (like the bars) and too far forward, as well as the left one being 2 in further to the rear than the right. But the highest praise was for the forks and frame, which 'hit the jackpot'. With the lowered seat height they found the chassis 'beyond criticism', and with the excellent fork and standard TT100 tyres it could be cornered very quickly indeed.

By **1973** Meriden had sorted out the oil-in-frame twin's appearance. There were new, more substantial chromed mudguards front and rear. The front one was supported on three 1970-type brackets looping around their outside and fixed in the old way, though now in chromed tubing, while the rear one bore a chunkier polished alloy mounting for its new squared-off Lucas L917 tail lamp, with the rear winkers moved forward onto the lifting

handle/grab-rail. The conical rear hub too was polished and lacquered rather than silver-painted as previously.

The front forks sported chromed top outer covers and were fitted with clipless rubber gaiters. The forks themselves had been redesigned with new top and bottom yokes, the former with additional slots permitting the stanchion top spigots to be clamped by hexagon-headed cap screws. The top lug had a boss to take the new disc brakes' hydraulic pipe junction. The sliders and stanchions were interchangeable with the T150 Trident disc-braked models, and like them, the left-hand leg had an integral cast lug for the caliper. The damper tube and valve assembly were as previously, and though a new spring was now specified, it was interchangeable with the previous one in conjunction with new spring top abutment threaded cap screws. Onto these were mounted the speedo and rev

**Left** *Hot pants to get the new 750 twins off with a bang. This one is a TR7V Tiger for 1973.*

**Right** *1973 also brought the front disc brake for twins as well as triples.*

counter brackets, which were retained by an additional top cap nut. The disc brake alloy sliders were now polished all over. Between the forks on the left side sat the 10-in Lockheed disc brake with its opposed pistons. Above the forks sat a traditional 'teardrop' chromed headlamp shell carried on conventional black brackets, and bearing an easy-to-use three-position toggle light switch, while the main ignition/light switch went back within reach on the left side fork cover.

The 4-gal tank was decorated with painted winged scallop-shaped panels which helped soften its squareness, while a new dualseat, with a chromed plastic rim round its base again, was uptilted at the rear for a livelier line and more of a sit-in effect for the rider. Testers found it comfortable. The pre-'71 seat catch and locating plunger were fitted again, and the side panels were made simpler, with the frame modified to suit. They were now a

plastic moulding and no longer featured the ornamental louvres; though still in two parts, these were now bridged by new name badges which replaced the previous transfer. Beneath them, the same basic elements and air boxes were fitted. New exhausts, still unfortunately push-in and all too prone to blow, were fitted, to carry, on the UK models, a longer, quieter silencer with for this year only a marked curve to its tapered rear portion, around redesigned internals. New handlebars were fitted to accommodate the front brake's master cylinder. With this revamped cycle, Meriden shook off the worst excesses of Umberslade, and much of the year's development would stay with the Triumph for the rest of the decade.

The twin was now offered both in 650 and, from engine no. JH15435, bored-out 750 form; though for the first four months, up to XH22018 in December 1972, the 650's

71 × 82 mm dimensions were only opened out to 75 × 82 mm, giving a capacity of 724 cc. (The reasons for this, and the rather unhapppy background to the 750, will be found in Volume 5). From then on, with new cylinder castings, the T140V had reached its final 744 cc (76 × 82 mm) form, burdened with increased vibration and a softly tuned engine, with the E3134 camshafts abandoned and fifties cam profiles adopted for the exhaust cam so as not to overstress the main bearings and what was essentially the 650's crankshaft. However the Spitfire cam profile was fitted on the inlet, with high lift and wilder timing. Cam followers were thus now $\frac{3}{4}$ in radius for the inlet but $1\frac{1}{8}$ in radius, still with the timed oil feed, for the exhaust. Bhp figures were no longer given: it was admitted that the output was lowered, though this was blamed on the new silencers, and power was undoubtedly improved in the middle ranges. Mute evidence of the change in tune can be found in the tappet settings, which changed from the 650's 2-thou inlet and 4-thou exhaust to 6 and 8 thou respectively for the 750, though some handbooks and manuals persisted in specifying the old settings in error. The early 750s ran at a catalogued 9.3:1 compression.

There were some positive aspects to the enlargement. The new cylinder head featured a second holding-down stud in the space between the rocker boxes, to cope with the necessarily narrower head joint in a 750 cylinder, making 10 studs in all. There were now also locating dowels between the head and rocker boxes to stop shuffling and protect the gaskets. The 750 head also had new cast aluminium inlet port adapters, still splayed, as well as a new manifold balance pipe. Within the head there were new valve guides, botton spring cups, pushrods, and pushrod cover tubes. This '10-stud' head, in conjunction with a new material for the holding-down bolts themselves, a special steel with a high expansion rate claimed to be more compatible with that of the alloy head, somewhat improved the twin's cylinder head sealing, though the rocker boxes proved leak-prone, and the ultimate head joint cure would come with the replacement of the copper head gasket fitted at this time by a composite one for 1978.

The cylinder block itself was shorter, which helped the fit of the engine to the frame. In addition, heavier section con-rods, $\frac{1}{2}$ in shorter, were fitted, with light pistons with strengthened crowns to counter collapse under stress. The pistons fitted Apex oil-control rings in their bottom grooves, as on the Trident; these wore quickly if oil changes were neglected. The new cylinder block also featured better oil circulation, from increasing the oil pump capacity and the size of the internal passages. The crankcase had been strengthened to withstand the extra loads: there was extra metal around the bearing housings, and these were given a new denser and smoother surface finish by means of a metal burnishing operation. On a new crankshaft with a balance factor of 74 per cent the previous flywheel was fitted, but with new bolts.

*T140 Bonneville for 1973.*

*1973 TR7V Tiger with 'comma' panel on tank and chromed guards.*

In the 750's transmission, $\frac{3}{8}$ in triplex primary chain replaced the previous duplex chain, and while stronger, this brought its own alignment problems. Thirty per cent stronger clutch springs and a redesigned clutch shock absorber spider were fitted. There was an extra tooth on the gearbox sprocket, making 20 in all, to take advantage of the mid-range torque.

*Motor Cycle* tested a T140 in February 1973 and were frankly disappointed. 'Somewhere along the way it seems to have lost its magic', they commented, concluding that the 750 twin was a rather unexceptional machine. Vibration was much in evidence, but if this Triumph was not smooth it was at least quite flexible, and pleasantly light for a 750 with a kerbside weight of just 427 lb. While the handling was unimpaired and the disc brake excellent, the efforts to damp down mechanical noise had not been successful. There was an irritating carburation flat spot between 3,000 and 4,000 rpm which produced reluctant acceleration from a 70-mph cruising speed, and the top speed was just 100 mph. (Harry Woolridge identifies the flat spot as megaphonitis, from cam overlap.) Doug Hele then took the test bike away for a day and breathed on it, after which it ran 112.6 mph!

The 650 continued in production from then on with a suitably modified version of the new crankcases and top end, and hence adopted triplex primary drive. The five-speed gearbox was standard for the 750, but remained optional for the 650, and for the 1973 750 a new high gear assembly (due to the lack of the previous high gear bearing, with a new gear to fit the new bearing) plus a new layshaft assembly were introduced. The latter, introduced to improve gear selection as there had been problems with jumping out of gear, brought in location of the high gear pinion by circlip rather than the previous pressed-on shoulder. But 1973 was also a troubled time for gear breakage, namely of the driving dog on the layshaft, and the gear conversion kit offered to counter this was fitted as standard later in the year. It involved new mainshaft first and second gears, plus layshaft first, second and third gears, as well as layshaft first gear selector fork and driving dog. Another welcome mid-season change was the fitting of the T150 operating camplate and indexing plunger, and hence the end of the leaf index spring which had been so difficult to fit.

Otherwise the 750's running gear differed little from the 650. Its frame carried a different headsteady, and for both capacities the 1973 steering head deleted its previous front fairing tubular lugs. The UK 750's 4-gal tank deleted its previous chromed trim rail and presented a smooth topped surface. All tanks were planished flat and had a new mounting method. The T140 carried the 650's 30 mm carbs, but with a main jet at 210. For both, the oil cap now carried an integral dipstick. Concern about the oil level was well founded, as the frame's 4-pt capacity was minimal and the o.i.f. twins did run hot. In fact, according to Norman Hyde, Meriden had to buy a new

156

thermometer while first testing their
lubricant's running temperature, as the old
one didn't go up high enough — 'The mercury
shot straight off the end of the scale'!

Finally, for the 650s, one unusual batch of
264 single-carb Tigers constructed early in
the 1973 season were T65 'BSA
Thunderbolts'. BSAs to satisfy their (overseas)
buyers, these (wisely) also specified the old-
style 1968–70 TLS drum brake at the front,
which meant extra machining to mate the '71
forks with the different torque arm location.
There were also Police 750 Saints and, in the
same way, these specified a 1970-style q.d.
rear wheel with a bolt-on sprocket, as well as
4.10 × 19 in wheels front and rear, a centre
stand with shorter legs and a strengthened
operating lever, lowered gearing, an extra
quiet silencer, and an RM21 alternator
arranged for high output. These would be
some of the final Police Triumphs for a while,
as the vibratory 750s were not popular with
the Traffic boys, who called them
'Haemorrhoid Specials', and by 1977 the TR7
was reported to be 'not acceptable in its
present form to the Met'.

Towards the end of the model year the rear
brake was revised again, this one being
identifiable by an annular groove. Up to then,
the rear brake cam and its liner had consisted
of a round shaft with two flats, but in the

interests of a stronger fit, the new one was
squared and tapered.

The **1974** model programme had hardly
begun when Meriden was plunged into
turmoil and ground to a halt in October 1973,
but revisions had been made to both the 750
and 650 twins, the latter continuing in limited
production. Machines were then blockaded in
Meriden and not released until July to
November 1974, and then in another batch,
which included the last 650s, from March to
May 1975. Luckily engine and frame numbers
of the B-range machines were faithfully
recorded and can be found in the engine
number section below. The stay in the
unheated, leaking factory did not do the
machines' finish much good. One of a batch
of 300 650s released late in 1974 and tested
by *Motor Cycle* was found to be 'shoddily
assembled and hastily retouched'. Even with
this year's restrictive silencers, it was fast,
however, returning 112-mph — just like the
750 T140 and indeed the TR7V, one of which
on test was a couple of miles faster than the
big Bonneville, emphasizing the desirability of
the fuss-free single-carb models. The Tiger
also ran a 13.8 standing quarter, very nearly
equal to a Trident.

1974 engine mods were few. The 750's
compression ratio had been quietly reduced to

*For 1973 the twins also became
available in the UK with styling
like this Tiger 750 at Ontario,
though with different silencers.*

*One of the final T120 650s, released by the workers' blockade during the summer of 1974.*

7.9:1, thought until 1978, 8.6:1 pistons would remain as an option. The new-style flat finned rocker boxes were revised, now each with two extra cover fixing screws, and improved gaskets; the 10-stud head and its rocker boxes had proved to be a potential problem to rebuild, since over-tightening of the rocker box bolts could loosen the main cylinder head studs. The oil pressure release valve was revised again to fit a finer mesh filter gauze, and there was a new nylon-loaded oil pressure indicator switch with an extended rubber cover. The junction for the large-bore breather pipe at the back of the primary chaincase became of black plastic. In the gearbox the final drive sprocket was amended, with its outer face now chamfered to suit a new sprocket nut lock-washer and O-ring oil seal.

On the cycle side, the most prominent feature for the Home models was the new and more attractive cigar-type silencers with a near-parallel tail section. They reduced noise levels while still producing an acceptably throaty roar, but they did have some stifling affect on the performance. In the light of some fractures, the chromed front mudguard was now attached to a thicker section mounting bracket on the fork leg. But the main change, and one that would carry over into the co-op era, was that for both 650 and 750 a version of the US export variant was now offered for the UK market, featuring that year's new and very shapely 2.8 (Imperial) gal 'teardrop' tank with its 'picture frame' badges, and matching 8-in rise cowhorn handlebars. Otherwise, for this year these machines were as the UK version, including gaiters on the forks. The tanks in practice gave a range of about 130 miles. Their radically waisted rear may not have been a good fit between the knees, and with the high 'bars meant that as usual speeds were restricted by wind pressure on the rider's spread-out body to the 70–75 mph range, but in that year's purple and white for the T120, or Cherokee Red and white for the T140, these machines did look gorgeous.

**1975** consisted, as mentioned, in the sell-off of existing 650 and 750 models once the Meriden co-op had been established.

The **1976** model year can be taken to have commenced in July 1975 with model no. HN62501, the first T140 produced with the left-foot gear-change which US legislation required after 1974, and with a disc rear brake. That was how the T140V, and the TR7V when it was reintroduced for mid-1976, were made from then on.

The background to these changes can be found in Volume 5. To make the new brake and left-foot conversion acceptable to NVT, who were marketing the Triumph twins at the time, Meriden had had to strengthen some brackets and address problems of stiffness in operation. The left-side conversion consisted of just a simple steel rod, cranked to give clearance round the clutch, between the rear of the gearbox inner cover and the operating pedal; the pedal itself was shorter, at $3\frac{3}{4}$ in against the previous $4\frac{1}{2}$ in. This did however mean new gearbox inner and outer covers and joint washers, and an appropriate spindle bush, operating quadrant and kick-start axle. The primary chaincase cover was modified to suit, and at the same time deleted the rotor inspection and timing cover, substituting a screwed inspection plug and fixed pointer assembly, with an O-ring now fitted to the ignition timing hole plug. For the traditionally minded, reconverting to right-foot shift was comparatively simple, requiring only a right-hand-type gearbox outer, a plug for the primary chaincase and a right-hand-type gearchange quadrant spindle. However, providing cross-over operation for the new rear brake was more complicated.

The main drawback with the new arrangement was that its position dictated that the footrests, which were now standardized where previously the left and right had been different, had to be positioned too far forward. This created a riding position which threw the weight rearwards in a way that became uncomfortable after an hour or so in the saddle, and which was also less than ideally suited for high-speed running. Another feature of the new gearchange was that on the handlebars the clutch featured a new operating lever assembly, and for some time from now on, clutch cables would prove to be short-life items.

The 10-in rear disc brake, with its right-side pedal, was announced as featuring a slightly thicker (0.235) disc, which the front brake also adopted to standardize, though Harry Woolridge says that brake discs were always recognized as being nominally .230 in from the start. The new right-side brake pedal was tucked rather too closely into the engine, and was too far from the rider's foot. Mostly the brake worked well enough, though once again not in the wet, and many riders would have preferred the belt and braces of a drum brake at the rear, especially if it had been mounted on a q.d. rear wheel. Changing the disc rear wheel was trying, despite the distinctively underslung caliper being easy to swing away. The disc meant a modified rear frame and swinging-arm, and attached to the

*A 1978 T140 Bonneville in the US spec. that many preferred.*

*Unsatisfactory Lucas switchgear, with the tacky stick-on labels on the headlamp shell visible in the background.*

frame were pillion footrests at the 45° angle to the rear which US legislation required, plus a modified battery carrier/coil mounting and a shorter tool tray, all to fit with the rear master cylinder. The rear mudguard was also altered to suit. Like the front brake, the disc itself was chromed, and as the chrome deteriorated it could chew up the pads. Skimming the chrome off the discs is a good move. In addition, Dunlopads should not be used with chromed discs, as their sintered composition wrenches off the chrome. Even after skimming, drilling the discs for lightness is not advisable as the discs' cast iron has a low tensile strength. At least one example of the rear brake which I tried was very ineffective, but though the rear disc often worked well in the dry, despite a certain woodenness, there would be one unhappy side-effect from its power: because of it, the 10-gauge rear wheel spokes then fitted had a tendency to work loose and ultimately snap.

There were other changes on the co-op 750, some aimed at oil-tightness. The oil pressure release valve was fitted with an O-ring, the oil pump junction block, feed and return pipes were revised, and in mid-year the fixing screws on the black plastic primary chaincase breather outlet stub were made

longer. The cigar silencers were revised internally to keep noise down, the new ones being identifiable by noticeably concave dished end plates and new left- and right-handed brackets to clear the rear brake hose. Induction noise was also tackled, with the filter elements now pierced to take intake silencer tubes, and their plastic covers bolted from the outside. The Concentric carburettors by now were from Amal's Spanish subsidiary, as indicated by their extended tickler buttons, and there were changes to their fuel feed banjo fibre washers. New petrol taps with 'on/off' and 'reserve' marks were fitted. These would prove to be rapid-wear items, as their internals were plastic and easily weakened by petrol.

In mid-year a new chromed front mudguard was fitted which did away with the previous centre and front stays, replacing them with a Trident-style central bridge piece. On the US versions, available in the UK from now on, fork gaiters were left off. The holes in the guard for a front number plate went, as this was no longer a UK legal requirement. The handlebars had new knurling to take new Lucas alloy switchgear, with the switch functions cast into the left-hand cluster, but with the important right-hand ones (headlamp flasher and kill button) only marked by tacky stuck-on labels, as were the lights and switches on the chrome headlamp shell, all to satisfy US legislation. New Smiths instruments were fitted, with the NVT symbol gone from their faces. The seat's pan was revised slightly so that its front and rear hinges could be the same, and the Triumph name was featured in gold at the rear of the seat.

*Bike* magazine quickly tested a co-op Bonnie in October 1975, and found it

reasonably quiet, just as quick as the previous ones with 111 mph top speed, and with excellent brakes, though they squealed. Not so good was the vibration, which they found continuous at 80 mph in a numbing, boring way, though with 70 mph representing just 4,000 rpm, cruising at that speed was possible. The new gearchange too was stiffer, notchier, and more difficult to operate. As would be the case from now on, electrical problems predominated, with a winker loosening off, the flashers going berserk at high speeds, and three blown fuses in a thousand miles. Inaccessible fuel taps and the choke control still down by the carbs were further niggles. But the machine was oil-tight, the great handling was intact, and on the left side the centre stand elbow on the test hack provided had been worn to a smooth flat. Ground clearance could in fact be a real problem, as *Bike*'s Mike Nicks found out the following year when he tested a green and white TR7V Tiger—the centre stand dug in on a bump, and he came off. Nicks nevertheless praised the combination of suppleness and firmness from the ride. Emphasizing the unevenness of the co-op product—you could get a good one or a bad one—this Tiger *could* be cruised at 80 mph/5,000 rpm, with the vibration in the background not 'of the worst order' as on the previous Bonnie. Mid-range pulling power was the strong suit, however. Single-carb fuel economy was a little better at 48 mpg than the Bonnie's 45.4 mpg. Despite his tumble and a rev counter failure, Nicks judged the Triumph 'a fine motor cycle to ride'.

The background to the problem of the co-op bikes' uneven quality is discussed in Volume 5. Broadly, lack of cash, outworn machinery, and sometimes attitudes within the factory were the causes. Not even the handling was exempt. Talking to T140 owners, I have been struck by widely differing versions of how good or otherwise the oil-in-frame handling could be, and as well as the condition of the swinging-arm and shock absorbers (the originals tired quite rapidly), I also found out recently that of five AV (anti-vibration) Police prototypes supplied to a Merseyside dealer, three had to have their frames cut and rewelded to get their rear wheels in line. The AV frames were admittedly all hand-jigged, but it gives an idea of potential problems. The majority of the co-op's twins handled very satisfactorily, however.

Imprecise machining from worn plant at this time often caused high oil consumption, pistons loose in the bore and cylinders requiring early rebores, though Harry Woolridge points out that all barrels were originally graded to .0003 in, but that piston distortion did occur until Hepworth and Grandage changed the form. The push-fit exhaust pipes frequently worked loose in the head. There were still occasional problems with rear frames fracturing. Head gaskets, fork seals and an epidemic of failures from the unprotected wheel bearings fitted at this time were additional troubles which would be addressed before long. The most persistent problems, however, remained electrical ones, with contact-breakers going off song, the damp- and vibration-prone Lucas switches being a constant nuisance, including the main ignition/light switch with its lack of positive contact, and the wiring harness containing too many bullet connectors and being too

**Left** *A 1977 Silver Jubilee Bonneville in UK spec.*

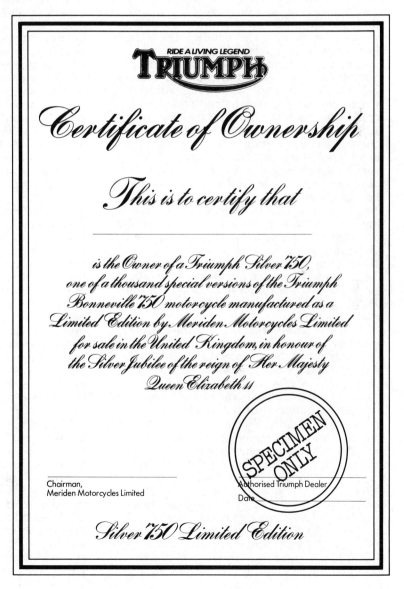

**Right** *And the certificate to prove it. Actually, rather more than 1,000 were made in the end.*

prone to shorting out. Eighteen per cent of a 1980 *Cycle World* survey of Bonnie owners had experienced electrical problems, the majority with shorts in the harness.

Around 20,000 machines were produced altogether during the two years of 1976 and **1977**, and during the latter year, in August, the Jubilee Bonneville limited edition was launched. Its background will be found in Volume 5. Since the Royal Jubilee involved was a Silver one, the basic finish was silver (though not a very impressive one, being too dark). This was embellished with red, white and blue — a blue seat with red piping, and silver-painted mudguards with blue, red and white striping which was echoed round the silver petrol tank's blue side portions, and even on the rear chainguard. Extra chrome on the fork section, timing and chaincase covers, and tail lamp housing, plus limited edition stickers on the side panels, completed a decor which was brash rather than charismatic. Dunlop K91 Red Arrows tyres with red pin-striping, 4.10 × 19 front, 4.10 × 18 rear, were fitted. The latter dimensions, incidentally, were as the other twins, since the 750's tyres had reverted to that size after 1974. Also at the rear came the first Girling gas shock absorbers, designed to be mounted 'upside down', with their spring load adjusters at the top. These would soon be adopted by the whole range. Many would find the gas Girlings too harsh in operation for comfort. The Jubilee came in either UK or US variants. Around 2,400 were built in all, many in the UK instantly being salted away as 'investments'.

**1978** saw some uprating, but the factory's priorities were production, plus the development of the 'E' model for 1979, so that they could continue selling in America when the new EPA laws came into force.

One of the most welcome changes for 1978 was the introduction of the 'eyeletted composition' cylinder head gasket in place of the previous solid copper one. In conjunction with the 7.9:1 pistons being standardized throughout the range, this set the seal on top end oil-tightness, as it had done for the Commando. It was vital, however, that the compound gasket should not be fitted upside down: it had to be placed on the barrel face so that two rings could be seen around the bores. On the front forks too, new 'self-aligning' fork oil seals and retainers greatly improved the situation there, and were

interchangeable with the previous parts. The US models fitted gas Girlings as standard from the start of the year, with the UK following suit in mid-year. Not before time, sealed wheel bearings were introduced, and on the rear wheel stronger nine-gauge spokes were specified to counter the previous breakages. In another welcome move a new headlamp unit, with a halogen main bulb and suitable holder, was fitted. The 6H horn was revised once again and, in mid-year, Lucas batteries were supplanted by excellent Yuasa equivalents. In mid-year, Smiths' inability to supply Meriden's needs (see Volume 5) meant a change to European Veglia instruments. In the rev counter drive box the driven gear thrust washer was modified to combat drive fracture.

Further detail changes included the fitting of a locking washer in place of the previous lock tab washer on the crankshaft rotor nut, and from engine no. 02690, the rockers and their adjusters adopted UNF threads. In the gearbox a gasket was introduced between the inner and outer covers. The mudguards on the UK models switched from chromed to painted, and fitted nylon washers to their fixing bolts. The UK colour schemes were half and half. There was an execrable Tawny Brown and Gold version, with gold panels lined in white and brown on the mudguards, and even a brown version of the dualseat. The seat itself was new that year and also came in black, both colours being available in broad- or narrow-nosed versions to suit UK or US models. Unfortunately, the upholstery was not very substantial and the seat uncomfortable on a long run, but the alternative Polychromatic Aquamarine and Silver colour scheme was very attractive. Finally, the side panels were now redesigned one-piece plastic items, fastened to each other by a small spring, and each with a circlip fitted on their fixing bolt.

**1979** brought the UK launch for the T140E. In many ways the new machine was worth waiting for, even if performance suffered due to US environmental demands.

Background to the E model can be found in Volume 5. Its main component was a new cylinder head, which with parallel inlet tracts left behind for ever the traditional Bonnie's splayed-head assertiveness. The new head featured slightly more metal round the ports, and a slightly reshaped combustion chamber. The crankcase breather was run to the air box,

*The 1979 E model, available in Bonneville form only and seen here in UK spec., the best red and black finish.*

while the oil tank breather went to a rocker box.

On the T140E's parallel inlet tracts were a pair of Amal Mk 2 Concentric carburettors, and since their dimensions did not permit a single-carb alternative, the Tiger stayed with a Mk 1, and thus was no longer for sale in America. Mounted on rubber stubs, the Mk 2 was a superior, square-bodied design with alloy PTFE-coated slides. They eliminated float tickling which many by now saw as either quaint or a messy chore: the EPA's concern was that no petrol or petrol vapour should vent to the atmoshpere, and previously the Concentric had vented its float chamber through the tickler. Otherwise the Mk 2 worked like its predecessor, though with a slightly improved airflow, as well as a new cold-starting enrichment jet controlled by a small vertical slide valve and operated by a small lever mounted on the carburettor and checked by a click spring, all rather similar to the controls on the Thunderbird's SU instrument in the '50s. This mean that the single-choke control lever, which the parallel carburettors permitted, was still mounted down on the carb, and could be set either on or off only. So though the Bonnie still started well, there could be awkwardness while it was warming up. A cable-operated alternative was available from Amal, and in view of

rider's preferences this would be fitted for 1981. While the Mk 2 was a refined design, it should be mentioned that Triumph specialist Les Williams considers that the instrument did not really suit the Bonneville, being difficult to set up to give clean mid-range response.

The new cylinder head, in conjunction with the Mk 2s, burned leaner and returned better fuel figures — 56 mpg around town was recorded by a T140E on test with *Which Bike?*, with 50.5 mpg on a run. Elsewhere in the engine, the timing side ball-bearing was finally replaced by an unusual SKF roller of similar dimension. This makes a worthwhile substitute if a previous 750 engine is being rebuilt, for not only does the roller take more load, but this one gave positive end location of the crank like a ball-bearing usually would. The outer cage was U-shaped: rollers were fed in and then a top-hat piece was fitted over, followed by a plain loose washer. When the crankcases were bolted up, crankshaft end float was then determined by the amount of play on the top-hat piece. Equally significant was the anouncement that the crankshaft was now 'machined differently', which in fact meant it was machined more comprehensively, a significant factor in reducing vibration.

The gearbox too came in for some revision. The camplate was re-profiled to improve

Lucas Rita set-and-forget
electronic ignition for the T140E
as standard.

selection, with its neutral indent deepened.
The gearchange was still notchy, but much
improved on the previous set-up, though the
clutch could still be heavy.

There was also plenty of new quality
electrical equipment. The most significant
item was Lucas Rita electronic ignition,
offered as standard. This system had been
under development for some years, and while
there were some early teething troubles, its
'set-and-forget' character and immunity to
vibration represented a great leap forward in
rider convenience as well as engine life and
smoothness. Behind a finned cover in the old
points position, basically a rotating metal bar
crossed two magnets and thence activated
both the spark and the degree of auto
advance. The system's amplifier box sat
beneath the right-hand side panel. The other
major item was a Lucas three-phase alternator
whose increased output was particularly set
up to be effective at lower rpm. This was a
real step forward, permitting daylight
headlamps and worry-free town running
where the constant drain of the brake light
and indicators could previously flatten the
battery. The system included a new Zener

diode and, it should be noted, a change for
the first time in nearly three decades from a
positive to a negative earth electrical system.

Further uprating was to be found on the
handlebars, with the last and best Lucas
control switches, black in colour bar the red
kill button, now all clearly labelled. This was
not perfection — the internals were unchanged,
and a *Motor Cycle* tester found that his left-
hand switch let in water while he was
washing the bike, and that after that the horn
sounded every time he turned the ignition on,
also noting that the indicator toggle
sometimes needed jiggling at the end of its
travel to make proper contact — but it was a
great improvement. The clearly labelled
indicator lights, for winkers, main beam,
ignition warning and a new green (and only
intermittently effective) neutral indicator, were
all now mounted, with the ignition switch, in
a neat Trident-style console between the two
instruments, which were themselves newly
encased in substantial rubber
binnacles — though they still sometimes
rotated within them. The headlamp was
rubber-mounted, though not effectively
enough to prevent blowing bulbs on most

test bikes. It also appeared that the halogen bulb was no longer fitted. Finally, the control levers, now pivoting on black blocks, had been redesigned to give less of a stretch, though riders still wanted dog-leg levers to solve that particular problem. The UK handlebars had been slightly narrowed from 29 to 27 in. Claimed dry weight of the T140E was down from 413 to 395 lb.

There had been some careful attention to the number of previous detail complaints. The seat was now lockable and beneath it were secured two helmet hooks. A neat little chromed parcel carrier was fitted: it had a recommended 15-lb weight limit, but scored on looks and convenience. Allen socket-head screws were used on the engine cases. Chromed mudguards were back for the UK models, while the US ones fitted fork gaiters again. The wheel hubs were now lacquered as well as polished, while the thickness of the discs was announced as slightly increased at 2.54 mm though Harry Woolridge is convinced they stayed at .230 in. The front tyre size standardized with the rear at 4.00 in, though the front wheel remained 19 in against the rear's 18 in; the tyres themselves

were TT100s. New, modern-style ribbed footrests were fitted with ready-chamfered edges encouraging maximum lean.

Tests on the E model, however, showed that ground clearance was still a problem. *MCM* had both the centre stand and the footrest digging in on the right, while *Motor Cycle* found that an over-long prop stand 'ate away most of the bike's cornering clearance on the left'. But all united in admiration for the new bike's sumptuous finishes, which included polished cases, a powder-coated frame, and a wide range of finish combinations, with black plus metallic red the best yet on the UK Bonnie, and silver and black extremely spiffy on the US. The chrome was good and the paint was applied in five coats and still hand-lined, but the powder-coated frames were to prove problematical, being prone to cracking which let water and subsequently rust in, and then to peeling off in strips.

It was a bit sad, then, that the E model proved a little down on performance compared to its rougher predecessors. It was initially trumpeted at 54 bhp, but this was quickly modified to a more realistic 49 bhp at

*A neat T140E touch, the 15 lb parcel rack.*

**Left** *UK spec. T140E Bonneville for 1979.*

**Below right** *1979 US spec. T140D Special, slinky in black and gold.*

6,500 rpm: the Tiger put out a claimed 46 bhp, though a 1977 *MCM* test with a dynamometer found the truth on their test machine was 41 bhp at the rear wheel. Naturally, maximum power and top speed were no longer the point, which was that lovely surging mid-range torque from as low as 1,500 rpm, but as *MCN* noted, a sudden drop-off at the higher end of the rev range gave a feeling of somewhat limited power though, as they concluded, all the power was at least stowed in the lower and middle range where it could be used. The riding position with the forward footrests, backward bars, and not very comfortable seat was a distinct limiting factor, but the E was smoother than many expected, and oil-tight.

In March 1979 came another variant which introduced a number of future developments for the range, namely the Bonneville-engined T140D Special. Another limited edition strikingly finished in gold-lined black and chrome and with handsome Lester seven-spoke black and cast alloy wheels, the D went beyond cosmetics. Early US-styled versions (by far the most handsome) featured an exhaust system siamesed in front of the bottom of the downtubes to pass beneath the frame on the right to a single special silencer. The pipes came straight out of the head and then turned through 90°. Months had gone

into tuning this exhaust system for both environmental acceptability, mid-range torque, and additional ground clearance. To accommodate it, and incidentally give better protection from road spray, the rear brake's caliper was now mounted above the disc, something which would shortly be adopted by the rest of the range. The single silencer not only contributed to a 25-lb weight reduction, it also made maintenance on the drive side considerably easier! In addition, the exhaust pipes were finally positively located in the cylinder head again, clamped into spigots screwed into the exhaust ports. This was particular to the 'D', though the pre-'71 system would shortly be adopted by the whole range.

Cosmetically the 'factory custom' D ran ungaitered, polished forks supporting both the extremely handsome black and chrome wheels and a truncated chromed mudguard held by just its central bracing strip. Both US and UK tanks carried the plain Triumph name badge and were gold-lined, as were the side panels which bore nameplates with 'Special' in red beneath the 'Bonneville'. But the bum note [*sic*] in terms of styling was the seat, a stepped, cross-hatched affair whose bulk was at odds with the skinny look of the bike's front end. It was also poorly proportioned, being wider at the base than at the top.

Meriden's intentions had been laudable in aiming to provide something comfortable and better positioned. Internally the seat featured new 'cold cure' inserts: fitting a whole seat with top quality foam was too expensive, so while the majority of the seat remained stuffed with foam rubber off-cuts, the rider did get the benefit of the superior inserts, though ironically the bulky pillion portion was not so comfortable. Behind the seat went a redesigned, squared-off grab-rail/lifting handle. The seat married well with footrests raised nearly 2 in to help the ground clearance, along with a redesigned centre stand which testers found no longer grounded. Both these features would be adopted by the whole range. At the rear, the D's back tyre was a slightly fatter 4.25 × 18 Dunlop TT100.

This last feature would in fact give rise to some problems, amplified by the US-spec handlebars. The larger cover was found to induce a speed wobble, which also affected earlier E models. Ds and later Es adopted a heavier section swinging-arm, but according to Harry Woolridge this was done mainly for looks, and return to a 4.10 rear tyre represented the real cure to the problem of weave. Another minus point for the D revealed on a *Bike* test was that while the modified stand and footrest worked well in increasing the ground clearance, the siamesed exhaust system grounded quite badly on the right-hand side, wearing paper thin on the test bike within two weeks. Later, UK Specials would be offered with the twin exhaust system, but the siamesed ones did do the job in improving mid-range power at around 4,000 rpm, where it pulled torquily. Top speed, however, was strangled by the silencer and down in the mid-90s. The final irony was that the Special's black paint job wore rather worse than the standard models.

Most of the remaining 20,000 or so Triumph twins built from the start of 1979 to the co-op's end would be variants on the E,

so this may be a good time to take a general look at the co-op's product.

On summer weekends throughout the '70s and early '80s, you would still see quite a few Triumphs on the road, often in company with two or three big Japs, because (while working) they could hold their own in general running, and there were still takers for what the Bonnie offered, a 'European alternative', quite a good all-rounder with considerable charisma and some real virtues. A litany of the latter became very familiar to British bikers, in face of the relentless mockery from the majority who had gone over to the faster and more reliable Japanese. The Triumph's handling still remained a strong suit, and both tractability and braking were aided by a strikingly light weight, at around 420 lb kerbside, when a Honda 750K was 110 lb heavier. Pop star David Essex bought a T140E in 1980 'because it's the only new bike left that sounds like a motorbike should', and though civilized, the deep rumble of the annular discharge silencers did have its effect.

Spares were cheap, whether they were genuine Meriden or pattern items. There were real savings to be made, for spares for Japanese machines—not only consumables like bulbs and cables, but items like handlebars and exhaust systems, the kind of things which suffered from a winter on the street, or from a tumble—sometimes cost three or four times as much to replace as their Triumph equivalents. That was when you could get the Japanese ones: though the shortages already mentioned in Volume 5 applied to Triumph too until the late '70s, motor cyclists were discovering that the fast turnover of new models from the Orient meant that after a few years, spares back-up for them could sometimes be less than satisfactory, while the oil-in-frame Triumph models were coming up to their tenth year in production, and 30 per cent of engine parts were interchangeable with even earlier models. The Triumph's petrol economy was reasonable by contemporary standards, hovering around the 50 mpg mark, though this could be offset by oil consumption ranging from 600 down to 200 mpp.

The other great economy argument was that the relative simplicity of the engine made doing your own maintenance possible, which was not always the case with the sophistication and massed carburettor banks of the Japanese. This needs qualifying,

however, as do-it-yourself was certainly possible, but not particularly quick or easy. When adjusting the tappets, to remove the inlet rocker covers you needed two different spanners and an Allen key. If the carbs were not removed, the job was difficult without a socket plus extension, a ring spanner plus an open ender, and small hands. Care was essential, too, because over-tightening the rocker box bolts could loosen the main cylinder head studs. (The Triumph Owners Club in fact offer a special tool to torque the rear bolts of the rocker box without disturbing the head.) If the carbs did have to come off, very often the mounting studs would come unscrewed along with their nuts, as was also the case with the studs for the sump oil filter. The push-fit exhaust could scarcely be removed by one person, and was an awkward job even with two. Adjusting the primary chain meant removing the left-hand footrests, one turn at a time, loosening and dropping the left-hand silencer, and then draining the oil from the chaincase via a combined adjuster and drain hole. Then you lay on your back fiddling with a screwdriver and a special extension inserted down the drilling into the crankcase, with residual oil running down your arm and onto the exhaust. (The primary chain adjusters themselves were vulnerable items, and were eventually redesigned for 1980.) Oil went down your arm also with the quaint concentric double level-plug/drain-plug in the sump for the gearbox oil. A silencer had to come off to remove the rear wheel spindle, and hence the rear wheel itself. And every time the cylinder head was removed (which could be frequently) it involved three gaskets and six oil seals. And so on.

But all that could be forgotten on a fine day on a good A-road, when you got the fun of the big Triumph's looks, lightness, brakes, handling, righteous sound and, above all, the brute surge of power when you grabbed a handful of throttle, a meaty response for which there was no substitute, until it was brought up short around 80 mph by the vibration. Crude it might be, but undeniably effective and exhilarating, even if the effect was somewhat muted on the sanitized 'E' variants.

**1980** saw Meriden's production quartered after the previous year's upheavals and redundancies, but also some positive improvements, as well as the Executive flagship tourer, and the introduction of the ES electric start models. As mentioned, the raised pillion footrest and exhaust and modified centre stand, as seen on the D Specials, were now found on all models, with ground clearance notably improved. One unfortunate side-effect was that with the raised pegs, the rider's foot was impeded by the kick-start lever, and when tired his foot tended to slip off the peg. The centre stand was finally more accurately located by two small brackets welded from the pivot tube to the main frame tube.

A simple but major breakthrough was the adoption of the four-valve oil pump. This finally laid to rest the long-standing danger of grit completely impeding the plunger pump's operation, with potentially disastrous consequences. The new pump, with its four instead of two-spring-loaded valves, was only interchangeable with the previous one in conjunction with a suitably modified timing cover. Another welcome detail improvement was a redesigned primary chain adjuster. The brake pedal forging was reinforced. Under the seat a larger tool tray was fitted. The indicator stalks were rubber-mounted, though this did not stop them still swivelling skywards as vibration took its toll. One unfortunate detail was the introduction of tin-shrouded spark plug caps. These were required by law as an anti-electrical interference measure, but they tended to trap any available moisture, and most riders quietly replaced them. Finally, the excellent Avon Roadrunner tyres were fitted;

this had started as a stop-gap arrangement while Dunlop were on strike, but they were found to suit the Triumph well.

In February, the T140E Executive was launched, in paint jobs of striking metallic-based Smoked Maroon shading to Ruby, which strongly echoed contemporary BMWs. While other versions of this finish never looked right when offered on the standard models, the Executive's maroon version was genuinely impressive. The model consisted of a cockpit fairing crafted by Brealey Smith Ltd in glass fibre and ABS leathergrain material, with a tinted screen and twin round mirrors, the latter soon to be offered for the whole range, mounted on large Police-model pull-back handlebars.. The seat was a more satisfying sculptured variant of the D Specials, with rider and passenger portions outlined in 'King and Queen' fashion. At the rear, mounted on a tubular carrier, were colour-coordinated Sigma panniers and top box, bearing the Triumph logo and providing a big 3.9 cu ft of luggage space. The panniers could be quickly detached, and they locked to the frame.

Shortly afterwards, by June, the model was available in the Electro Executive variant, though the first Electro machines on offer were Bonnevilles, soon followed by Tigers. Background to the electric start story and its early troubles can be found in Volume 5. Here it can be added that the Lucas M3 starter motor selected had at one time been fitted to Reliant three-wheelers, and was now made

*T140ES Executive, a co-ordinated tourer with electric foot.*

under licence in India. With Norton's notorious Mk III Commando effort in mind, the Meriden men had done their homework carefully. Exhaustive testing in a cold room emphasized the need for a $14\frac{1}{2}$-amp. hour Yuasa battery in contrast to the standard 11 ah item, as well as a higher-output Lucas RM24 180-watt alternator and triple Zener diodes. To fit the bigger battery, a small bump had to go in the underside of the seat pan. A higher-output pulse sensor went in the electronic ignition circuit to produce a fatter spark at lower rpm. A final development problem had concerned the rubber blocks in the cush drive being affected by increased heat, and this was dealt with by a new mix.

After years of chiding Triumph for not updating themselves, some now queried the necessity for an electric foot which increased the machine's price by £100, its all-up weight by around 30 lb (the T140 Electro's dry weight was 430 lb), and distorted the line of the timing side crankcase cover. The electro timing chest had to be widened, and the wider chest was adopted for the kick-start variants also. What the critics ignored was the existence of an electric foot on every large-capacity Japanese machine for over a decade, which had bred a generation of riders who

would be seriously embarrassed if a stall at the traffic lights had to be followed by kick-starting.

The Electro's starter motor was mounted behind the cylinders in the old magneto position. Direct drive to the clutch was rejected in favour of a reduction gear system linked to a Borg Warner sprag clutch which drove onto the intermediate timing gear. This timing gear ran on improved bearings, with bushes now in both the crankcase and the timing cover. A panel was cut from the rear portion of the timing cover which, when unbolted, gave access to the bolts securing the motor. The reduction drive, unlike Norton's at 20:1, was kept deliberately low at 15:1, to assist cold weather starting. This proved pretty reliable, and in service the starter's only real problem was occasional wear on the idler bush, which would then need replacing. At first the kick-start was sensibly retained, just in case. Around half the models produced for the next two-and-a-half years would be Electros.

**1981** saw the co-op having scraped through another financial crisis and with its workforce again severely curtailed. But even so, in mid-year they were offering three new models—the economy TR65 Thunderbird 650,

*The 1981 Electro Bonneville.*

the Tiger Trail bikes in both 750 and then 650 form, and a limited edition Royal Wedding Bonneville.

Several useful improvements were incorporated. The action of the clutch was significantly lightened by modification to the operating mechanism and by the use of lighter springs, as well as by dropping one of the bonded driven plates, which left six in all. Together with the use of more waterproof nylon-lined cables, this diminished the problem of snapping cables and very heavy clutches, though the clutch remained a serious pull. The T140's Mk 2 Concentrics fitted larger needle jets, and their choke was now controlled by a handlebar-mounted lever. Early in the year the Bonneville's gearing was also raised a little by the use of a 45-tooth rear wheel sprocket in place of the previous 47-tooth item. In the engine, the wear-prone inlet valve guides were fitted with oil seals, and this simple measure could lower oil consumption to 800 mpp. New rubber-mounted footrests were fitted, and a new anti-vibration fork shroud permitted the use of a 60/45-watt sealed beam light unit. The round handlebar-mounted mirrors appeared on all models, and seats became the same style as those on the D. Claimed oil capacity

was now 5 Imperial pints, but this seems to have been only a paper improvement.

The brakes' poor wet weather performance also came in for scrutiny. The brake calipers became Dural forgings on some models. In addition, twin cast-iron AP Racing front discs were offered as an option. They were a desirable one, not so much for extra braking power as for their balanced operation, so that fork twist was kept to a minimum. In mid-year cast-iron discs (the same as before but not chrome-plated) were adopted for all models, and Dunlopads could then be standardized for the range.

Making a virtue of their small size and limited production runs, the whole range was now offered in 'FFC' or Factory Fitted Custom mode, meaning that you could order your machine in US or UK spec., in any one of six colour finishes, which now included a rather dingy metallic blue or red, and with or without electric starter (though a kick-start now cost extra with the latter), cast wheels or the double front discs. You could also now order it in side-car trim, though as will be remembered, at the time of the oil-in-frame's introduction it had been described as unsuitable for use with a side-car. This trim involved stiffer fork springs, a steering

*Black paint for economy on the new 650 in mid-1981, the TR65 Thunderbird.*

*The TR65 Thunderbird's economy instrumentation, with the ignition switch and warning lights going in the rev counter's binnacle.*

damper, 18-in not 19-in front wheel, and lower gearing via an 18-, not 20-tooth gearbox sprocket.

In mid-year, with the April 1981 announcement of the TR65 Thunderbird, came changes for several of the range's ancillaries. Morris cast wheels replaced the previous Lester ones. For the Executive, a new CLP full frontal fairing, developed for Police models, was offered, and this permitted the use of crash bars for the first time, since the bars were attached to the fairing and did not put the oil-bearing frame at risk. The T140's carburettors changed to Type 94 Bing constant velocity instruments, produced in collaboration with Amal. Direction indicators progressively changed to squared-off German ones with black bodies and stalks, so the days of skyward-pointing winkers were at an end. As production of British petrol tanks ceased, new 4-gal tanks took their place. These were made in Italy, with Monza-type flip-open caps, circular petrol taps (though still unfortunately mostly plastic), and deeper rounded sides and a smoother profile. The tanks were first seen on the Thunderbird. Somehow their shape lacked definition. By June all models were fitting the high-output alternators, but only Electros fitted the bigger battery.

The new 650, the TR65 Thunderbird, was essentially a cost-cutting exercise. To take advantage of preferential insurance rates for the lower capacity, as well as to beat the vibes, the 750's 76 × 82 mm dimensions simply had their stroke shortened to an oversquare 76 × 71.5 mm by the use of a new crank, new barrel with one fin less, pushrods to suit, and the Bonneville pistons with more metal on the top. Bonneville cams and a Tiger head kept other modification to a minimum, with just slight alterations in the machining of the crankcase castings. At £200 less than the 750, the Thunderbird was offered in kick-start form only, with points ignition, matt black finish for the crankcase covers and for the siamesed exhaust system, ungaitered forks with black sliders and covers, the new 4-gal tank and square winkers and, like the Trail, warning lights and ignition switch in the binnacle where the rev counter would have been.

At the rear a 7.5-in SLS brake based on the pre-o.i.f. 650's non-q.d. drum was fitted, and in a faint wave at the glorious past, the side panel badges bore the old Thunderbird logo. Aimed at the first-time big bike buyer, this was something like the economy model many had been urging, and came with an insurance deal which knocked £40 off fully comp. cover in London. With the Bonnie having cracked the £2,000 barrier, however, even the TR65's £1,829 looked like luxury time, when that year £1,841 would get you a four-cylinder Suzuki GSX 750. Still, the new Thunderbird was a pleasant all-rounder, a smooth runner that vibrated a lot less than the 750 and would prove itself robust. With 9:1 compression producing a claimed 42 bhp at 6,500 rpm and a top speed close to 100 mph, on test with *Classic Bike* the TR65 was found to have both exceptional low-speed pick-up and good throttle response, and at faster engine speeds 'an almighty surge of power flowed in'. An excellent town bike, it was marred only by economy Dunlop Gold Seal tyres, including a narrow sectioned 3.25 × 19 in front one which affected the handling, by a lack of mid-range grunt compared to the big 'un, and by a lack of rider comfort due to a combination of hard suspension, with gas Girlings perhaps tailored to a heavier load than the Thunderbird's 395 lb dry weight, plus an uncomfortable economy dualseat. Only around 400 were to be made.

Launched at the same time was the 750 TR7T Tiger Trail, with a TR6T Trail 650 version joining it briefly in October. The bright yellow 750 Tiger was a hastily conceived lash-up, aimed at a road/trail posture for Europe. Basically a Tiger 750 with single Mk 1 concentric carb and without even the gearing change, the Trail was fitted with Avon Mudplugger tyres (4.00 × 18 rear, 3.00 × 21 front, on steel Radaelli rims) on a road-bike front end with a high-mounted sprung plastic mudguard and a 6-in headlamp, with fork trail modified from 110 to 104 mm. The Trail featured an unattractive and vulnerable black exhaust system with a massive black chrome zigzag silencer diagonally mounted on the left, an inadequate bash plate and tatty finishing touches like a plastic rear number plate which was hit by the back tyre when the suspension was on full compression, and T-motif transfers on the US-spec. tank which peeled easily. A 7.4:1 c.r. engine produced a claimed 40 bhp, but the Mudpluggers were a poor on/off road compromise, all too prone to skid on wet tarmac and skittish on the dry, and 80 mph was the recommended safe maximum speed. Electronic ignition was one plus point, but the three-quarter-length seat

*The disappointing TR7T Tiger Trail for 1981.*

*The 1981 UK spec. Royal Wedding Bonneville, a handsome beast.*

was uncomfortable and ruled out passengers. Far too heavy at 380 lb, the Trail had an impractically wide turning circle and over-firm suspension, despite Marzocchi units with longer travel at the rear, which also sported the TR65's drum brake. Only good enough on a straight dirt trail, this was no Adventurer or Trophy, and the bright green 650 was no better. Only some 250 were built before the end in 1982.

July 1981 brought the limited edition Royal Wedding Bonneville, in either UK or US form. Just 250 were built, each with a certificate of authenticity. They were basically Electro Bonnevilles and now sported the Bing CV carburettors and Marzocchi remote-oil-reservoir shock absorbers at the rear, which featured a sealed air chamber and five-way spring pre-load. The UK variant fitted Morris mag alloy wheels, twin front discs on ungaitered forks with black sliders and top covers, Royal badges on the side panels, a black headlamp shell, and a new-style dualseat. The engine was finished in matt black with polished cylinder fin edges set off by a silver grey frame, but the really magnetic feature was the chromed 4-gal petrol tank, embellished with upper and lower gold-lined black wings which were echoed by the upper half of the gold-lined side panels. The chromed US tank was finished the same way but its wings were smokey blue-black and it bore a royal wedding badge on its top. It featured a mini-style 'King and Queen' seat with light-coloured seat portions, chromed headlamp and brackets, a chromed brake

pedal, highly polished engine and forks, single disc and wire wheels. Each machine carried a special head stem plate showing its limited edition number and the (Palace-approved) words 'In celebration of the wedding of Prince Charles and Lady Diana Spencer'. The UK version was very good-looking.

**1982**, despite being very nearly the end for Meriden, brought yet another two 750 models, the TSS eight-valve and the TSX factory custom.

General improvements for the year included longer side panels, now fastened by a single Allen bolt and dispensing with the connecting spring, (finally) dog-leg control levers which were a genuinely easy reach to operate, stainless steel mudguards, a new seal on the petrol filler cap, twin circular mirrors fitted as standard, a new seat filled with moulded inserts (not very effective), and a bigger tool kit—though it lacked an Allen key to unfasten the side panels.

This year's Thunderbird 650s showed some relenting on the austerity front. They were now offered with dual chrome exhaust systems, and a proper rev counter where the instrument binnacle had been.

The TSS had been brewing for a long while, being a development of the Weslake 8-valve conversion for 650 Triumphs in the late '60s: for background see Volume 5. The crankcases and gearbox were as before, the changes to the standard engine starting with a new, stiffer crankshaft, which like the standard one was a one-piece forging with a substantial flywheel but had narrower and fatter big-end journals to reduce flexing and, it was hoped, vibration, and which allowed the side-webs to be widened. The crank ran on roller bearings and was machined all over to help reduce vibration. Above it was a new alloy cylinder block, a first for production Triumphs for over 20 years. The distance between its bores was widened by $\frac{1}{2}$ in to allow better air space between the cylinders, which had steel liners. To allow this increase, the alloy con-rod's little-end eyes were offset 3 mm to one side. The con-rods were dowelled to give positive alignment. Of the 10 holding-down studs, four ran straight through into the crankcase, and the two centre studs were also long, threading into the base of the block. Due to the restricted space because of the wider-set bores, in place of a head gasket a pair of circular steel Cooper sealing rings fitted into annular bands in the cylinder head. The alloy block, which was squared off and fitted more fins than the standard one, saved 8 lb weight and of course greatly improved engine cooling. Versions of the alloy barrels were intended to follow shortly for the conventional twins.

The eight valves in the redesigned TSS head were operated by the usual two pairs of pushrods in the familiar tunnels, though the latter now fitted improved sealing rings. But each pushrod operated a pair of rockers, since the latter were forked. Adjustment was by screw and lock nut. The TSS rocker shafts were carried in the head casing, so that the covers did not have to take any valve gear loadings from the levering action of the pushrods. Both exhaust and inlet tracts were parallel, and the inlet cam milder than the T140's, while the exhaust cam was fiercer: really wild lifts and timing were not necessary, due to the efficiency of the new head design.

For within the head, in contrast to the previous hemispherical chamber and dome-topped pistons, the combustion chamber was shallow and the valves symmetrically placed at a 30° angle, much narrower than the conventional twins' wide and restrictive arrangement. The new design not only breathed much better but allowed 12 mm plugs to be fitted centrally, giving more efficient combustion. Another bonus was that the new design allowed the use of flat-topped pistons, with valve cutaways, which gave 9.5:1 compression yet still ran cooler than the conventional twins. The engine produced a claimed 57 bhp at 6,500 rpm.

The TSS engine, finished in black above the cases, was not very attractive, lacking the jut

*The eight-valve TSS 750 for 1982, flawed but fast.*

**Left** *The eight-valve, electric-start, double front disc TSS on test in Cornwall.*

**Right** *The 1982 TSX factory custom. Nice bike, shame about the stripes.*

of splayed ports or the definition of the other twins' angled head. It breathed through 34-mm Amal Mk 2s, fitted a halogen headlamp, and was available in electric start form only. Otherwise running gear was as for the UK T140, with Marzocchi Stradas at the rear and optional double discs on forks with black sliders and shrouds. Finish was a gold-lined black, though the upswept pinstriping and the line of the tank still didn't look quite right. Claimed dry weight was just 415 lb, and vibration, if not eliminated, was reduced

below speeds of around 85 mph: *MCN* felt that even higher gearing would have pushed the vibration period beyond reach. For with a 43-tooth rear sprocket, gearing was higher than with the current Bonneville's 45-tooth, and a standing quarter of 14.28 sec indicated that power was mostly at the top end. But the engine proved fairly flexible and unfussy, though it was happiest above 2,500 rpm.

The TSS was substantially quicker than the T140, with test speeds in the 120s when the rider was prone. Fuel consumption was up at around 40–45 mpg. The uncomfortable Triumph feet-forward riding position was intact over any distance, and the TSS's high speed revealed a slight front end lightness on bumpy bends, but it stayed on line and was exhilaratingly ready to rev. Sadly, though, the TSS was prone to many teething troubles. As is well known, the initial batch of cylinder heads proved to be porous. *MCW*'s Chris Myers suffered from this and many other problems on a TSS he had on extended loan. There was also trouble with the Cooper rings blowing frequently. This proved to be due to the liners slipping down the barrels. Rapid-wear cams and broken valve springs also played a part.

With all its faults, however, *Bike*'s Brecon Quaddy enjoyed the mid-range power, and found that with the centre stand removed and the Marzocchis suitably adjusted, he was

cornering as fast on the TSS as he had ever done before. The TSS was intended to be offered shortly in the AV frame, but time ran out for Meriden before that.

In April 1982 came the factory custom twin-carb TSX, the background for which can also be found in Volume 5. Internally, as with the TSS, the crankshaft bobweights were machined on their sides, in contrast to the Bonneville's plain castings. Aiming for 'that low-slung West Coast look', the TSX led with ungaitered chrome front forks carrying Morris cast wheels, a 19-in Avon Speedmaster Mk II front cover matched by a fat 16-in Roadrunner on the rear, both tyres with their lettering picked out in white. Mudguards were painted and very short, while the chromed headlamp was held on a bent-wire frame. A smooth, flowing look was achieved by blending the rear of the US tank into the front of a special stepped dualseat with a grab-rail behind it, and by positioning the slanted Paioli rear shocks some 2 in to the rear, with their lower mountings directly above the wheel spindle.

The look was completed by unlinked exhaust pipes and compact stubby megaphone silencers with sanitary internals to satisfy US legislation. The rear chainguard was chromed, and angled metal TSX badges went directly on the side panels. The engine, which breathed through 32-mm Bing

*One that never was. A new version of the Executive, with a stylish fairing, intended for 1983.*

carburettors, was painted black above the crankcases. It was a fair package, but I cannot have been alone in discounting it due to the screaming vulgarity of the curved yellow/orange/red go-faster stripes on tank and side panel, though the basic gold-lined metallic red colour was nice. On test, *MCS* found it a generally well finished, comfortable and relaxing bike to ride, happy cruising anywhere between 60 and 85 mph, with a top speed in the mid-90s probably limited by the shortie silencers with their pleasantly burbling, chugging engine note. One drawback was that with petrol consumption around 47 mpg, the tank proved to give a range of only about 110 miles, with less than 5 miles in reserve. *MCW*'s man John Simcock took one on a run to the Continent and suffered misfiring from a duff coil, and then the bike sticking in top gear as he arrived abroad, which meant that one of the selector mechanism plungers had to have two high spots eased off with emery paper. But he still appreciated the TSX's excellent handling and laid-back character.

Several new variations were scheduled for **1983**, including AV versions of the Executive and the TSS, an eight-valve TSX, and new 599 cc twins in Daytona twin-carb and Thunderbird US form (see Volume 5), but actual production ceased at the end of 1982. The co-op went into liquidation, John Bloor bought the Triumph name and licensed Les Harris to produce the existing 750 for five years, and new Triumphs did not roll again until June **1985**. The only machines produced by Harris were kick-start Bonnevilles in either UK or US spec.

Bloor had insisted that Harris stick strictly to the original specification, so plans for alloy barrels and TSS crankshafts on the Bonneville were vetoed, though apparently some of the former slipped through; much retooling was necessary, and many components now derived from Italy. Tyres were still Avon Roadrunners, but wheel rims were by Radaelli. The 38-mm stanchion front forks and the rear dampers were both made by Paioli, with the fork yokes stamped with an M to identify their adaptation to fit the calipers that grinded the twin front discs of the 260-mm brakes by Brembo. The Brembo rear brake pedal involved a slight alteration to the frame cradle: the pedal was a TSX type, with smaller diameter pivot. Switchgear and the front master cylinder were by Magura of Germany. New stainless steel mudguards and an underseat fuse box with car-type cartridges were fitted, but, as *MCW* noted, the cartridges faced vulnerably upwards under the seat. Carburettors were now Amal '1$\frac{1}{2}$s', which were Mk 1 Concentrics with Mk 2 cold start slides, mounted on rubber sleeves with clip fixings. Instruments were still Veglia. Side panels were the late type, bisected by a swooping gold line and with slanted name badges. They were now secured to each other, however, by a single rubber band!

Internally the crankshaft was in essence the custom TSX one with the bobweights machined on their sides (the work being done in Italy, in fact), though the balance factor remained at 73 per cent and it was interchangeable with the previous Bonneville's crank. The oil filter at the base of the frame's spine was taller, and now incorporated a 2.5-cm plain steel section at its base, as a dam to inhibit the filter picking up sludge directly. The Lucas Rita electronic ignition had its pick-up pegged to the parallel ground end of the exhaust camshaft, where previously this had been tapered. This required a deeper end cover, and the first ones fitted were unribbed. The wiring harness was only altered by the bonding of the fuse block to the front of the tool box. During the two-year production run, a side stand cut-out switch was fitted.

One of the best innovations from the rider's point of view were the new Lafranconi silencers, which were carried on slightly upswept exhaust pipes. These reduced noise output to well below their required 85 db, and carried the added bonus that the centre stand could be positioned even higher, giving yet more useful ground clearance for left-hand cornering.

Testing a Harris Bonnie in 1986, *Classic Bike*'s Mike Nicks found the engine had a tighter, tauter feel, which he thought might possibly be ascribed to the more accurate machining tolerances of modern CNC machinery. He found it better than the Meriden Bonnevilles in the areas of braking (front double discs as standard), suspension, switchgear and instruments. The picture wasn't all idyllic. Oil consumption was down to 200 mpp, there was an annoying mid-range carburation stutter, and at 80 mph and 5,000 rpm there was still 'an irresistible urge to ease the throttle', though Nicks found that this was due to the riding position rather than vibration, since this one was 'smoother than earlier 750 Bonnies'. The discomfort was a pity, as handling and manoeuvrability were

*And another that never made it, the twin-headlamp eight-valve TS8-1.*

*The last Bonneville, from Les Harris in Newton Abbot, in US spec. Around 1,200 were made between 1985 and 1988.*

intact, spares were as cheap as ever and the best top speed was up at 115 mph.

Writing in *BBM*, Peter Crespin also celebrated the joys of his own late-model Harris Bonnie. He found the originally stiff gearbox eased with time, as did the initial daunting vibration, which steadily disappeared with the miles. The same was true of a wooden feeling in the Brembo brakes. Interestingly, while investigating a flat-spot between 3,000 and 4,000 rpm, he found out that, in order to pass noise tests yet maintain a minimum of 45 bhp, the last Bonnevilles had been fitted with a hot Spitfire-profile inlet cam, coupled with a low-lift Speed Twin-type exhaust cam which was less than a perfect match for it. Replacing the latter with something more suitable, he wrote, transforms the bike. His machine also fitted the Nikasil linerless alloy barrels (available as after-market equipment for around £300) and never overheated however hard it was ridden. He found the chrome lasted well, but this was not the latest word from Jim Grant in *Classic Bike*, who wrote that 'Discussion with owners [of Harris Triumphs] suggests that reliability and finish can be desperately poor', and went on to cite dealers speaking of wholesale replacement of Italian suspension components, and of excessive rusting.

*BBM*'s Crespin concluded that 'It's a Bonnie with a capital B and if you always meant to buy one but didn't, you should have

done. Too late now', since he was writing a year after the last of some 1,200 machines (no. JN001258) had been produced, in March 1988.

Today the oil-in-frame Triumphs are not held in very high esteem. They caused a lot of problems and grief on their introduction for the Triumph Engineering Co., and after that for many riders, and their reputation has suffered accordingly. They are, however, probably the most practical big Triumph to use regularly on the road. In the course of a long production run most of the problems were sorted out, and spares are plentiful. This means that with regular attention, most o.i.f. twins can be made into practical motor cycles, though a concern for detail, which the factory should have shown but often didn't, is therefore a must for the individual owner.

Many of the problems have already been mentioned, and retroactive solutions can be applied progressively, as and when needed, to keep costs down. In the first line would probably be late-type head gaskets and fork seals, together with Rita or Boyer electronic ignition. On the cycle side, skimming the chrome off the earlier brake discs would be a good move, as would repositioning the centre stand pivot ears on a pre-1974 machine and welding the pair of brackets between the frame tubes and pivot ears on a pre-1980 twin. Suitable Koni suspension units are the quality but expensive option when replacement becomes due, and on pre-'79 machines, the timing side bearing can be replaced with the later roller when the time comes, as can the oil pump with a four-valve one. Charlies of Bristol do a replacement for the top-hat oil filter at the base of the frame's spine, with a more efficient micronic element. An oil cooler and thermostat can help with the hot running from the minimal oil capacity, and are just about essential for runs abroad.

Many find that the 750's recommended Champion N3 sparking plugs are too hard for everyday use, though good for sustained high speeds, with an N5 or equivalent being the better all-rounder. Those concerned with performance are advised to jet the carburettor(s) up by at least +.10, and possibly more if the air filters are removed, and to fit an after-market exhaust system — the Dunstall one, siamesed low down in a Y, with the single silencer on the right of the machine, has been well spoken of, and was claimed to produce an 18 per cent power increase. Some discard the centre stand, and for a more suitable riding position, flat handlebars and rear-set kits for the left-foot shift machines have been available from Wassell, Unity and from Norman Hyde. The latter also offers a sports seat as well as a brace for the front forks.

Most, however, like the big Triumphs for their character rather than outright performance, their looks, well-tried simplicity, and fast but agile handling which offers an easier and less intimidating alternative to much Japanese machinery. The commendably low weight obviously contributes here, and for the same reason the lower Series Cs and later oil-in-frames can make a good ride for girl rockers. Because of their indifferent reputation among enthusiasts, the prices of oil-in-frame Triumphs have remained fairly reasonable (though the situation may change now 750 production has ended) and this is particularly true of the neglected 650s which, with later additions such as a disc front end, can be made into very nice machines, though the pre-o.i.f. unit 650s are more attractive as well as undeniably more solid. So while not perfect, most of these twins are at least affordable, and provided they get careful regular maintenance, are very rideable — and hence firmly in the Triumph tradition.

## Triumph: The Unit 650 and 750 twins, oil-in-frame (1971–88) — production dates and specifications

### Production dates
TR6R Tiger—1971-73
T120RV Bonneville—1971-74
TR6RV Tiger—1972-73
T140V Bonneville—1973-74
T140 Bonneville—1976-78
TR7 Tiger—1977-83
T140 Jubilee Bonneville—1977
T140E Bonneville—1979-83
T140D Special—1979-80
TR7VE Tiger Electro—1980-83
T140E Executive—1980-83
T140ES Bonneville Electro—1980-83
TR65 Thunderbird—1981-82
TR7T Tiger Trail—1981-82
TR6T Tiger Trail—1981-82
T140 Royal Wedding Bonneville—1981
TSS 8-valve—1982
TSX Custom—1982
Harris T140 Bonneville — 1985–88

### Specifications
**T120, TR6R, T120V, TR6RV**
Capacity, bore and stroke—649 cc (71 × 82 mm)
Type—ohv twin
Ignition—coil
Weight—T120 (1971) 387 lb; T120V (1974) 413 lb
**T140, TR7, TSS, TSX**
Capacity, bore and stroke—744 cc (76 × 82 mm)
Type—ohv twin
Ignition—coil (1979-on, electronic)
Weight—T140V (1974) 413 lb; T140E/TR7 (1979) 395 lb; T140ES (1981) 430 lb; TSS (1982) 415 lb; Harris T140 (1986) 410 lb
**TR65, TR6T**
Capacity, bore and stroke—649 cc (76 × 71.5 mm)
Type—ohv twin
Ignition—coil
Weight—TR65 (1981) 395 lb

### Triumph: engine and frame numbers
Engine and frame numbers should usually correspond, but engine numbers are usually preceded by model codes (i.e. 5TA, T100 S/ S) while frame numbers until 1969 bore prefixes as follows:

| Frame prefix | Model |
|---|---|
| TC | 3T |

| TF | Rigid 5T, T100, 6T and TR5 |
| S | Swinging-arm pre-unit models |
| H | Unit C-range from 1957–69 |

## Engine/frame numbers

**1950**
Pre-unit 350, 500, 650

| from | 100N |
| **1951** | 101NA–15808NA |
| **1952** | 15809NA–25000NA, then |
| | suffix discontinued so 25000–32302 |
| **1953** | 32303–44134 |
| **1954** | 44135–56699 |
| **1955** | 56700–70929 |
| **1956** | 70930–82799 |

**1957**

| Pre-unit 500, 650 | 0945–011115 |
| C-range unit 350, and from, 1959, 500 | H101–H760 |

**1958**

| Pre-unit | 011116–020075 |
| C-range | H761–H5484 |

**1959**

| Pre-unit | 020076–029363 |
| C-range | H5485–H11511 |

**1960**

| Pre-unit | 029364–030424, then D101–D7726 |
| C-range | H11512–H18611 |

**1961**

| Pre-unit | D7727–D15788 |
| C-range | H18612–H25251 |

**1962**

| Pre-unit | D15789–? |
| C-range | H25252–H29732 |

**1963**

| Unit 650 | DV101–DV5824 |
| C-range | H29733–H32464 |

**1964**

| Unit 650 | DV5825–DV13374 |
| C-range | H32465–H35986 |

**1965**

| Unit 650 | DV13375–DV24874 |
| C-range | H35987–H40527 |

**1966**

| Unit 650 | DV24875–DV44393 |
| C-range | H40528–H49832 |

**1967**

| Unit 650 | DV44394–DV66245 |
| C-range | H49883–H57082 |

**1968**

| Unit 650 | DV66246–DV85903 |
| C-range | H57083–H65572 |
| TR25W | from C101 |

**1969**

| Unit 650 | DV85904–DV90282 |
| C-range | H65573–H67331 |
| TR25W | C5001–? |

Early in the 1969 season, commencing with JC00101, an entirely new system was introduced, with a two-letter prefix for every machine, the first letter being a month code, the second letter a year code. This prefix was followed by engine numbers in series irrespective of models, and thus included the Trident whose number began at 00101 and by the start of the 1970 season had reached 03601, while the TR25W by the 1970 season start had reached 00388, rising to 05146 by January 1970. There were inconsistencies in the numbering: the unit 650 numbers had reached 36585 in January 1970, then reverted to 30001 with the start of the oil-in-frame machines.

### Date Code

| Month | Year |
|---|---|
| A = January | C = October 1968–July '69 |
| B = Febrary | D = August 1969–Aug '70 |
| C = March | E = September 1970–Aug '71 |
| D = April | G = September 1971–Aug '72 |
| E = May | H = September 1972–Aug '73 |
| G = June | J = September 1973–Aug '74 |
| H = July | K = September 1974–Aug '75 |
| J = August | N = September 1975–Aug '76 |
| K = September | P = September 1976–Aug '77 |
| N = October | X = September 1977–Aug '78 |
| P = November | |
| X = December | |

Hence the commencement under the new system of the T100SS/T100T at NC00100 indicates October 1968.

### Start numbers

**1970**

| Trident | –03601 |
| Unit 650 | JD24849 |
| C-range | KD27866 |
| TR25W | – |

**1971**

| Trident | – |
| Unit 650 | HE30001 |
| C-range | KE00001 |
| T25SS | – |

**1972**

| Trident | – |
| Unit 650 | HG30870 |
| C-range | JG32303 |

**1973**
| Trident | — |
|---|---|
| Unit 724 cc | JH15435–XH22018 |
| Unit 747 cc | XH22019 |
| Unit 650 | JH15366 |
| C-range | JH15597 |

**1974**
| Trident | — |
|---|---|
| Unit 750 | GJ55101–NJ60032 |
| Unit 650 | GJ55101–KJ59067 |
| C-range | JJ57337 |

**1975**
| Trident | — |
|---|---|
| Unit 750 | —to EK62239 |
| Unit 650 | —to NJ60070 |

NB The 1974 and 1975 numbers refer to machines released for sale by the Meriden co-op during those years.

**1976**
| Unit 750 | HN62501 |
|---|---|

**1977**
| Unit 750 | GP75000 |
|---|---|

**1978**
| Unit 750 | HX00100 |
|---|---|

**1979**
| Unit 750 | HA11001 |
|---|---|

**1980**
| Unit 750 | PB25001 |
|---|---|

**1981**
| Unit 750/650 | KDA28001 |
|---|---|

**1982**
| Unit 750/650 | EDA30001 |
|---|---|

**1983**
| Unit 750 | BEA33001– AEA34393, ends |
|---|---|

**1985**
| Les Harris Unit 750 | EN000001 |
|---|---|

**1987**
| Les Harris Unit 750 | SN001258, ends |
|---|---|

NB 'FFC' engine number prefix, on some models made by Meriden from winter 1980 onwards, denotes 'Factory Fitted Custom', indicating built to customer's personal specification of colour and ancillaries.

### Triumph: colour schemes
(In the following descriptions, 'cycle parts' includes oil tanks and front forks unless otherwise mentioned, and the usual parts—headlamp rim, exhaust systems, petrol caps, etc.—are chromed.)
**1950** *3T* Black cycle parts, wheel rims chrome with ivory-lined black centre strip, mudguards black with ivory-lined black centre stripes, petrol tank black. *5T* All Amaranth Red, wheel rims chrome with gold-lined red centre strip.

*T100* Black cycle parts, wheel rims chrome with blue-lined silver sheen centre strip, mudguards silver sheen with blue-lined silver sheen centre stripe, petrol tank silver sheen. *TR5* Black cycle parts, wheel rims chrome with blue-lined silver centre strip, mudguards silver with blue-lined black centre stripe, petrol tank chrome-plated with blue-lined silver panels. *6T* All Thunderbird Blue (blue-grey), wheel rims chrome with gold-lined blue-grey centre strip, mudguards blue-grey with gold-lined centre stripe, petrol tank blue-grey.
**1951** *3T, 5T, T100, TR5* As 1950. *6T* As 1950 but colour now light Polychromatic Blue.
**1952** *5T, T100, TR5, 6T* As 1950.
**1953** *5T, T100, TR5, 6T* As 1950.
**1954** *5T, TR5, 6T* As 1950. *T100* Colour now Shell Blue, with mudguard stripe white-lined black. *T110* As T100.
**1955** *5T, T100, 6T* As 1954. *TR5* Black cycle parts, wheel rims chrome-plated, mudguards Shell Blue with white-lined black centre stripe, petrol tank Shell Blue.
**1956** *5T* As 1950. *T100* Wheel rims chrome-plated only. *TR5* Headlamp shell now chromed. *6T* As 1950, but colour Crystal Grey. *TR6* As TR5. *T110* As T100.
**1957** *3TA* Most cycle parts black, but front forks, panelling, mudguards and petrol tank Shell Blue. *5T* Cycle parts now black, wheel rims chrome-plated only, mudguards and petrol tank Amaranth Red. *T100* Standard colour now Silver Grey, mudguards Silver Grey with white-lined black centre stripe. Alternative scheme black cycle parts, mudguards Ivory with gold-lined light blue centre stripe, petrol tank Ivory top, blue lower, with gold dividing line. *TR5* As 1955, colour now Silver Grey. *6T* Cycle parts now black, wheel rims chrome-plated only, mudguards Burnished Gold with white-lined black centre stripe, petrol tank Burnished Gold. *TR6* As TR5. *T110* As T100, including alternative.
**1958** *3TA, 5T, TR5, 6T, TR6, T110* As 1957. *T100* Standard as 1957; alternative as 1957 but upper tank and gold-lined mudguard stripe colour now black, lower tank Ivory.
**1959** *3TA, T110, TR6* As 1958. *5TA* Amaranth Red including stands, engine plates, footrests, front forks and panelling. *T100* Standard as 1957; alternative as 1958 but upper tank Ivory, lower tank black. *6T* As 1957 but colour now Charcoal Grey, with mudguards' stripe gold-lined black. *T120* Black cycle parts, mudguards Pearl Grey with

gold-lined Tangerine stripe, petrol tank Pearl Grey upper, Tangerine lower with gold dividing line. Mid-season as 1960.

**1960** 3TA As 1957. 5TA As 1959 but colour Ruby Red. *T100A* Cycle parts black, mudguards black, petrol tank upper black, lower Ivory, with gold dividing line from rear of knee-grips. *6T* As 1959, but including black inner mudguard and Charcoal Grey rear panelling. Also black and Ivory option as T100A. *T110* As T100A. *TR6* Cycle parts black, mudguards Ivory with gold-lined black centre strip, petrol tank Ivory upper, Aztec Red lower with gold dividing line from rear of knee grips. *T120* Cycle parts black but oil tank and battery box Pearl Grey, mudguards Pearl Grey with gold-lined Royal Blue centre stripe, petrol tank Pearl Grey upper, Royal Blue lower with gold dividing line from rear of knee grips.

**1961** 3TA, 5TA As 1960. *T100A* Cycle parts black, front mudguard and rear panelling silver, inner rear mudguard black, petrol tank upper black, lower silver with gold dividing line from rear of knee grips. *6T* As T100A, with bottom fork members finished in silver. *T110* Cycle parts black but upper fork legs and nacelle Kingfisher Blue, front mudguard and rear enclosure silver, petrol tank upper Kingfisher Blue, lower silver, with gold dividing line from rear of knee grips. *TR6* Cycle parts black, mudguards silver with gold-lined Ruby Red stripes, petrol tank Ruby Red upper, silver lower with gold dividing line from rear of knee grips. *T120* Cycle parts black, but oil tank and battery box silver plus headlamp shell now chromed, mudguards silver with gold-lined Sky Blue stripe, petrol tank Sky Blue upper, silver lower with gold dividing line from rear of knee grips.

**1962** 3TA, 5TA, 6T As 1961. *T100SS* As T120 including chromed headlamp shell, but Kingfisher Blue in place of Sky Blue, including T100SS rear panelling. *TR6* As 1961 but Polychromatic Burgundy in place of Ruby Red. *T120* As 1961, but battery box and oil tank now black.

**1963** 5TA As 1962. 3TA As 1957, but with optional colour of Silver Bronze. *T90* Cycle parts black but headlamp shell chromed, rear enclosure and front mudguard Alaskan White, latter with black-lined gold stripe, petrol tank Alaskan White. *T100SS* As 1962, but Regal Purple in place of Kingfisher Blue. *6T* As 1961 T100A. *TR6* As 1962 but Regal Purple in place of Polychromatic Burgundy. *T120* As T90, with rear mudguard Alaskan White with

black-lined gold stripe.

**1964** 6T As 1963. 3TA Cycle parts black but forks Silver Bronze, front mudguard and rear enclosure Silver Bronze, petrol tank Silver Bronze. *T90* As 1963, but petrol tank top now gold with black dividing line from rear of knee grips, rear enclosures deleted so tool box black, rear mudguard as front. *5TA* Black cycle parts but silver sheen fork lower members, silver front mudguard and rear enclosure, petrol tank black upper, silver lower with gold dividing line from rear of knee grips. *T100SS* As 1963, with Hi-Fi Scarlet replacing Regal Purple, rear enclosure deleted so tool box black, rear mudguard as front. *TR6* As 1963 but Hi-Fi Scarlet replaces Ruby Red. *T120* As T90.

**1965** 3TA, 5TA, 6T As 1964. *T90* Cycle parts including tool box black but headlamp shell still chromed, mudguards silver with gold-lined stripe, petrol tank Pacific Blue upper, silver lower, with gold dividing line from rear of knee grips. *T100SS* As 1964 with Burnished Gold replacing Scarlet and Alaskan White replacing silver for lower tank and mudguard colour, with mudguard and rear tank lining now black. *TR6* As T100SS. *T120* As T90.

**1966** 3TA As 1965 T90, with 3TA rear panelling now gone. Gold lining on rear of tank now begins from rear of new 'eyebrow' tank badges, with lower colour now continung above knee grips, or sometimes below them with T100 and TR6. *T90* As 1965 but Grenadier Red replacing blue and Alaskan White replacing silver, and tank gold lining as 1966 3TA. *5TA* As 1965 but rear panelling deleted so rear mudguard as front, tool box black, and petrol tank gold lining as 1966 3TA. *T100* As 1964 T100SS with Sherbourne Green replacing gold for petrol tank top and mudguard stripe, latter now gold-lined again, as is petrol tank, like 1966 3TA. *6T* As 1963, but rear panelling deleted so rear mudguard as front, tool box black, and petrol tank gold lining as 1966 3TA. *TR6* As 1965 but Pacific Blue replacing gold mudguard and petrol tank lining (latter as 1966 3TA) now gold again. *T120* As T90.

**1967** *T90* As 1966 but HI-FI Scarlet replaces red and Alaskan White replaces silver. *T100, T100T* As 1966 T100 but headlamp shell chrome-plated, and Pacific Blue replaces green. *TR6* As 1966 but Mist Green replaces blue. *T120* As 1966 but Aubergine (purple) replaces red and gold replaces white, with previous gold lining for tank and mudguards replaced by white.

**1968** *TR25W* Cycle parts black, headlamp shell chrome, side panels black, mudguards and petrol tank Flamboyant Red. *T90* As 1967 but Riviera Blue replaced Scarlet and silver replaces white. *T100S, T100T* As 1967 but Aquamarine replaces blue and silver replaces white. *TR6* As 1967 but Riviera Blue replaces green and silver replaces white. *T120* As 1967 but Hi-Fi Scarlet replaces Aubergine and silver replaces gold, still with white lining for tank and mudguards.

**1969** *TR25W, T90* As 1968, but *TR25W*'s colour now Hi-Fi Scarlet. *T100S, T100T* As 1968 but Lincoln Green replaces Aquamarine and White replaces silver, with previous gold lining on mudguards and petrol tank replaced by silver. *TR6* As 1968 but Trophy Red replaces blue, with previous gold lining on tank and mudguards replaced by white. *T120* As 1968 but Olympic Flame replaces Scarlet, still with white lining for tank and mudguards. *T150* Cycle parts black, but headlamp shell chrome. Side panels and mudguards Aquamarine, as was petrol tank. Mudguards centre stripe silver with white lining.

**1970** *TR25W* As 1969. *T100S, T100T* As 1969 for T100T but Jacaranda Purple replacing green and silver replacing white, with 1969's silver lining on mudguards and petrol tank replaced by gold. *T100S* (and some *T100T*?) All Jacaranda Purple tank. *TR6* Cycle parts black, mudguards Spring Gold with white-lined black stripe, petrol tank Spring Gold with white-lined black centre stripe. *T120* Cycle parts black, mudguards Astral Red with gold-lined stripe, petrol tank Astral Red, with gold-lined Silver Sheen side sections. *T150* As 1969, but alternative colours now Olympic Flame dark orange in place of Aquamarine, and Silver Sheen in place of white, with Silver Sheen centre stripe for mudguards white-lined. For Aquamarine scheme, mudguards with gold-lined white centre stripe, petrol tank with gold-lined white side panels.

**1971** *T25SS, T25T* Cycle parts black including matt black exhaust system, forks polished alloy, headlamp shell chrome, mudguards red with gold-lined black centre stripe, petrol tank red with gold-lined swept-back scallops above gold-lined black Triumph name transfer. *T100R* Cycle parts black, mudguards Olympic Flame with white-lined black centre stripe, petrol tank Olympic Flame

with white-lined broad black waist band. *T100C* Cycle parts black, mudguards stainless steel, tank Olympic Flame. *TR6* Cycle parts black including side panels, forks polished alloy, headlamp shell chrome, mudguards Pacific Blue with gold-lined white stripe, petrol tank either 3-gal US type with gold-lined white swept-wing scallop panels above and below tank badge, or later 4-gal with central broad gold-lined stripe in white, and gold-lined lower horizontal tank band. *T120* Cycle parts black including side panels, forks polished alloy, headlamp shell chrome, mudguards Tiger Gold with white-lined black centre stripe, petrol tank Tiger Gold, either 3-gal US type with white-lined black swept-wing scallop panels above and below tank badge, or later 4-gal with central broad white-lined stripe in black, and white-lined lower horizontal tank band. *T150* Cycle parts black including side panels, forks polished alloy, headlamp shell chrome, mudguards Spring Gold with white-lined black centre stripe, petrol tank Spring Gold, either US type with white-lined black swept-wing scallop panels above and below tank badge, or 4½-gal Spring Gold with white-lined black side panels. Alternative scheme Black, with black mudguards and gold-lined white petrol tank side sections.

**1972** *T100R* As 1971 but colours Cherry Red and gold-lined Cold White. *T100C* As 1971 but tank upper colour Cherry Red and lower gold-lined Cold White. *TR6* As 1971, 4-gal tank only for UK, but Blue with black-lined white stripes. *T120* As 1971, 4-gal tank only for UK, and though main Tiger Gold maintained, secondary colour became black-lined white. *T150* As 1971, 4½-gal tank only for UK, mudguards chrome, side panels and petrol tank Regal Purple.

**1973** *TR5T* Cycle parts black including side panels, and front brake plate matt black, with chromed plastic winkers, matt black silencer, mudguards chrome, petrol tank polished alloy with gold-lined swept-wing panels in red or yellow with gold-outlined black Triumph name transfer. *T100R* Cycle parts black including side panels and matt black front brake plate, chrome headlamp shell, mudguards chrome, petrol tank Astral Blue with upper only swept-wing scallop panels in black-lined Gold. *TR6* Early models as 1972 but later with chrome mudguards, 4-gal petrol tank with 'comma'-shaped panels in black-lined white. *T120* Early models as 1972 but later with chrome mudguards, 4-gal petrol tank Hi-Fi Vermilion with 'comma'-shaped panels in white-lined Gold. *TR7* As TR6, but tank panel gold-lined, and white referred to as Opal. *T140* As T120. *T150* As 1972 but tank black with scallop-shaped gold-lined Red tank panels with twin swept-back wings above and below knee grips. *X75* Frame black, headlamp, rear chainguard and mudguards chrome, seat–tank unit red with twin black-lined yellow stripes.

**1974** *TR5T* As 1973. *T100R* As 1973, colours Argosy Blue and gold-lined Ice White. *TR6* As 1973, and if in US spec. for UK, gold-lined swept-wing scallops in Cold White from above tank badge, with tank in blue. *T120* As 1973 but petrol tank colours Purple and gold-lined Cold White, with US spec. for UK as TR6 but with base colour Purple. *TR7* As 1973 but petrol tank colours Green and gold-lined Cold White, with US spec. for UK as TR6 but with base colour Green. *T140* As 1973 but colours Cherokee Red and gold-lined Cold White, with US spec. for UK as TR6 but with base colour Cherokee Red. *T150* As 1973, but petrol tank side panel colour white-lined gold.

**1975** As 1974. *T160* Cycle parts black, headlamp shell and mudguards chrome, petrol tank either Cherokee Red with swept-wing scallops from above and below tank badge in gold-lined Cold White, or tank Cold White with gold-lined Sunflower Yellow flashes.

**1976** *TR7* As 1974 but petrol tank, either UK or US style, in Jade Green, with gold-lined Cold White panels. *T140* As 1974 but petrol tank, either UK or US style, in Polychromatic Red or in Blue, with gold-lined Cold White 'comma' or upper 'swept-wing' panels.

**1977** *TR7, T140* As 1976. *T140 Jubilee* Cycle parts black and chrome as T140, but side panels silver with special badges, wheel rims chrome with Blue centre stripe, Red outer and White inner lining, dualseat cover Powder Blue with Red piping, rear chainguard Silver with Blue styling stripe with Red outer and White inner lining, petrol tank UK silver with blue 'comma' panel, lined with narrow white inner, broad Red middle and broad White outer lines, US Silver with Blue upper swept-wing panels lined similarly.

**1978** *TR7* As 1976, but with alternative schemes—for UK, mudguards Silver, with Red U-shaped styling bands on forward section of front guard and below lifting handle on rear guard, bands lined with narrow gold inner and black outer lines, side panels silver with

red- and black-lined red 'hockey-stick' stripe along their base, UK petrol tank red with narrow gold inner and black outer lining for silver 'comma' panelling. US tank red with gold- and black-lined silver 'swept-wing' scallops, and chrome mudguards. Alternative Gold in place of red, and Silver as silver above, but with black outer- and blue inner-lining. *T140* As 1976, but with alternative colour schemes—for UK, mudguards Poly-chromatic Tawny Brown, with Gold U-shaped styling bands on forward section of front and below lifting handle at rear, bands lined with narrow brown inner and white outer lines, dualseat cover brown, side panels painted brown with white-lined gold 'hockey stick' stripe along their base, petrol tank brown with narrow brown inner and white outer lining for Gold 'comma' panelling, for US brown with brown and white-lined Gold 'swept-wing' scallops and chrome mudguards. Alternative Aquamarine Blue in place of brown, silver in place of gold, with Aquamarine outer and gold inner lines and black dualseat.

**1979** As 1978 but new side panel and petrol tank colour schemes. UK *T140* variants now with 'zig-zag' tank panels, choice of black side panels and tank with gold outer/black middle/gold inner lining and Candy Apple Red tank panel; or pale metallic yellow-gold side panels and tank, with white outer/gold middle/black inner lining and deep Metallic Gold tank panel, also with brown seat cover; or (also for *TR7*) Astral Blue side panels and tank, with gold outer/astral blue middle/gold inner lining. US variants, either black side panels and tank with silver upper wing-shaped scallops lined gold outer/black middle/gold inner; or Candy Apple Red side panels and tank with black wing-shaped scallops lined gold outer/black middle/gold inner; or as above but with silver scallops lined in same way; or Astral Blue side panels and tank with silver scallops lined gold outer/blue middle/gold inner. The *T140D Special*, with cast alloy wheels with spoke recesses in black and rim section polished, US tank black with portions above and below lined in gold, side panels black with two horizontal gold lines beneath badge, UK as above but with 'zig-zag' petrol tank panel lined gold outer/black middle/gold inner.

**1980** As 1979, but for UK *T140* an all-black tank available with 'zig-zag' petrol tank panel lined white outer/black middle/white inner.

**1981** *T140 Electro and Executive UK or US*

As previous but side panels in Smoked Burgundy or Smoked Blue darkening from bright to near- black, UK with single L-shaped gold line at lower front of tank, US with silver upper scallops with single gold line. For *T140* UK, white-lined black variant, or the black and Candy Apple, or pale Metallic Blue side panels and tank with black tank panel lined black outer/blue inner, or Gold side panels and tank with Candy Apple Red panels lined black outer/gold middle/black inner. US *T140* Astral Blue and silver as 1979, with a further variation as the latter but colour Olympic Flame with gold-lined white upper scallops. Also now pale Metallic Blue side panels and tank with gold-lined black scallops, or black with gold-lined Candy Apple Red scallops, and Metallic Grey with gold-lined black scallops, the wing-shaped scallops on these variants now extending back from both above and below the tank badges. *TR7T Tiger Trail*, black frame, forks, headlamp shell and exhaust system, with mudguards, side panels and tank yellow (see text for details). *TR6T* As TR7T, but colour bright green. *TR65* black frame, engine cases, lower forks, headlamp shell, exhaust system, side panels, petrol tank now of different shape and with 'boomerang' double gold lining tapering to join at its ends and not joined at upper rear.

**1982** As 1981, with models adopting new side panel 'tick' curved gold line beneath tank badge, and UK tanks with 'boomerang' lining as 1981 TR65. *TSS* Black frame, headlamp shell, side panels and tank, both with lining as above. For Royal Wedding and TSX models, see text. TR65, as 1981 but exhaust system now chrome and engine cases polished.

**1985** *Harris T140* As previous, stainless steel mudguards, black side panels with gold 'tick' lining, UK black petrol tank with single side gold lines now not joined at lower rear, plus gold lining on tank top, US black with gold-lined Candy Apple Red scallops above and below name badge.

**1986 and 1987** As 1985.

**Triumph: some approximate modern colour equivalents**

| | |
|---|---|
| Amaranth Red | BL Damson (as on Dolomite) |
| '58 Thunderbird optional Polychromatic Blue | Ford Blue Mink |
| 'Twenty One'/3TA Metallic Blue | Ford Cosmos Metallic Blue |
| '59 Thunderbird Dark Gunmetal Grey | Jaguar Dark Grey |
| '66 TR6 Trophy Metallic Mist Green | Vauxhall Metallic Jade Green (Holts aerosol AV53) |
| '66 TR6 Trophy Alaskan White | Ford Diamond White (Carplan aerosol) |
| Pre-unit Tiger 100 silver | Volkswagen Silver Metallic or Lancia Silver Fox |
| '61 T110 Kingfisher Blue | Peugeot Blue |
| '61 T110 Silver Sheen | Rover Silver |

M.S. Motorcycles, r/o O'Briens Buildings, 203–269 Foleshill Road, Coventry, CV1 4JZ (01203 552300) provide accurate duplicate colours for most years and models based on extensive research with original paint chips.